# MEXICAN NATIONAL IDENTITY

# MEXICAN NATIONAL IDENTITY

*Memory, Innuendo, and Popular Culture*

## WILLIAM H. BEEZLEY

The University of Arizona Press   Tucson

Again, for Blue
and our friends Joe and Fay Hobs

The University of Arizona Press
© 2008 The Arizona Board of Regents
All rights reserved

LIBRARY OF CONGRESS CATALOGING-IN-PUBLICATION DATA
Beezley, William H.
Mexican national identity : memory, innuendo, and popular culture /
William H. Beezley.
p. cm.
Includes bibliographical references and index.
ISBN 978-0-8165-2689-5 (hardcover : alk. paper) —
ISBN 978-0-8165-2690-1 (pbk. : alk. paper)
1. National characteristics, Mexican.
2. Popular culture—Mexico.
3. Mexico—Social life and customs.  I. Title.
F1210.B34 2008
972—dc22       2007035057

Manufactured in the United States of America
on acid-free, archival-quality paper.

13  12  11  10  09  08     6  5  4  3  2  1

# CONTENTS

## *"Small Deeds, and Vulgar Rumors"*

After spending time at the court of the Emperor Maximilian and the Empress Carlota, José Zorrilla, the author of the classic Spanish drama *Don Juan Tenorio*, composed a poetic travelogue of his experiences in Mexico. He created an alter ego, whom he called *un loco*, to write a brief prose essay to introduce his poetic recollections. The loco explained that the poet Zorrilla saw only Mexico's grandeur—its light, beauty, and fecundity that God had created—and it inspired his poetry about his temporary home. On the other hand, the loco informed readers that he offered "only homemade details about domestic matters" and "the small deeds, and vulgar rumors, almost always disdained by statesmen and diplomats, and almost never well appreciated by great historians."[1] The same might well be said about the book that follows. I provide homespun descriptions of the small deeds, rumors, and everyday matters that constituted life in the nineteenth century and contributed to the way people thought about themselves, their countrymen, and their nation.

National identity in the nineteenth century developed primarily in response to popular curiosity about the territories and peoples that Alexander von Humboldt and others praised as the richest colony in Spain's empire and that had become independent in 1821. The response to this curiosity came in various popular forms, and the national identity that it fostered stressed, above all, cultural and physical diversity. Government officials across the nineteenth century altered this emphasis on regional and ethnic variety, and increasingly narrowed it, limiting what ethnic and racial groups were included in national society. Those excluded were ignored or trivialized or criminalized in everyday practice and mocked in theory. Nevertheless, a widespread popular sense of national diversity persisted. This is the story of how it happened.

In the exploration of these themes, the goal has been understanding national identity and popular memory, and the risk has been attempting to tell a good story. Each of these purposes requires some discussion. In reverse order, my thinking on these topics goes as follows: What is a good story? And is there anything wrong in telling one? The questions respond to the often rather patronizing remark that someone has only written a good story. It reflects the assumption that history should be more scientific. This is to say, these critics decry the lack of blatant references to fashionable theories, the lack of scientific rigor presumed to result from the use of theoretical jargon, and the lack of clear, often political, objectives. These critics seek monographs that can be read with little thought, because they lack subtlety, allusion, or indirect references. All good stories have narrative structures that can be identified, and good historical stories have theories embedded in them for those who take the time to locate them. Not stating the theoretical argument is not the equivalent of having no theory.

The book that follows has a clear thesis: that the emerging political, economic, social, diplomatic, and population ideals and attitudes during the nineteenth century found a consensus in the cultural expressions that came to constitute national identity. This interpretation rests on the discussion of widely accessible cultural forms and the general population's reaction to them. In the narrative, the discussion could, but will not, dive into the cold, deep waters of historiography. The general theme examines how national identity and popular culture overlap in significant ways that form a reliquary of everyday detritus of personal and family memories combined with the habits and traditions of community life. The argument focuses on some of the popular sources of national identity. These include the ephemera of independence festivals, the folk art of children's games, contents of annual almanacs, and performances of itinerant puppet theater, and they serve as the themes of the chapters that follow. Based on these and other popular sources, nationalism as collective memories emerged slowly in the nineteenth century. Its story follows.

National identity overlaps with popular memories. Thinking about the way individuals and groups amend memories into a workable past that molds national identity could profitably begin with Maurice Halbwachs, whose work has been selected and translated as *On Collective Memory*.[2] Halbwachs argued that individuals as members of groups construct collective memories and that each group has different ones. The most important of the social groups for the construction of memories begins with the family, friends, and coworkers. Moreover, he concluded that memories, if they are to remain vivid and useful, need to be reinforced by celebration, with festivals or monuments, for example. These collective memories serve as the building blocks of national identity. Halbwachs included in his theories a discussion of the importance of landscape, so that geography has intimate connections to memories. He inspired the work of numerous historians, as the historiography turned to the study of mentalities and the memorialization of national events.[3] These trends provided the context for new attention to questions of nationalism and national identity.

Benedict Anderson, in his analysis of the international rise of nationalism beginning in the early nineteenth century, examined the imagined community—the nation of unseen, unknown individuals who shared common values, for the most part promoted by the printed word.[4] This masterful analysis nevertheless remains twice removed from a complete conclusion: First, because low rates of literacy outside of western Europe and North America (and even there for much of the nineteenth century) made literacy an unreliable index. This opens the difficult but fascinating question of the relationships among orality, literacy, and memory.[5] Performances in theaters, and in the street, especially during festivals, seem more common and more influential in the transmission and repetition of cultural values.[6] Second, reliance on literacy begged the question of what people read that urged them to imagine their compatriots. Discussion of performance, of course, has the same weakness. Understanding the surge of nationalism requires knowing what writers wrote that was read, what performers performed that was seen, and what revelers celebrated in the street. The writers and the performers in Mexico, for the most part, dealt with Mexican subjects because they had the specific goal of satisfying a paying audience, whose purchase of admission or printed words would enable them to meet the needs of daily survival. They often reached conclusions about subjects for their dramas based on what they saw in the streets during fiestas.[7]

Making a living and identifying national characteristics coincided in nineteenth-century Mexico. These activities were more than congruent, because they were essential to both; they were more than incidental, because these desperate individuals had to search for something elemental that politicians and priests could ignore, and often did. Once national traits were identified, the artists and artisans created images as abstractions, that is, synecdoches, of these sentiments, often in new ways, in new frameworks, or in new contexts but never completely departed from what could be recognized as community values. They adopted as their guiding rule, the rule of commerce: "Never disappoint expectations."

These fundamental values, some may argue, represent general human concerns rather than ones uniquely Mexican. This prompts the question, How could universal human issues promote Mexican national identity? One answer says that individuals equated human and Mexican values, and denied them to others, especially strangers, foreigners, Protestants, and, on occasion, indigenous peoples. But this answer may be too easy, too much the result of reflexive postmodernistic thinking, using dreadful neologisms such as "othering." We must also recognize that one specific characteristic of national identity came from its unequivocal location, its sense of place. Perhaps it is this, the national cultural, physical, and political geography, that Mexicans yearned to know about and through this interest first acquired a popular sense of their nation. The space contained the only environment in which Mexican identity could emerge.

Mexican national identity had a surprising provenance. Despite official efforts by eager politicians, army commanders, and schoolteachers, and despite the rise of particularistic community expressions of rights and patriotism, national sentiments received their enduring promotion from persons concerned about something more immediate than creating national identity. Individuals attempting to earn a living became the purveyors of the new patriotism. Peddlers, actors, artisans, writers, and performers sought popular appeal so that they could secure a livelihood. The surest market for their goods or performances required a broad audience. This came when they touched some widely held, if unexpressed, sentiment, or presented a well-known homily in a slightly new way, or explained some obvious but mysterious attribute of daily life. This could be summed up by saying they attempted to respond to the widespread curiosity held by Mexicans about themselves and their country.

In the comments he uses to criticize memory, and here by implication ideas about national identity, James Sallis (in a gloss of Walter Benjamin) defines the strengths, weaknesses, and arbitrary nature of history as a good story. Memory, and by extension narrative, he tells us, "cannot arrest the flow of time. It can only re-create set scenes, encapsulate privileged moments, arrange memories and incidents in some arbitrary manner that, word by word, will form a book." This has overwhelming results, he concludes, as he continues, "The unbridgeable distance between act and language, the demands of the written text itself, inevitably and insidiously degrade faithfulness to reality into mere artistic exercise, sincerity into mere virtuosity, moral rigor into aesthetics. Endowed with later coherence, bolstered with clever continuities of plot and resonance, our reconstructions of the past will always be a kind of betrayal."[8]

Now a good story, in fact, does many of the things that Sallis accuses it of, but it also accomplishes many of the things that other critics think it does not. The significant characteristic of the good story is that the author respects both the past and the reader. Scientists as they test theories exchange shorthand notes for others to test. Quasi-scientific historians, I believe, prefer this form because it allows them to publish what can be generously called technical papers, or in a less charitable way, rough drafts rather than historical essays. By either name, these works press the past into theoretical frameworks and show no respect for readers, as the authors leave unrevised the arcane, jargon-ridden, and often obvious theoretical discussions. Of course, there exist readers who prefer the so-called theoretical form, because it is easier than paying attention while reading the text. A good story that shows respect for readers liberates them from the cage of theories by challenging them to think about the narrative, encourages them to evaluate the events and actors by making the theory implicit in the presentation, and inspires them to think through its implications or just to enjoy the account of real people in the past. A good story allows the reader to recognize the ways that history serves as a liberating, humanistic discipline. Even conceding Sallis's point that perhaps all reconstructions are to some extent a distortion of previous events—a betrayal, in his words, of the past—one must recognize that to give Mexican lives dignity by recognizing their humanity through artistic exercises, virtuosity, and aesthetics achieves enough. In fact, it accomplishes a great deal and, consequently, as a good story, is history at its best.

# ACKNOWLEDGMENTS

Earlier versions of these essays were presented in various seminars, including ones early on at the Latin American Centre, Saint Antony's College, Oxford; another at the Latin American Centre, Cambridge University; and another at the Instituto de Estudios Históricos, el Colegio de México, and later at the University of Houston, the University of Chicago, and El Colegio de San Luis Potosí. My thanks to Alan Knight, David Brading, Guillermo Palacios, John Hart, Emilio Kourí, and Sergio Cañedo for arranging them. I thank as well the participants at these seminars and at others for their helpful comments. Additional colleagues, especially my *tocayos*, the other two Guillermos (Palacios and French), Colin MacLachlan, Dina Berger, Amanda López, and Elena J. Albarrán, have commented on this manuscript at varying stages of its development. The faculty and fellows at the Oaxaca Summer Institute and members of my graduate seminars have made incisive criticism. Carmen Nava Nava provided companionship in many archives and acted as a most reliable source of information on popular culture.

Ricardo Pérez Montfort provided stimulating discussions on popular culture and folklore. Both Francisa Miranda, from the Centro Nacional de los Artes, and Carmen Espinosa V., from the Colegio de México, offered extraordinary help in locating critical materials on puppet scripts and lotería images, respectively.

In discussions with these individuals, perhaps in some cases I listened unduly and in others not enough. Nevertheless, I regard these scholarly interlocutors as accessories before the fact, because they share the responsibility for what is good about this book, and they are partially guilty for any mistakes of fact or errors of interpretation. Scholarship remains a joint endeavor.

Some information in this book has appeared in different form in two other publications, and I thank the editors for permission to use material that appeared in *Historia mexicana* and the publisher, University of London Press, for information that appeared in Garath Jones (ed.), *The Creation of Public Space in Mexico*.

Because the focus of this book examines the constant reshaping of attitudes about the national community and its sense of identity, the subtitle includes both *memory* and *innuendo*, inspired by felicitous lines in two mystery novels, Stephen Greenleaf's *Southern Cross* (23) and John Dunning's *The Bookwoman's Last Fling* (183). The title means to suggest that Mexicans constantly revised their memories of the past events, relationships, and locations that made them Mexican, and that often these memories became gestures, signs, or objects that served as mnemonic devices of their national identity, ones that offered innuendos of who they were.

# MEXICAN NATIONAL IDENTITY

## CHAPTER 1

# How El Negrito Saved Mexico from the French

## The Popular Sources of National Identity

Napoleon III, the ambitious parvenu emperor of France, dreamed of world empire based on his leadership of those European countries and their former colonies that shared a Roman heritage. Justifying his plans for the Western Hemisphere, his advisers coined the phrase *Latin America* to express the goals of the campaign. He identified Mexico as the cornerstone in this projected sphere of influence and ordered an invasion in 1862. Despite the stunning Cinco de Mayo (May 5, 1862) victory by Mexican soldiers at Puebla, the French troops soon overwhelmed the defending armies and occupied Mexico City in 1863. Napoleon III then dispatched his puppets, Maximilian and Charlotte, who Hispanicized her name to Carlota, to rule his client Mexican empire.

During the French intervention and empire (1862–1867), as the allied foreign invaders and Mexican conservative armies attempted to defeat Benito Juárez and his liberal forces in the north, the Emperor Maximilian and his ministers tried to build popular support for the foreign regime in occupied regions. Nevertheless, critics persisted. For example, the Oaxacan poet Manuel E. Rincón, living in Mexico City, wrote a one-act comedy about the regime called Cosas del Día. Hoping to avoid the censors, he opened the play in the provincial town of Orizaba, but imperial authorities closed it after one performance because of its satirical references to the French. The comedy was never again performed, but the script as a pamphlet sold well under the table, especially in Oaxaca and other provinces outside the capital city.[1]

The emperor and empress worked to increase the popularity of their government, if not loyalty to it, by attempting to appear Mexican and expanding the holiday list. They turned to a campaign of appearances and celebrations. Besides adopting the Spanish Carlota for Charlotte, the empress posed for a painting wearing the white tunic and tricolor headdress to represent "la patría Mexicana."[2] The emperor devised a kind of imperial "circuses" campaign, proclaiming more elaborate celebrations of Independence Day, for example, and he added new holidays, such as his and his empress's birthdays, to the calendar. He tried to promote entertainment favorable, or at least neutral, to the regime. In his effort to find more acceptable diversions, he named José Zorrilla, the famous playwright and poet, who was in Mexico to escape his unhappy marriage in Spain, as the director of the imperial theater and court poet. Zorrilla in 1865 directed the Mexico City premiere of his now classic *Don Juan Tenorio*.[3]

Despite the emperor's efforts at censorship of his critics or the distraction of them with imperial-sponsored entertainments and holidays, his endeavors failed to eliminate several forms of popular satire. Newspapers, most notably *La Orquesta* and *La Chinaca*, published political caricatures. Above all, puppet shows continued unabated in their sarcastic commentary about Maximilian, just as puppeteer Louis Lemercier de Neuville mocked Napoleon III in France.[4] Mexican puppeteers formed part of a long-established tradition in which puppets served as social critics. In 1823, marionettes had appeared in *Seis noches de títeres mágicos*,[5] making satirical attacks on the first emperor, Agustin I. The tradition has continued to the present.[6]

During the years of the French intervention, one extremely popular puppet show in this tradition was a two-act performance called *The Pastry War* that by implication criticized the French-supported emperor. Guillermo Prieto, a popular newspaper columnist, saw the melodrama and reported the action of the puppets as follows:

> The curtain opened on a dense forest, where several repulsive monkeys with long, curling tails were making horrible faces and shrieking. Into this wild scene wandered El Negrito, the personification of the Mexican people, carrying a sword in one hand and

with the other behind him. He was dressed in charro trousers buttoned down the side of each leg, a short jacket, and sombrero with a tricolor hatband.

When the monkeys saw him, they huddled together, and sent one to question him.

El Negrito, mistaking the approaching monkey for the devil, shouted, "In the name of God, what do you want?"

The evil-looking monkey replied, "That you pay me for my pastries."

"You'll see how I pay you," answered El Negrito, as he hoisted the Mexican flag that he had held behind him.

Immediately the scene changed to the city and coast of Veracruz under attack by French cruisers and troops. The French charged the defenders of the Fort San Juan de Ulúa. The battle raged with bursting rockets and cannon shells, as flags waved, and drums and bugles sounded. The puppet French troops advanced, broke into the fort, and gradually began silencing the Mexican guns. El Negrito remained indefatigable, attacking, fighting, and killing Frenchmen. Nevertheless, he soon recognized that the battle appeared lost, so he grabbed the national flag and climbed to the highest point of the fortress. There he knelt, made the sign of the cross, and prayed, "Alas, Most Holy Mary of Guadalupe!"

At that moment the back of the stage was lit by sparklers, as gold and silver confetti rained down. The Virgin, surrounded by the archangels, descended. When she and her entourage touched down in the fort, the French immediately turned and retreated, throwing down their guns as they heard Mexican trumpets signaling charge. As they ran to their ships, these French soldier marionettes turned back into ugly, snarling monkeys.

At that moment, El Negrito proclaimed:

> Alas Veracruz, Veracruz,
> Alas unhappy Veracruz
> What a scare Santa Anna gave
> to Admiral Baudin![7]

And the curtain rang down.

Now before someone raises questions about this being a top-down social analysis, he or she needs to consider that a puppet company was not just an enterprise. It was much more; it was a family's livelihood. To say its goal was to make a profit does not capture the urgency of the endeavor. Puppeteers did not try to make a profit, but to make a living—an entirely different proposition. As a result, puppeteers had to be completely sensitive to how their shows played with audiences. Public opinion polls were not necessary. If puppeteers did not gauge their audiences correctly, the people did not return for the second night of performances.

The audience who watched, stomped, and applauded[8] as El Negrito defeated the French represented a cross section of the city's residents. Spectators of all ethnic and social groups watched the puppeteers perform in regular theaters or on temporary stages on street corners or in town squares, especially at the Salta del Agua and alongside the National Cathedral.

The motley audiences, as diverse as the residents of the capital, enjoyed the entertainment, especially the action that displayed the puppeteers' dexterity. With puppets, action predominated everything, followed closely by sarcasm.

Most of those watching understood the implied satire of Maximilian's regime, and probably so did the police. These authorities generally tried to contain disrespectful behavior by both performers and audiences within theaters rather than close the entertainment. Complaints about audience disorder and performers who violated legal and community standards appeared regularly in outraged letters to officials. Perhaps the police did not want to act without literal violations, and these dramas relied on allusions and innuendos. Or perhaps the police may simply have wanted to avoid hearing the public jeers that would accompany a reputation as the officer who arrested a puppet.

Beyond the sarcasm, individuals in the audience, no doubt, identified other common themes. The spectators who joined the commotion of the battle by howling, clapping their hands, stomping their feet, and pounding on the benches and railings of the theater's seats, demonstrated that they recognized the protagonist, El Negrito, and knew how to call him to action. In some cases, members of the audience also recognized themselves, because within the play were allusions, references, implications, and allegations aplenty.

For these reasons, *The Pastry War* offers unusual access to the popular history and culture of the mid-nineteenth century. Some puppeteers as they entertained audiences recognized or assumed a popular curiosity about the new nation. They saw an opportunity to tell Mexicans about Mexico. The directors of various companies, for example the Rosete Aranda family, wanted to present a marionette-guided tour of the country. The puppets offered *tableaux vivants*, or nearly *"vivants,"* of holiday celebrations of Independence Day, the Virgin of Guadalupe Day, Semana Santa, and other festivals of national importance; regional variations of these festivals; and other popular activities such as bullfights and dances. Moreover, the puppeteers presented regional social types as well, such as the China Poblana and the women of Tehuantepec. The puppet theater included folklore and geography familiar to the people through observation and oral tradition.

Examining *The Pastry War* reveals the role of puppets in the creation of an unofficial history that contributed to the popular sense of national identity. Furthermore, it demonstrates the powerful use of satire for which Mexicans should be famous.[9] In the effort to ridicule the French occupation and the puppet emperor, the drama focused on another intervention, that of 1837–1838, in which the French, at least in Mexican eyes, looked absolutely foolish. This brief episode developed when the French officials seized the opportunity created when Antonio López de Santa Anna lost Texas and left the Mexican government in disarray. The French demanded repayment of loans and additional financial claims. The Mexicans pled poverty. In response, the French government dispatched naval vessels to blockade the port of Veracruz. Mexican government officials, as a temporizing measure, agreed to review the claims and discovered one for 200 pesos, submitted by a French baker in Mexico City who swore soldiers during a military coup d'état had eaten his entire stock of cakes, cookies, tarts, and turnovers. Although they initially rejected the demands, ultimately government officials had to pay the French, including the baker, a total of some 8 million pesos. Moreover, the French decided to provide an object lesson: their navy bombarded the port of Veracruz—and coincidently, shot off one of Santa Anna's legs as he galloped across the beach to save the city. Thereafter, Mexicans satirically referred to the episode as the Pastry War.

The puppets created a version of the battle at Veracruz to mock the French, with their willingness to give up their lives for both tasty confections and their Emperor Maximilian, through the fanciful depiction of the Pastry War. The elements of the performance contributed to this ridicule. The play contained exceedingly rich references and allusions to the fundamental events, commonplace myths, and essential stereotypes that constituted popular national identity.

The drama began with a reminder of the demons who threatened the nation and its way of life. When the curtain went up on the monkeys, many in the audience immediately recognized the performance as a political satire that identified the evildoers seeking to dominate the society. The vain monkey, El Mono Vano, with its horrible face, shrieks, and long curling tail, served as one of the first and most pervasive caricatures of politicians. The image first appeared in 1808 and became common shortly afterward in the popular almanacs published by José Joaquin Fernández de Lizardí with illustrations by José María Torreblanca, best known as the engraver who created the nation's official seal. The Mono Vano, the howling, ugly politician, appeared in cartoons and puppet shows, and even became one of the cards in the illustrated table game similar to bingo, lotería de figuras. During the Wars of Reform, 1858–61, the reference became more specific as liberals used as their rallyng cry the song "Los Monos Verdes" (the green monkeys), which mocked the conservative troops in their green uniforms. The liberals continued to sing this bitingly sarcastic description of the conservatives, who sided with the French, during the intervention.[10]

Conservative politicians, whether domestic or French, were represented as evil, a curse on society. The monkey appeared nearly human—ugly and with other flaws, yes, but the image was like that in the mirror of a carnival funhouse, with distorted human features. Consequently, El Negrito confused the French politicians and evil monkeys with the devil. The French troops who had invaded Mexico in 1862 had received encouragement from the country's conservative politicians. Liberals saw them as evil, vain monkeys, the devil incarnate. The monkey puppets damned both French invaders and conservative domestic politicians.

As the minions of the devil, the monkeys appeared in the iconography of popular religion that reached back to the medieval era. In religious art, they often represented the devil's unredeemed henchmen and the unrepentant sinners who clawed at the faithful. In this way, the monkey puppets, with their many allegorical valences, allowed easy identification by audiences. For anyone who missed the reference, when the French troops ran from the fort and turned back into monkeys, in one of the most popular and technically difficult tricks performed by puppets,[11] it became evident.

The people, at least the Liberals, had their heroes. Opposed to the French stood El Negrito, one of the most famous marionettes of nineteenth-century puppet theater. He appeared as the symbol of both national and local traditions. He represented the people of Mexico in general and the Jarocho region of Veracruz in particular. By the 1860s, his reputation had been well established through his encounters with the aristocratic criollo puppet Don Folías as a daring, satirical, and humorous character. Many of their domestic imbroglios climaxed when El Negrito told Don Folías that his wife had cuckolded him. In this way, he revealed himself as daring as the witting messenger reporting the adulterous wife, as satirical in his seeming concern for marriage propriety, and as humorous in his joyful dance of pleasure at Folías's discomfiture.

Of course, many in the audience knew El Negrito's role and his trademark foot-stomping performance from these plays, so that when the scene in *The Pastry War* shifted to El Negrito's battle with the monkey soldiers in Veracruz, the audience imitated his distinctive behavior with foot stomping of their own. This represented a call for their champion to claim victory against the French, just as he succeeded in other melodramas against his high-society nemesis, Don Folías. Foot stomping as a form of communication recalled for some the prohibition by the Spanish colonial officials of drumming by African and Afro-Spanish slaves because the Spaniards feared the drums communicated conspiratorial messages. Hand clapping and foot stomping replaced the drums for the black population in both Cuba and Mexico, especially Veracruz. It reminded the audience that blacks, once before, had succeeded against imperial laws and leaders. Moreover, El Negrito succeeded against all odds and thus, no doubt, encouraged the audience against the occupation by French troops and the pretensions of Maximilian and Carlota.

These characteristics suggest that El Negrito, the puppet, developed from the model or in concert with the widely popular El Negrito, the poet. The latter held sway in the eighteenth century as the most popular satirist and wit of the Bourbon era. Born in Almolonga, Puebla (near Xalapa), as José Vasconcelos to slave parents brought from the Congo, his early life remains unknown, especially how he learned to read and write and how he secured his freedom. He developed a strong relationship with the Jesuits, perhaps as a lay brother, and that may explain his learning. He was alleged to have said in verse that if he'd been given the chance to study, he would have been the equal of the Jesuit savant Samudio. In the capital city, he earned a living by his wits, composing limericks, winning verbal duels, and surviving linguistic snares prepared to trap him in blasphemous or traitorous declarations. His wit made him supremely popular; his many verses had a touch of satire on politics and the Spaniards that skirted blasphemy.[12] As a confirmed bachelor, he argued that marriage offered a man nothing but a wife who would only cause worry and jealousy. In one of his triumphs, he rhymed the phrase "your hairs hang from" that had eluded even sor Juana Inés de la Cruz. Although he died in 1760, his reputation and poems remained well known, and his great popularity had an impact on popular culture. For example, the humorist, novelist, and publisher of almanacs José Joaquín Fernández de Lizardi often used epigraphs that quoted El Negrito, and Lizardi included references to him in his novel *El Periquillo Sarniento* (*The Mangy Parrot*). Rival publisher Simón Blanquel, beginning in 1860, included anecdotes about El Negrito in each year's almanac, with actual or apocryphal poetry and witticisms. During the same decade, puppeteer Soledad Aycardo, known as don Chole, had a small theater in the capital city's Alameda, where he staged plays that included El Negrito Poeta. Throughout the nineteenth century, the vendors in the archways in Puebla sold hand puppets of El Negrito Poeta.[13]

The poet's popularity in history and folklore probably extended to the puppet. Nevertheless, at first glance, El Negrito appeared an unlikely and curious champion in the land of great indigenous cultures and the nation of the so-called cosmic race forged from the mixing of American and European peoples. Two explanations obtain: first, the drama demonstrated that ethnicity counted less than clothes and behavior. El Negrito dressed as the quintessential Mexican, spoke like the quintessential Mexican, and acted like the quintessential Mexican, so he made his pigmentation irrelevant. This puppet implied that the opportunity existed for individuals to mold their identities, rather than live out the condition in which they were born. It represented the possibilities offered by liberalism, especially the opportunities and obligations faced by each person. El Negrito, with the Virgin's help, defeated the French. The marionette showed what one person with initiative, daring, and courage could do. A second factor bears on the situation. By accepting El Negrito, the audience rejected a European symbol for the Mexican people; they rejected the Mestizo, the living product of European subjugation of the indigenous peoples; they rejected an indigenous figure, because Benito Juárez had become the Indian symbol of the nation, leaving no political space for another[14]; they rejected, we should note, a woman because of mid-century gender views. El Negrito, in the circumstances of the time, offered the significant alternative to other ethnic choices.

In identifying El Negrito as the personification of the people, the audiences chose a parodic symbol with racial overtones. He can be compared to another black puppet with a completely different character, who appeared at roughly the same time in English theater. The British puppet lacked the power of speech and could only mutter "shalla-balla." In 1836, the character became known as Jim Crow, after the popular song sung by Thomas Rice, an English minstrel.[15] On the contrary, the Mexican marionette spoke eloquently and acted bravely. Puppeteers often indicate class or social importance by the size of the puppets, and El Negrito always appeared equal in size to other puppets, indicating that he was a serious and significant actor in the national culture.

Implicit also in El Negrito's confrontation with the French was an allusion to the Haitian rebellion led by Toussaint Louverture, in which this independence leader had successfully driven French troops from what became the island nation of Haiti. The uprising of slave and free blacks had overwhelmed the French and provoked the fear of similar revolts among European colonizers through the region.[16] The Haitian rebellion had signaled the end of the French colonial empire in the Americas that the French troops had arrived in Mexico in the 1860s to repair. El Negrito, by his presence, alluded to this previous, humiliating defeat.

Less apparent allusions mocked Maximilian's international policies that contained racist characteristics. The emperor extended diplomatic recognition to the Confederate States of America, fighting to preserve slavery, and, after the United States won its Civil War, he permitted migration by Confederates with their slaves to Mexico. Mexicans knew well the issues, because they had legislated the abolition of their slaves in 1827. During the years just prior to the French occupation, puppets regularly performed another drama that had allusions to the issues of the U.S. Civil War, *La cabaña de Tom, o La esclavitud de los negros*.[17] As the Union troops defeated the Confederates in the United States, El Negrito symbolized the prospective defeat for Maximilian.

El Negrito represented Jarocho culture, with its liberal traditions in Veracruz. His dress, recognized as a charro costume, came from the Jarochos, especially the region's cowboys, who were often Afro-Mexican. Veracruz state had Mexico's largest percentage of Afro-Mexicans in its population, the largest real number, and, at independence, perhaps the largest number of free blacks in the Americas.[18] They had an indelible impact on Jarocho culture in both cattle raising and plantation agriculture, and in popular activities, including music and dance. Even without the Jarocho clothing, the audience associated El Negrito with coastal Veracruz. Still today a residual expression of the importance of the Afro-Mexican population appears during Carnaval in Veracruz with the large-scale figure (a puppet!) of El Negrito de Batáy; and in the Ballet Folklórico de

México, Amalía Hernández included the dance of this same character with Cuban roots with its specific music.

As a representative of Veracruz, El Negrito reminded some audience members that when the new emperor and empress arrived by ship in Veracruz, they received a silent reception. The audience no doubt relished the way residents of the port had insulted Maximilian and Carlota as they remained inside their houses, with the doors and windows closed to the French-imposed monarchs. Any verbal or visible reference to Veracruz recalled this act of defiant disrespect.

Moreover, in accepting El Negrito, the people in the audience acclaimed him as their champion. Thus he represented the typical community figure called the cacique, or the local *valiente*, often identified by outsiders as a social bandit,[19] who appeared in broadsheets and games of lotería de figuras. This protector and spokesperson represented the community's shared values, challenges, goals, and rural roots, and most often was not a politician or bureaucrat, but an individual known for wit, strength, and courage. Generally, these valientes, or local heroes, held few political offices or party affiliations, but like the militiamen of the era, they served their community.

Nevertheless, as an Afro-Mexican, El Negrito continued to cause disquiet. Reflecting the typical Mexican discomfort with ethnicity, especially questions of pigmentation, the puppeteers, newspaper reporters, and recorded audience reaction always referred to the black puppet in the diminutive, never as El Negro, which would leave no doubt about the character as a black adult. Rather the diminutive form made ambiguous the skin color (perhaps, a little black) and projected a certain patronizing attitude at the same time that the term expressed endearment. These contradictory attitudes remain embedded in the culture and became news in 2005 through the statements of President Vicente Fox and the release of a postage stamp honoring the 1940s mischievous black comic-book hero, Memín Pinguín, whose features and antics were called racist by U.S. civil rights groups. President George W. Bush declared the stamps offensive, with "no place in today's world," and civil rights leader Rev. Jesse Jackson wanted the Mexican government to remove them from circulation. Sixto Valencia, the Memín cartoonist, declared, "I drew him without intending to offend anyone." Some Mexicans agreed the stamps were insensitive, but many others attacked the United States for hypocrisy in its treatment of blacks in the past and of Mexican illegal immigrants today. Certainly, a multitude of convictions and stereotypes were stirred up by this Afro-Mexican puppet with each performance.[20]

Throughout the play, the green, white, and red national flag, or the "tri" for *tricolor*, symbolized liberal national government in Mexico City. The paradox of liberalism—increased individual freedoms under increased centralized political control—comes across clearly in the flag's symbolism. Its colors come from the banner of San Hipólito, initially the patron saint of the city of Mexico. The national image of the eagle, snake, and nopal had served as the allegorical expression for the founding of Tenochtitlán, the capital of the Aztec Empire.[21] These were symbols for the centralization of the nation under Mexico City—exactly what the liberals of Benito Juárez, after driving out the French, wanted to accomplish.

El Negrito's actions with the flag in the second act of the play recalled a fundamental legend of national resistance. The legend of the Niños Héroes, the boy heroes, told the story of the brave cadets who defended the fort of Chapultepec against the U.S. Marines during the U.S.–Mexican war. When the battle was clearly lost, the last six cadets, rather than surrender, took the flag and went to the highest parapet, where Juan Escutía wrapped himself in the banner and the six plunged to their deaths.[22] During the play, when El Negrito took the national banner to the highest spot in the fort, it recalled for the audience this widely repeated story of national heroism.

At this point in the play, there was a break in the action, in which El Negrito and the Virgin of Guadalupe offered the audience another fundamental cultural tableau. The image of El Negrito on his knees before the Virgin recalled hundreds of church altar screens, prayer cards, and religious paintings representing Mexico's most popular legend of the appearance of the Virgin of Guadalupe to San Juan Diego. Moreover, the appeal to the Virgin referred to plays, dances, and puppet shows used to justify the conquest and the evangelization of Mexico. The appearance of the Virgin, in one advocation or another, had defeated the enemy; for example, she had appeared to

scatter the Moors at Granada, the final battle of the 700-year recon-
quista in 1492. Moreover, the appeal to the Virgin for assistance forms
one of the most pervasive of narratives in Spanish literature. Gonzalo
de Berceo, one of the first Spanish authors to write in the vernacular,
composed *Milagros de Nuestra Señora* sometime between 1246 and
1252, and it was often performed with puppets. From that time, the
narration has remained the same: after suffering a grave injustice, or
a terrible wrong, the victim appeals to the Virgin, who reverses the
situation.[23] From early in the colonial period, the friars used stories,
dances, and dramas that demonstrated the Spanish success based on
the intercession of the Virgin, an appeal to Santiago, the help of San
Hipólito (the Spanish conquered Mexico City on his day), or some
other miraculous assistance.[24] The scene reminded audiences that
Mexicans, in this case El Negrito, could appeal to their Virgin and
receive her assistance. In doing so, the puppets offered nothing new,
but an embellishment to the stories of intervention by God, the help
of the Virgin, or the saints, that formed the basic structure of much of
local, informal, unofficial community histories with which all of the
members were familiar.[25]

The Virgin of Guadalupe in the play merged local or vernacular
religion and nationalism. An appeal to the Virgin of Guadalupe
makes a connection between El Negrito and Padre Hidalgo, between
the struggle against the French and the struggle for independence.
An appeal to the Virgin demonstrated the old saying, "Sixty percent
of all Mexicans are Catholic; 95 percent of all Mexicans believe in the
Virgin of Guadalupe." In other words, liberals in their struggle against
the official, hierarchical Roman Catholic Church and its pervasive
institutional presence in everyday life did not give up their personal
devotion to the Virgin of Guadalupe. Of course, we should also note
that the virgin in this advocation of Guadalupe appears clearly as a
Mexican and not as a European personage.

This melodrama considers the practice of *curanderismo*, that is,
the use of local curers who perform folk medicine. An allusion appears in El Negrito's use of prayer in an appeal to Guadalupe to cure
the Mexican body politic of the French sickness. This appeal brought
the Virgin with a group of archangels, and, most assuredly, one of

them was San Miguel, the conqueror of the devil and evil. The French occupation was the illness of the Mexican civil society; the French disease—or syphilis—was the malady of unfortunate individuals, in this case of the Mexican nation. San Miguel, one of the archangels who descended with the Virgin of Guadalupe, is one of the principal saintly figures in expelling evil and defeating the devil. The suggestion of French illness made a veiled but effective comment on rumors throughout the country about the emperor. Gossip widely reported that Maximilian suffered from syphilis, thus accounting for the fact that he and Carlota had no children and explaining why they had separate bedrooms. The absence of an heir resulted in the imperial couple adopting the grandson of Emperor Agustín de Iturbide during their brief reign.

Besides these allusions, the play contains a direct reference to the practice of curanderismo in the verse proclaimed by El Negrito as a conclusion. He declared, "What a scare" Santa Anna gave to the French admiral. What he said exactly was "What a *susto*" Santa Anna gave to the admiral. A *susto* is much more than a scare. It describes a condition that combines deep sadness, appetite loss, and fitful sleep. This experience causes the soul to be separated from the body. It might be noted that Freud identified a connection between loss, bereavement, and depression. Anthropologist John M. Ingham found in the town of Tlayacapan, Morelos, that about two-thirds of all susto cases involve children. The typical child suffering from fright illness was a boy, timid, melancholic, and overprotected by a mother who centered her life in her children. The prospective victim of the susto was thus a mama's boy, likely later in life to be dominated by his wife. In other words a *mandelón*, or, in English, a man tied to his wife's apron strings. The admiral who suffered a susto clearly appeared as a *tímido*, a timid or cowardly person. The only cure for susto was by a folk healing, called variously a *limpio*, an *agua de espanto*, an *escapulario*, a *poner la sombra*, or *evangelios*. The last calls on the help of San Miguel to expel the evil and return the soul to the body.[26] El Negrito, in the play, accused the French admiral of being a mama's boy or intimidated by his wife, certainly not a real man. Moreover, for all the French science and medicine, the only cure for his condition was folk healing practices. In this way, as the puppet saved Mexico, he made a statement about the efficacy of local knowledge versus imposed science,[27] about Mexican cultural experience versus the European imposed civilization brought by the French and their imported emperor.

Finally, the puppets in the play made a clear statement of beliefs about right and wrong, about good and evil. Conquest, greed, and imperialism were wrong; community, religion, and individuals with ethnic and regional diversity were right. This axiomatic binary expressed in this Manichaean form expressed a fundamental view of romantic nationalism,[28] and it became one of the foundations of the emerging national identity

This puppet drama provides a beginning point for the discussion that follows of how people, after independence in 1821, began to think of themselves as Mexican and what they meant when they referred to *la república*, or *mi patria*, or *mi tierra*. We know that when they said *México*, then as now, they meant Mexico City.[29] What Mexicans thought about their identity grew from a host of official, institutional, informal, and familial forms that taught values and fashioned nationalism in the nineteenth century. Museums, for example, served as major institutions for teaching, in an informal, visual way, national history.[30]

Fiestas, almanacs, popular art, and puppet theater—each of these offers a point of entrance for understanding the creative, satisfying, and fundamental character of national popular memories. Both civil and religious elites attempted to use officially sponsored celebrations for didactic purposes. While officials presented the public with numerous civic and church displays, each festival had a popular character as well that included ephemeral art and artisanry, and customary practices. The civic and religious fiestas included floats, arches, and other ephemeral paraphernalia.[31] Three other unofficial media served an important, perhaps more significant, role in the shaping of popular memories in the nineteenth century. These were cheap almanacs, called *calendarios* for much of the century; children's games, especially lotería de figuras and *juego de la oca*, and other forms of popular art; and itinerant puppet theater. These forms also served a didactic purpose, usually only incidental to the entertainment they offered. In these cases, the almanacs, games, and popular public performances, in particular puppet theater—each relied on mnemonic devices that recreated specific accounts of the past. These images formed the improvisational lexicon used in discussing the popular, local versions of the nation and its citizens.[32]

Each of these forms served as reference points of memory and identity. During fiestas, the images and other ephemeral items such as food, gifts, and mementos created individual memories associated with the celebration. The *troqueles*, or wooden tortilla presses, for example, used to make multicolored tortillas embossed with the national seal, the Virgin of Guadalupe, or some other patriotic symbol, were common in the *bajío*. Of course, each fiesta had toys or items associated with it. Holiday practices associated with the particular location that often included memorials, statues, monuments, and relics, and even the buildings and neighborhoods that form the destinations and the stages for the celebrations all served as mnemonic devices for the memories of ordinary people. Independence Day, for example, during the nineteenth century celebrated Padre Miguel Hidalgo, and tied the struggle for independence to sacrifice by arranging for the appearance of veterans of this struggle and later of other national struggles.[33] Almanacs identified the dates for all the significant events and generally provided explanations of meanings for the holidays, monuments, and practices.[34] The games repeated in symbols the popular story of the passion of Christ,[35] the icons of great patriots, and the stereotypes of society. The puppets performed the most common human conflicts and expressed the most human concerns, such as domestic life, everyday faith, erotic interests, social criticism, self-caricature, picaresque humor, and adventurous spirit.[36] They acted out the stories of day-to-day life and ordinary people with their problems involving family, work, politics, *caciques*, and romance.[37] Taken together these activities provided the common popular sources for the formation in the nineteenth century of popular national identity.

CHAPTER 2

# Tightly Knotted Nodes of Possibility

### Almanacs and Lotería

*When you look back at your life, you discover, or you invent, points in time that seem to be tightly knotted nodes of possibility. Out of the seemingly endless options that present themselves in a given situation, you choose one in particular, and your life and the lives of those around you start moving relentlessly toward a particular outcome.*

—Walter Satterthwait[1]

Independence in 1821 meant little at first. The distant Spanish monarch, Ferdinand VII, no longer ruled, but the king had meant next to nothing in practical ways since 1808. The incessant fighting ended in 1821, but the loyalty of different armies to either royalist or patriotic causes had been mostly in name only since 1815. Commanders from both sides now cooperated and took charge of the new nation. Together they devised plans to preserve some parts and change others of the colonial legacy. They issued decrees that declared that the Viceroyalty of New Spain had become the Empire of Mexico, and made laws that replaced the colonial society arranged by family, ethnic, and occupational prestige with one people called Americans. Little agreement existed on these ambitious pronouncements, which were read aloud in villages across the country; soon the former colony split into a dozen political arrangements and separate nations, and although official documents ignored ethnic designations, the old social divisions endured. Contradictions abounded, perhaps best illustrated in the national ambitions of republican Father Miguel Hidalgo and the monarchical General Agustín Iturbide, the two men who initiated and completed the struggle, and who had nothing in common beyond a desire for independence. The new leaders thus failed on both counts—to establish by mandate both a new regime and one people—and their goals remained the essential stakes for much of the nineteenth century: to create a workable national government and to engender a common national identity.

Neither goal would be accomplished by the ambitious utopian decrees issued by government officials or by cherished popular sentiments held by the residents in their local communities. Each required identifying and fostering the political and social practices that together best expressed what was ideally and recognizably Mexican. During the first decades after independence, leaders repeatedly planned and failed at creating a new national government, and these same leaders sporadically and unsuccessfully attempted molding a national identity.

The leaders of the kaleidoscopic governments, during the first four decades after independence, sought inspiration for their political organization and their national identity in various familiar models, especially the Spanish Constitution of 1812. Old leaders with new duties formulated ideas of national identity in a more or less official campaign along two lines: (1) Most politicians and planners turned to the definition of a people based on Spanish language, Catholic religion, geographic origin, and historic heritage; (2) but a few, constituting for the most part the small, nascent scientific community, turned for their plans to the new discipline called social mathematics. Both groups looked to Alexander von Humboldt's well-known treatise on New Spain,[2] while the scientifically curious also found inspiration in the work of the Parisian astronomer Adolphe Quetelet, who promoted what he called social physics.

Quetelet's application of mathematics to society came in the 1820s, with special interest in compilations of the frequency of crime, disease, and illiteracy. He created tables of deviations from the normal or typical behavior as he searched for natural laws that governed individuals. In creating normative statistics, he identified individual characteristics and tabulated them, not to describe universal human nature, but to establish the national type. He introduced, in this way, a dramatic change in thinking about nationalities—from the idea of races (for example, the Spanish race) to national types. The former rested on language, religion, history, and geographic origin, and the latter emerged from the society's physical and behavioral characteristics. This innovation, called social mathematics, invoked new conceptions of society based on the national type, the human expression of national identity, and suggested social reform. From these tables, he argued that government officials could determine the kind of society that existed, then devise laws that would modify individual behavior to achieve the society they wanted.

Mexicans trained in science and mathematics soon became familiar with Quetelet's tables of deviation for Paris as an introduction to normative statistics. A few Mexicans, who had already compiled some population tables, organized their efforts to collect and publish a statistical portrait of their country. They created the National Institute of Geography and Statistics in the 1833, which brought together a diverse group of individuals interested in national characteristics. It included politicians hoping to define the people, scientists wanting to manipulate statistical tables to improve the people, and military officers seeking knowledge of both the countryside and the population to prepare the defense of the nation.

These individuals formed a community until 1848 that collected and published statistical tables. Their formulation of statistical categories and identification of deviant behavior represented the conception of national identity based on collective individual physical and moral features. This differed dramatically from the broad description of a community based on religion and language. This elite formulation was optimistic in its analysis of the people and positive in its predictions for the future. This confidence collapsed in the general malaise that swept over national leaders and smothered national optimism following the disastrous war with the United States (1846–1848).[3] Nevertheless, many of these characteristics, no longer advocated by officials, remained in existence, even if they lay dormant. Rather, other individuals from different levels of society, as popular entertainments revealed, picked them up and promoted them.

In the years from the beginning of the struggle for independence to the end of the U.S.–Mexican War (1810–1848), popular forms of identity emerged and continued to develop across the nineteenth century. These grassroots expressions of identification with the new nation reflected both a legal initiative and a moral economy. The legal impetus to a growing sense of community came in the Spanish 1812 constitution that directed all settlements of 1,000 persons or more to arrange formal organization as municipalities. Municipal status gave communities control over local lands, taxes, and militia service. Local community vitality received additional encouragement, because the struggle for independence over the course of the decade of violence had as one major effect the decentralization of authority. This made the municipality the most vital level of administration. Over the course of the succeeding decades, especially during the disastrous 1840s, when Mexicans experienced the U.S. invasion and occupation, localities developed new community-held sets of values that have been labeled folk liberalism.[4]

These grassroots liberal attitudes emerged from the community members' understanding of their rights, in other words, the moral economy of the municipality based on constitutional provisions and community contributions to the nation.[5] This moral economy, the basis of folk liberalism,[6] had a specific, community character that could not be transferred to another village or town.[7] The community's rights, its sacrifices, such as the loss of militiamen fighting against foreign invaders, and its struggles to protect communal lands and to resist outside taxes were particular to each community. Members of different communities might think of themselves as having common characteristics, but at first they did not necessarily identity with other Mexicans, even though many were curious about their fellow citizens, and about their new nation.

In response to this interest, a popular sense of geography took shape that included the landscape of specific physical features and the population of distinctive peoples. Mexicans recognized their quintessential natural feature represented in the twin volcanoes Popocatepetl and Ixtaccihuatl that dominated the capital city and the central valley. Images of these volcanoes appeared everywhere, announcing to travelers that they were arriving at the country's center, orienting residents of the city moving around town, and representing the country to all Mexicans, seeing them or their representations. Especially striking is a nineteenth-century painting of Monterrey, Nuevo León, actually fitted against the striking mountain known as the Saddle, but as painted the Saddle is overshadowed by Popo and Ixta. Thus, Monterrey, as presented by one painter, marked its identity as part of Mexico. Moreover, the legends surrounding the volcanoes penetrated the popular knowledge of the nation's peoples. Popo and Ixta, in folklore, were an indigenous lord and his sleeping lady; in another version, Ixtaccihuatl had died following a false report that her suitor Popocatepetl had died in battle. Pictures of these two persons in an astonishing array of garments—Romanesque with feathers, idealized Aztec in togas, semi-European, and indigenous raiment—became commonplace.

Along with the volcanoes, maps portrayed an abstract of the nation's various physical features. The diverse landscape echoed the human diversity presented in this popular geography. The population comprised an array of individuals, who were all Mexicans. This became the popular essence of performances and folk art, to display diversity without abandoning the fundamental Mexican qualities of the people. As the identification of national characteristics emerged, the popular geography concerned regional characteristics. Regionalism across the nation built on most of the same everyday attributes, but in different mixtures in different places that appeared as local or vernacular culture. This collage of national and local community symbols formed a collective memory that appeared most explicitly in folk art and fiestas.[8]

Maps, like symbolic physical features and regional individuals, portrayed Mexico with diversity as the salient attribute. During the late colonial period, Enlightenment practicality inspired Bourbon bureaucrats to produce new maps furnishing useful information. Two late-eighteenth-century examples were prepared specifically for clerical travelers, offering itinerant priests information on altitude (as symptomatic of climatic conditions) and language (as expressions of ethnicity). These sketches lacked distance scales or physical features, indicating instead the connecting communities from the capital city center. These two maps were "El Plano con indicaciones linguísticcas. Siglo XVIII. El Valle de México, Michoacán, Guadalajara, Río Verde" and "El Mapa geográfico del arzobispado de México." José Antonio Alzate drew the latter in 1772. Cartography entered a new era of representation with the map of New Spain produced in 1807 under the direction of Alexander von Humboldt. Nevertheless, only in 1856 did Manuel Siliceo, the secretary of development (Fomento), organize a commission to publish an "atlas nacional." Moreover, the commission, which included José Fernando Ramírez, Manuel Orozco y Berra, and Francisco Díaz Covarrubías, among others, never completed its work, although Orozco y Berra did direct the preparation of a map. Later, in the nineteenth century, Antonio García Cubas became the nation's most important cartographer, known especially for his map, based on the 1807 Humboldt map, of the central valley.[9]

Even with early maps and accepted symbols, during the first decades after independence the sense of nationalism remained provisional. Provisional, first of all, because of the blurred character of the nation's boundaries. In both the north and south, hazy borders existed: Where did the United States and Mexico meet? In the south, did the state of Chiapas form part of Mexico or Guatemala? And in southern Yucatán where did the borders separate the overlapping British, Guatemalan, and Mexican claims, all of which ignored the unified Maya culture of the divided region? The Maya who refused to bend to Mexican culture in the southern peninsula and the various nomadic peoples who ignored Mexicans in the northern marches added to the provisional character of the nation and nationalism. This question of borders had political significance, and both cultural and social dimensions as Mexicans believed the boundaries divided their civilized society from the barbarians beyond. Thus, borders formed the critical framework for the popular geography that provided an essential part of national identity.

National officials succeeded in marking the boundaries only in the latter part of the century. The Porfirian regime (1876–1911), with its companies of army surveyors, largely fixed borders, boundaries, and names of locations. At the same time, the preeminent Porfirian artist, José María Velasco, painted landscapes extraordinary for their eloquence in the incorporation of national features. Both the survey plats and the Velasco landscapes attempted to create a national standard and replace the multiple popular versions with an official geography.[10]

Moreover, the provisional nature of the national regime that teetered between republic and monarchy left Mexicans uncertain whether they were citizens or subjects. The society also had a conditional character, despite the prohibition against using noble titles and efforts to reduce corporate "fueros" or legal privileges for high churchmen, military officers, and city councilors. Despite decrees, constitutions, and laws, Mexicans remained divided by geographic origin, ethnicity, occupation, and family.

Individuals had a major role in the shaping of early nationalism. Mexicans turned to outstanding men and women as metonyms or, perhaps better said, as synecdoches for their community. Recognition of these individuals was no simple recourse to great men or great women as the makers of history, but an effort to recover the ties of community that existed between leaders and followers. As a result, different individuals served as heroes of different communities. Who personified independence? Hidalgo? Or Iturbide? Who expressed the politics of the nation? Alemán, Gómez Farías, or Santa Anna?

## Almanacs

Many of these individuals, along with the salient geographic features, appeared in the so-called *calendarios*, or almanacs. As a source for popular or local history and collective memory, these cheap, annual publications had a significant role.[11] They expressed a great deal of common knowledge. They first appeared in the colonial era with information on Holy Days of Obligation, the days of fasting and other days with required attendance at the mass. These feast days had special indications for Indians and non-Indians. The custom of indicating holy days by ethnicity continued until the 1880s. Almanacs also contained accounts of the lives of the saints and martyrs, and frequently had an image of each individual. Of course, they related the story of the Virgin of Guadalupe and showed her image. Besides religious themes, the colonial calendars presented information on the stars—the astral knowledge used in astronomy and astrology. At the beginning of the nineteenth century, almanacs acquired a political character when they published the images of King Fernando VII and Queen María Isabel. These images joined those of popular saints and the Virgin of Guadalupe in most almanacs. For the rest of the nineteenth century it was customary to print the images of political leaders. Because of this practice, today we know something about the appearance of political leaders, such as Hidalgo, Morelos, Juárez, and others, before the introduction of photography.

As the colonial era ended, two publishers changed the contents of almanacs. These new volumes greatly affected the emerging popular memory. The two new publishers were José Joaquin Fernández Lizardi and José Mariano Ramírez Hermosa. Lizardi added fables and poems to his almanacs, and he decided to include illustrations by José María Torreblanca. One of the most popular characters drawn by Torreblanca was El Mono Vano, the vain monkey, as a political caricature.[12] Lizardi also included images, that is, engravings, of the heroes of the Wars of Independence, such as Padre Hidalgo, and other political leaders. He published what he identified as the symbols of liberty, independence, and the nation, and provided a caption that explained the significance of each image and allegory. In this way, Lizardi taught the public primary lessons of civics.

José Mariano Ramírez Hermosa, after 1822, used his almanacs to introduce new patriotic and scientific ideas. He combined the historical chronology of the church and state. He began his chronology with precise dates for the creation of the world, followed by the time of the Great Flood, and the landing of Noah's ark. He included the lives of the saints and the origin of popular devotions such as the Virgin of Guadalupe. Moreover, he added the history of the Aztecs, again with dates for such events as the election of Moctezuma and the fall of the Aztec Empire. He reported the history of the Spaniards in New Spain and the events and individuals of the independence movement.

Soon another publisher appeared. Mariano Galván Rivera began publishing almanacs in 1826 and quickly surpassed his competitors in the business. His became well-known as the *calendarios galvanescos*, still in existence today. One historian spoke about their distribution and significance when he said that the almanac became the "vehicle of culture even in the most remote regions of the country." These almanacs contained articles concerning religion, science, literature, and history. All of the Galván almanacs had numerous sections: (1) reporting the popular events that occurred on different days—called *los efermérides*; (2) identifying politicians; (3) portraying ecclesiastical authorities; (4) naming military leaders; and (5) describing the commercial class. The latter, according to Galván, had become a major force improving life in the principal cities. These volumes also had a didactic character. The Galván and other almanacs, for example, taught geography, providing information on the distances between places, offering descriptions of cities, and identifying cultural centers, such as information on schools and fencing masters.

Galván attempted to publish almanacs for special markets. He offered, for example, almanacs for women. His *calendario de las señoritas mejicanas* appeared in the years 1838–1841 and again in 1843. These calendars, in reality, were books of some 300 pages. Because few bought them, this enterprise failed. He tried another idea, calendars for common people that were smaller and cheaper, even though the regular calendars cost only a few *reales*. These almanacs had two parts. One section provided a list of days with political notices—the history of pronouncements, a section that might be called "today in history" for each date (los efemérides) that included events of great interest, such as the date of the burial of the popular singer Enriqueta Sontag, the procession in supplication against the cholera epidemic, and the public execution of infamous criminals. The second portion of the almanac offered a religious section that contained a history of churches and their famous bells, biographies of the popes, and notices of Mexican girls who had made their first communions in Rome.

Many other publishers issued almanacs in the first fifty years after independence and experimented with ways to increase sales of their publications. Some also printed broadsheets with popular songs, devotional images, and invitation and congratulation cards; most included innovations to make the volumes more popular. Besides increasing sales, some of the publishers also had the goal, as one said, of "reforming the conventional customs through the virtuous example of heroic individuals."[13] José Joaquín Fernández Lizardí, in both his novels and his almanacs, attempted to promote what he understood to be good moral behavior. Mariano Galván in 1829 became the first to include statistical tables in his almanacs. These represented the expression of national identity and of optimism in the nation. Francisco Ortega in his almanac of 1836, for example, expressed his confidence in reason and science, political toleration, and material progress. One of the new elements in the almanacs came in 1843 with the introduction of lithographs. These engravings were illustrations with a romantic, sweet, and often melodramatic character. These kinds of pictures continued as part of calendars up to the present day. In 1852, political cartoons appeared in the almanacs for the first time. These had been featured earlier in broadsheets and in periodicals such as *El Calavera*.

For this popular form of communication, sales remained the crucial issue. Simón Blanquel, who used the pen name El Pícaro, "the rogue," sold his almanacs from his shop in the capital city. In addition, each year he traveled to the great fairs at San Juan de los Lagos and throughout the Bajío, and to others even in the far north, such as Saltillo. He also regularly visited pilgrimage sites to peddle his books. Another major way of selling them was by the street vendors of miscellaneous goods. These salespeople sold a variety of everyday items and always carried a few almanacs. When they sold them, they would return to the publisher for two or three more.

Blanquel, in an effort to increase sales, developed a line of almanacs for the middle class. Three of these became well known: *El calendario mágico de suertes*, *El calendario de las profecías de la Madre Matiana*, and *El calendario de rústica Bertoldo*. As the titles reveal, he developed these almanacs so that they intersected with popular interests and well-known characters. The almanacs produced for women and domestics after 1850 frequently included recipes and additional useful information for housewives. He appealed to the long-standing literary and fictional tradition of Bertoldo, the hero and buffoon of popular eighteenth-century translations of the seventeenth-century Italian novel.[14] In another of these almanacs, he tried to capture the widespread interest in prophecies of the nation's future.[15] In the nineteenth century, perhaps the most famous prophet was Madre Matiana, supposedly an eighteenth-century domestic in various Jeronymite convents who had visions in which she spoke to the Virgin. According to various accounts, the Virgin Mary had taken Madre Matiana to visit hell to witness the cause of God's impending wrath. Matiana saw a meeting of the devil with his demons, where they composed constitutions and legal codes to circulate on earth. According to pamphlets and almanacs, Madre Matiana then correctly predicted, among various riots and political upheavals, the Wars of Independence and the foreign invasion of Mexico (understood to mean the U.S.–Mexican war) as God's response to the political documents associated with republicans and the "dragons of the apron," that is, the Freemasons. She had emerged as a people's prophet par excellence by the mid-nineteenth century, and her prophecies circulated widely across the country. By 1861, a pamphlet claiming to contain her original predictions went through numerous editions, and by the last years of the century, chapbooks with her prophecies were sold in various religious venues, including distant Oaxaca at the fairs related to the pilgrimage to the Virgin of Juquila. These resurrected prophecies seem clearly related to the Liberal Revolution of Ayutla, the Wars of Reform, and the French intervention as the principal campaigns to separate church and state and to establish a secular society.[16] The almanacs captured the strain of popular apprehension at the same time they celebrated the collective experiences that created national identity.

At the end of the 1870s and the beginning of the 1880s, calendars adopted their modern form, and the annual handbooks became almanacs. Moreover, the latter began to include photographs that represented the national physical reality. These photographs included the national cathedral, the Guardiola Plaza, and the national museum; each of the three locations served as a repository of material cultural that represented the national identity.

Almanacs, whether they were short-lived like the *calendarios por mexicanitas* or more enduring like the *calendarios galvanescos*, stored everyday history, folklore, and gossip, and had an influence on the popular memory and the formation of national identity. First, the almanacs provided readers, or those who heard them read aloud, with a strong sense of place, that is to say, a description of the nation's immense size and its physical wonders. Examples included the volcanoes Popo, Ixta, and Orizaba and the waterfalls at Tula. The almanacs provided information on the size of the country as it provided the distances between cities and the maps of the states and cities such as México, Guadalajara, and Veracruz. Later almanacs featured photographs of national scenes that illustrated Mexico's physical character and beauty.[17] Second, the almanac provided knowledge that Mexico was a land of impressive architecture from the pre-columbian, colonial, and independent eras. The almanacs included as examples some discussion of Aztec relics, the fortress of San Juan de Úlua, the National Cathedral and other colonial churches, and *El caballito*. Third, the publishers offered information on patriotic symbols; the creation of the national flag and that of the national seal are two examples.[18] Others explained the national icons of the eagle and Lady Liberty.[19]

This is one of the ways that the almanacs taught civics. Leandro J. Valdés, for example, in his second *Calendario de la democracia dedicado al pueblo mexicano* (Calendar of Democracy Dedicated to the Mexican People), for the year 1852, featured a civic catechism. It consisted of questions and answers for readers to memorize; in part, it read:

> What is political liberty?
> The common independence;
> Power exercised with violence not only is an injustice, it is a sacrilege.
> What is authority and what is domination?
> The first commands for the good of all,
> the second is absolutism;
> the first keeps us from danger; the
> second degrades us.[20]

Besides providing explanations of politics, the publishers of the almanacs also judged politicians. For example, the almanac editor Abraham López said that the nation's problems came from the self-importance that each politician adopted. He said that each state governor thought of himself as more important than a king. López concluded, "Cada gobernador se cree igual a un bajá de tres colas. No obedece leyes ni las ordenes que dimanen del centro"; that is, "each governor believes he is equal to a pasha with three tails. He does not obey laws or orders that come from the central government." Moreover, in various almanacs, editors took care to explicate the difference between the rights of human beings and the rights of citizens. According to one, every individual had the right to live free, with security and protection of life and home; the citizen had these rights, and the additional rights to own property, to vote in the election of government officials, and to carry arms.[21]

The almanacs, in the effort by the publishers to increase their popularity and therefore their sales, often also offered a catalog of common, often entertaining, knowledge. Thus, the prophecies of Madre Matiana had a broad following that continued into the twentieth century. The everyday information encapsulated in the almanacs reflected, and ran parallel to, the general popular, unofficial narratives that were often incorporated into the popular board game la lotería de figuras.

## Lottery Cards

While the almanacs presented local information and encouraged civic participation, folk art often offered a popular history of society, identifying individuals who had an important role in the community, displaying activities of everyday life, recalling events and holidays with special meaning in the locality, and identifying the attributes of vernacular religion. This expression of the collective popular memory can appear in various forms, especially in untrained art, often described as artisanal painting, or sculpting in either ceramic or wood, and in the products, foods, dances, and other ephemera of annual celebrations. *Arte naïf*, or naive art, represents daily life through the achievements, struggles, romances, and failures of the artist's community. In Guatemala, for example, Óscar Eduardo Perén from Comalapa, whose paintings appear in the UNESCO–sponsored publication *Arte naïf:*

*Guatemala*,[22] said that he began painting in the 1980s to preserve for future generations the social life and traditions of his community, and later, especially during the military's repression of his countrymen, to conserve the history of Comalapa.[23] The same can be said for much folk or popular art in nineteenth-century Mexico: artisans recorded in paint or pottery the unique history and specific traditions of their communities.

Mexicans, after independence, developed a fascination with the people of their country. A great deal of information about the individuals who made up the society, their community standards, and their popular history appeared in games for children and adults. Lotería de figuras, for example, offered a taxonomy, an index, of the nation's social types, much like the *casta* paintings of the Bourbon period or the *costumbrista* paintings of the late nineteenth century. This impulse to register the members of society resulted in early-nineteenth-century lithographs by foreigners, and more explicitly in such publications as *Los mexicanos pintados por sí mismos*, and such performances as the so-called theater reviews that featured typical urban characters of the capital city. Nevertheless, the most common representation of national types, the folkloric, occupational, and stock characters, came in board games, either juego de la oca or lotería de figuras.

Lotería, or lottery, developed during the colonial period and appeared in two forms after independence. The national lottery, a form of numerical gambling, was initiated in 1769 by colonial officials as the drawing of lots to raise money for various charitable projects, and was reestablished after independence to provide national assistance to social campaigns. Lotería also referred to a board game much like bingo, which used either numbers or, in the more common form, pictures of different people, places, and things typical of daily life. It was played at home and in local fairs. This game, unlike cards used for gambling, which had an ambiguous place in colonial and republic society because it seemed to represent a vice of the poor, fell into the category of *eutrapelia*, a recreation offering rest and relaxation.[24]

This game originated in Italy, probably in Naples, where it was known as *Mercante in Fiera*. From there, this game and others spread to the royal court in France, where they had widespread popularity in the sixteenth century, with the first card game introduced in 1526 and the first lotería game published in 1539. The games moved from Paris to Madrid and the Spanish royal court.[25] Influencing the board game in Spain were the folded papers with illustrations called *aucas*. The sheets, especially popular in Barcelona, offered images with a simple text that told both religious and civic parables in something like early comic books. Even with their blatant educational purposes, they became popular with children, who avidly collected them in the eighteenth and nineteenth centuries. Alonso Remón published the first Spanish guide to games in 1623, entitled *Entretenimientos y juegos honestos y recreaciones cristianas*. Further information about the game's early history comes from a small book, whose second edition appeared in Valencia in 1830, entitled *Nuevo arte de jugar a la lotería. Colección completa de los mejores tratados sobre este juego*. It contains internal evidence that the first printing, a translation from Italian to Spanish, appeared in 1763. The extant second edition contained images, such as "*luna lotérica,*" "*la cábala de Rutilio Bonicasa,*" and "*hesmorfias italianas,*" whose meaning and significance cannot be readily deciphered. The so-called *hesmorfias* or dictionary provided a key to the ninety numbers used in the lottery and their relationship to the figures of the game.

From Madrid, lotería and other games reached colonial Mexico. The former in particular had great popularity both in homes and in fairs celebrating parish patrons, such as El Cristo Negro de San Ramón in Campeche,[26] and it assisted in the evangelization process.[27] Evidence of the game's early appearance in Mexico includes some figures and locations. For example, the image of "don Ferruco in the Alameda" was typically Mexican.[28] Finally, evidence exists that the game was clearly established in Guatemala by the mid-nineteenth century, suggesting, because of trade patterns for Spanish imports from the peninsula to Veracruz to Guatemala, that it had wide popularity in Mexico as well.

Local artists in the nineteenth century usually painted the game cards and boards with local images, including individuals.[29] The standard game set included the cards for the dealer or caller and playing boards. The sets typically had ninety images, although a few had two decks with only fifty-four, with the boards done in five ranks and five columns of images; as many as twenty persons could play.[30] Each card had both a figure and a number, but the numbers had an association with the images only in certain versions of the game. The figures in different sets had different numbers, such as the number on the death figure. Artists often drew the game boards on tin, much like the ex-votos, the popular painted accounts of miracles given in thanks and taken to the parish church, with paper cards for the dealer (fig. 1). A few nineteenth-century examples remain of paper game boards that someone drew by hand to use at home. More detailed were the playing boards embroidered on cloth. These attractive examples of handiwork show imaginative images for the cards that represent the national and social stereotypes.[31] For the fairs in the nineteenth century, dealers used wooden game boards and had wooden pieces to call out the numbers or images. By mid-century, printing companies in both Mexico City and Guadalajara began producing the game boards and cards on heavy paper. Probably companies that manufactured playing cards first printed the lotería cards as well. The popularity of the game was revealed by the decision of the Buen Tono Cigarette Company, and other competitors, such as La Esperanza in Mérida, Yucatán,[32] to give away versions of the game during the 1890s as an advertising promotion.

Lotería had both its greatest popularity and several outstanding promoters of the game in the port of Campeche during the nineteenth century. The images on the game cards featured well-known individuals and locations of the community, and the Campeche version soon appeared throughout the country. Among the most prominent of the game's producers, José María Evia Grignel decided in 1891 to create a special lottery set to promote the sale of cigarettes in the community. The Evia Grignel version of the game featured (and still does today) ninety images that originally appeared in his cigarette packages. Those who collected all ninety received cash prizes. Evia Grignel began to produce game sheets with the ninety pictures always associated with a particular number, such as seventy-two, "the tree of the Noche Triste," and thirty-four, "the republican eagle." This version of the game used markers or chits that players drew from a wire basket or from a cotton bag and called out. Individuals won with five images in a horizontal, vertical, or diagonal line, as well as with designs such as the cross, the

**1.** Lottery games in the nineteenth century offered players the opportunity to tell stories that revealed popular religion, local history, and national identity. *Lotería* game board painted on tin, from the Champion Folk Art Collection, Tucson, Arizona. Photograph by Cheryle Champion.

large cross, or full card. At the same time, Guadalupe Hernández, a silversmith, devised his own version to promote at fairs and in homes. Families of both would later register the images with the patent office and claim to be the inventor of the Campeche version of the game.[33]

Despite the success of the Campeche lotería, the most prominent entrepreneur of the game was Clement Jacques. A French immigrant, Jacques arrived in Mexico City in 1880, and by 1887 had established a thriving business providing corks from forests in Campeche to the bottling industry. He soon diversified his activities into food processing, for which his name is still recognized today. His products included chiles; olives and olive oil; sauces, including mole; beans; fruit juices and jams; and honey. He expanded his cork business to include lumber and other wood products. After some consideration, he also determined it was cheaper to buy a print shop than to contract for labels and advertising. He aimed to expand domestic sales and develop export markets for his bottled foods. With the latter goal in mind, he decided to exhibit his products at several world's fairs. At the exhibitions in Chicago (1893) and St. Louis (1904), he won several gold medals. As a promotion, he printed decks of playing cards to advertise his bottled jalapeños.

Jacques soon found that the printing of playing cards, both for Spanish and for American (poker) games, had become profitable. His decks of cards included several with images that featured his adopted nation, especially the set called "National Cards," featuring Aztec warriors and Spanish conquistadors. This encouraged him to turn to other printing activities to increase sales, and he decided to produce board games, especially lotería. He adopted most of his images from either individuals and places he knew in Campeche or from the Campeche version of the game, just as he adapted many images from Spanish decks of cards in his own. His initial version featured two sets of fifty-two images, called the old and the modern series, sold together. This suggests that he sold the game so it could be played either as the Italian *Mercante in Fiera* (which required two decks of fifty-two cards) or as lotería. As his trademark, he adopted *el gallo*, the cock, the national image of his native France, and under the name Pasatiempo el Gallo he copyrighted the images of his lotería game in

1913. Later, during the 1950s, his company produced a new game set that featured such images as the airplane, the automobile, the telephone, the train, and the television. Today Pasatiempo del Gallo, now located in Querétaro, continues to print playing cards and calendars, uses the paper trimmings for confetti, and manufactures the lotería for both domestic and foreign, especially the U.S., markets.[34]

Other nineteenth-century entrepreneurs produced versions of the game that sometimes used the images on the decks of Spanish playing cards,[35] but with up to ninety images needed for the game, artists soon turned their creativity to images of social stereotypes, well-known individuals, and recognized locations and objects. The individuals featured in the lotería game came from everyday life, reflecting the same persons as those in popular collections of wax figures engaged in such everyday activities as working and cooking, and at weddings and funerals. One collection of twenty figures made of Campeche wax provided an index of work and life in the nineteenth century.[36] This interest in the activities of the ordinary people after mid-century reached the theatrical stage. Dramas featured the same characters who appeared in lotería, most notably in the *Revue of 1869*, first performed January 30, 1870. Probably modeled on the Spanish *La gran vía* that had premiered in Madrid on July 2, 1866, it used the street as the backdrop for the cavalcade of passing individuals.[37] The show featured stock community members such as the lottery ticket salesgirl, the drunk, the arrogant foreigner, the fat politician, the corrupt cop, the stool pigeon, the duplicitous mestizo, and the country bumpkin. This kind of performance with both actors and marionettes quickly became popular, and soon featured performers in regional costumes and regional music.[38] A constant interaction occurred, trading characters back and forth between the stage and the lotería games.

Besides social stereotypes, other images in the lottery games represented the material and domestic culture of everyday life. The humble tools of trades, such as the hammer and the ladder, as well as such domestic animals as the horse, mule, sheep, rooster, and hen have identifiable roles in community life, personal subsistence, and daily activities. Familiar domestic items associated with the family and home life also included the cat, chair, razor, and a variety of fruit. The image of the parish bell—whose sound marked time, gave alarms, signaled sacraments, and indicated life's passages for the community—recalled home and neighbors. Villagers recognized its voice and usually gave it a name. In many ways, the image of the bell served as the metonym for the community and its church.

Many of these homey objects represented vernacular Catholicism as well. Everyday religion included the story of Adam and Eve, with the apple that made sinners of everyone, and the snake, who offered the temptation. All these images often appeared in the game, but if not, certainly the apple and the serpent did. The latter also evoked the national seal with the eagle that devoured the snake and the representation of St. Michael, who defeated the devil who appeared as a snake. The popular story of Noah, the ark, and the Great Flood found its most common representation in the dove that Noah sent to see if the waters had receded, but sometimes cards featured the ark itself. Lotería sets always included the dove. The basket in most sets, for those who wanted a biblical reference, could be used to recall the story of the child Moses being saved from death.

Perhaps more common were images that offered popular versions of the life of Christ, beginning with the Nativity. These images can be seen clearly in the "Advocations of San Gregorio," a key to common images that express popular religion. Folk stories expanded on biblical accounts to provide memorable details, especially for the story of Jesus. Nativity stories, often repeated or built on community *pastorelas*, included the animals, especially the sheep and donkeys, who spoke on Christmas Eve.[39] Miniature nativity scenes, with figures in ivory or wax, appeared in the eighteenth century, becoming increasingly common as family possessions during the nineteenth century. The sets included sheep, hens, horses, bulls, and other animals, and both biblical personages and local individuals, such as washerwomen and water carriers, whimsically added to the scene. Many also featured the characters that appeared in the lotería games. Again, as with many objects and activities of the popular culture, the origin of these nativity sets seems to be Naples. Beyond the Christmas season, home altars that were becoming more popular and more elaborate in the nineteenth century included the same or similar figures.[40] Players of lotería could weave into the game the Christmas story, if they chose.

Popular versions provided embellishments to biblical accounts or provided devices for remembering religious stories. For example, the image of the hand, from this religious perspective, recalled representations of "the right hand of God," "*la mano mágica*," or the "hand of power," which identified Mary, Joseph, Ann, and Joachim, the parents and maternal grandparents of Jesus, showing the importance of genealogy and family.[41] The keys and the trumpet, for the religiously inclined, referred to San Pedro and the gates to heaven, and the trumpet of Gabriel.[42] Other important stories from the Bible could be read into the lotería cards, such as the images of the grapes or wine barrel, both of which could be used to recall the story of the miracle at the wedding of turning water into wine and, from the family perspective, establishing a sanctified marriage. The Bible, rarely found in private homes, reported the crucifixion; popular religion provided details about Roman soldiers nailing Jesus to the cross, wounding him with a spear, then rolling dice for his cloak, and climbing a ladder to remove the body, so that the hammer, nails, dice, cloak, and ladder all had religious references for those who knew the stories. The cock, for example, in religious discussions referred to Peter's denial of Christ. Stories developed that in those spots where Christ's blood dropped during his crucifixion, roses appeared and bloomed overnight. From this legend, the rose became the symbol of Christ's blood and his crucifixion. The rose has been associated with Christ's suffering, the five-petal rose associated with Christ's wounds, since the early period of Romanesque art beginning in the twelfth century, and in the early fifteenth century the white rose appeared in paintings of the Madonna, because of its popular association with virginity. Rolled-up rose petals served as the early rosaries.[43]

Flowers played a prominent role in the board sets. The game reflected a collection of popular attitudes, including ideas about the language of flowers and plants. The cards commonly included six or seven botanical images, always the rose, and usually the nopal, the pine, the palm, and the cypress. The card for the flowerpot (*la maceta*) showed roses or other flowers growing in it. The pear, the apple, and the watermelon often appeared. The widespread nineteenth-century effort to identify the secret and romantic use of flowers as symbols of meanings resulted in the publication of numerous volumes on this subject. The most widely known volume was Charlotte de Latour's *Le langage des fleurs*, published in 1819 and widely translated and circulated throughout Europe and the Americas.[44] For romantic and social meanings, Latour and a host of others claimed that they had discovered oriental or ancient significance associated with flowers and, occasionally, herbs. The language of flowers apparently was the creation of the French middle class and was adopted in those places,[45] including Mexico, where the French had cultural influence. Beyond this language of courtship, seduction, and friendship, flowers had religious associations. The rose, lily, and marigold in Mexico served as floral associations of Christ's blood as well as the Virgin of Guadalupe, of the Holy Mother, and of all the souls in purgatory, respectively.

The flowers could be read also by others to find political meanings. Of these plants, the nopal has the most important national character, as it forms part of the symbol of the Aztec heritage (from the foundational myth of Tenochtitlán, the capital city) and part of the seal of the federal republic. The red rose, for another example, had become a symbol of the Socialists in France, because of its color and the color of the party's flag. Carnations developed an association with the culture of Andalusia, the flamenco, the bullfight, and gypsy life.[46] The use of flowers, especially the marigold and the coxcomb, during *muertos*, the Days of All Souls and All Saints, also resulted in symbolic identifications. The appearance of these flowers on the game cards could be interpreted in a variety of ways. Of course, for some players the images may have recalled nothing more than a literal recognition; pictures of dice and roses to these players meant nothing but gambling and flowers. For others, they served as mnemonic devices for the popular crucifixion story or recalled the four appearances of the Virgin of Guadalupe.

The lottery callers, as they chanted the cards, voiced folk wisdom, commonplace truisms, and stock riddles, mixed occasionally with *albures*, or double entendres.[47] The cards included images that recalled romance, seduction, and sexual allusions. The guitar was the essential instrument for "Las mañanitas" on birthdays and the serenades used in courtship. It was the preeminent instrument of the mermaids made famous in the *Odyssey* who lured sailors to their deaths and since ancient times have lured unwary men to the same end. The lyre, the classic instrument of poets, recalled both Mexico's and Spain's rich poetic literature and the romantic sonnets offered as gifts to a lover. The caged songbird and handkerchiefs also fit in this category. Besides romantic and literary references, the image of the lyre could serve as well as a mnemonic for both biblical (King David) and classical (the Muses) stories.[48] The various melons provided physical references for those who had a preference for double entendres.

These games taught or recalled the common knowledge of the family, community, and religion. They differed from the domestic games in the eighteenth and nineteenth centuries adopted by the British middle class. The English games had a more formal, specific educational purpose, just as did the stream of exhibitions across England. The English cards often portrayed world geography, non-European animals, and Asian, African, and American peoples.[49] These lessons helped to foster imperial attitudes and, perhaps, satisfaction with the empire among the English bourgeoisie.

## Humiliation, Satire, and Social Control

Rather than teaching imperialism through self-righteous geography and self-serving physiognomy, lotería images often mocked some social types and celebrated others. The former pattern built on a tradition of the social use of satire. Public humiliation had its origin in classical Greek society. The invention of satire had an early connection with curses and other magical powers relying on the "potency of abuse ... with the most violent language."[50] Even before Aristotle, Archilochus, first satirist of record, devised iambic verse that, according to Ovid, could be used to wage ruthless warfare. Archilochus invoked it as a technique to wreak vengeance and death on his betrothed, who had broken their engagement, and her father. Satire, as a form of searing public humiliation, became a well-used weapon.

Satire from the classical era onward was a social weapon aimed at vices and follies. The concern with family honor and related practices of shaming those who violated the social order, that is, the practice of humiliation, developed in the Italian city-states. Especially in Florence, shaming civil transgressors took the form of painting the name of the guilty person on the walls of public buildings. Inscribing the name in full view of the community humiliated the family and the individual, whether present or not. The name represented the person as surely as effigies would in other instances. Moreover, the Italian brothers Carracci first developed caricature at the end of the sixteenth century. Their sketches transformed physical features and exaggerated eccentricities in order to ridicule someone. From Italy, the practice spread throughout Europe, reaching both France and England during the seventeenth century. The earliest satirists proposed to ridicule their victims and thus to shame them into conformity with what was regarded as proper social behavior. Rabelais and Pope both turned their prose on persons who exhibited anticommunity traits, such as stinginess, inhospitality, pride, and excessive authoritarianism by those who ruled. At the conclusion of Englishman Ben Jonson's play *The Devil Is an Ass* (1616), the protagonist declared that the proper treatment of scofflaws was not punishment, but shame. Later, during the years of the French Revolution and the wars between the French and the English, the English Loyalists held regular festivals to burn effigies of Thomas Paine.[51]

Society in the Iberian peninsula, even earlier than the development of satire in France and English, elevated and combined the intense family and civic values from both Roman and Muslim practices. The Siete Partidas, the basic Spanish law code, made despoiling a person's honor a capital crime. Spaniards used effigies as a means of public punishment of civic and religious deviants, by dishonoring his or her reputation.[52] The Inquisition burned effigies of absent unrepentant heretics. In what is probably a sixteenth-century engraving entitled *Los fines de la desobediencia y los desastres del vicio* and designed for parents to use to instruct their children, drawings showed punishments from humiliation to execution.[53] Communities regularly burned Judas effigies on Holy Saturday, which were identified as specific persons or as archetypical characters who threatened the social order, such as drunks, adulterers, gluttons, or bad community officials.[54] Once a Judas figure had been placed on display, the effigy might be beaten with canes or paraded on a donkey, as it was in Cuenca and Toledo; in the province of Guadalajara, the tradition called for hanging placards describing the inappropriate behavior around the effigy's neck or tossing it in a blanket smeared with excrement. Proverbs, satirical verses, ribald songs, and especially apocryphal last testaments constituted other vehicles of popular censorship in Spain.[55] Even when people were punished in the Inquisition's autos-da-fé, the guilty wore both placards that announced their sins and conical caps called the Sanbonitos, whose colors identified the transgression to the spectators, whose presence created the humiliation for those on parade.

Public humiliation long served as the Mediterranean community's truncheon to punish deviants, the Spanish avenger's weapon of choice, and the Inquisition cleric's scourge of apostates. The participants and audience in the first case and the audience in the second two cases drew satisfaction (and perhaps lessons of behavior) from the reaffirmation of community values and the humiliation of those who defied its mores. Besides church- and civic-sanctioned humiliation, on other occasions community members took informal action to shame the behavior of individuals who transgressed local standards. Typical were actions similar to the charivaris in France. Usually consisting of local folk and neighbors surrounding the dwelling of the transgressor and making noise, such as beating on pots and pans, this community practice in the United States was often called making someone "dance to rough music." In Mexico, one way to describe ridiculing or mocking someone used the phrase *hacer bailar*, to make him or her dance.[56]

Humiliation as a method of enforcing social order, in whatever culture, requires shared values. As one of the forms that James C. Scott has identified as the "weapons of the weak,"[57] it functions only in communities where the values are deeply entrenched and widely honored. In those circumstances where the shared set of local values has crumbled, say, an incipient revolutionary situation, they do not work. The existence and especially the vitality of low-level forms of resistance indicate the vigor of the community rather than the presence of social fissures that serve as omens of incipient revolution. These acts of resistance only accumulate when they fail to serve as a corrective. In a tightly knit community, these actions provide ritual shaming for individuals, which ameliorates the situation. These weapons of the weak that include the forms of ritual humiliation reveal both the nature and the vitality of community mores, rather than indicating some gradual but inexorable movement toward a popular uprising as suggested by Scott. In several cultures, the community even provides sanctioned occasions, during both civil and religious rituals, for these satiric presentations to take place. Moreover, these episodes of public humiliation may be counterproductive to the extent that people use them to substitute for more direct and necessary actions to confront their problems.

In Spain and the regions it colonized, the practice of using popular holidays for carnivalesque activities expanded during the imperial years. These included turning the world upside down and ritual humiliation, such as burning effigies. These occasions occurred especially with Corpus Christi processions that featured iconic or stereotypical representations of the Seven Deadly Sins, common vices, and threats to the community. Burning Judas figures—that is, effigies of individuals who threatened the social order—took place during Holy Week or on different towns' saint days. They were burned not just in the Spanish kingdoms, but also in Central Europe. Across Spain at this time it became customary early in Holy Week to hang a grotesque straw or cardboard figure that the people often called Judas. Then, after a week of ritual public display of the figure, they burned the "Judas" after the Gloria Mass on Holy Saturday. The practice continues in Spain to the present.[58]

From the peninsula, Spaniards brought the custom with them to the Western Hemisphere. This practice and other satirical forms were firmly established by the middle of the seventeenth century. The construction of papier-mâché figures intended for immolation occurred as part of the welcoming ceremony for the new viceroy, the Marques de Vienna, of New Spain in 1640; and later whole scenes would be fabricated from papier-mâché for burnings, such as the Monte Paranaso constructed in 1789–1790 in Mexico City.[59] Throughout the nineteenth century, Judas burnings served as part of a community's ritual shaming as a means of social control. Today, Judas burnings have moved to Easter Sunday, and in some communities, despite the Revolution's disruption of the process, the shaming continues with either Judas figures or Judas's Last Will and Testimony, which mocks community members, especially local officials.[60] The Judas figures from colonial times to the present included effigies recognizable by their caricature of local personages and by their adoption of typical mnemonics of social types.[61]

## Lotería Redux

Lotería cards projected the general pattern of satire as a social corrective relying on public humiliation. Mexicans since the colonial period have used numerous methods for directing ritual satire not only at the behavior of political leaders, but also at the activities of community characters who disrupted or threatened the social order. They have reproduced these individuals as stereotypical Judas figures that were burned on the Saturday of Holy Week. Often these characters or caricatures appeared in other popular forms, including poetry and children's jingles and games, such as juego de la oca and, especially, lotería.

Often the most disruptive characters in community life, represented in symbols, were manipulated in various popular forms. One of the best-known images, used as a Judas figure and in the lottery games, was El Catrín, also called the Lagartijo, a member of the idle rich, a typical *flaneur*. *Lagartijo*, from the word *lagarto* (lizard), referred to the habit of these men to lounge idly for hours in the sun. Such a dandy was ironically called El Catrín, "the gentleman," to exaggerate his pretensions. This pejorative term was used for the first time shortly after independence, by José Joaquin Fernández de Lizardi, who, under the pseudonym El Pensador Mexicano, wrote the picaresque novel *Don Catrín de la Fachenda*. He described the title character as a poser, a fop who believed the world owed him a living. The lagartijo and the *catrín* shared the conceit to inhabit the upper levels of society and to adopt European manners and fashions. Many of these individuals lacked money. They dressed as the boulevardiers of the day, with top hat, frock coat, high-button collar, and imported shoes, but the *catrines*, so it was said, often wore shoes with holes in the soles and shirts with frayed cuffs, and had no underwear to wear at all. At restaurants they never paid. The gossip about them indicated the gap between their aspirations and reality, and alluded to their shifty existence. The catrines appeared as features in many drawings and engravings of the nineteenth century. These characters, during the Díaz years, enjoyed making promenades along Mexico City's Plateros (now Madero) street and drinking in private clubs. They were clearly illustrated in Posada's engravings, especially the broadsheet called *Repelito de catrines* (Hand-me-downs of the Dandies). The catrín was, and still is, often interpreted as the devil himself in disguise, offering the powerful temptations that threaten family, community, and orthodox life.[62]

While the catrín represented an aristocratic individual fallen on bad times, usually of his own making, or someone with upper-class pretensions, he was a rogue nonetheless. The lower-class equivalent was the drunkard, who as the Mangy Parrot himself described, got drunk, fought, and made love in the streets or pulque stands.[63] This social stereotype always appeared in the lotería games, from the earliest sets, as El Borracho. As one of the most common images, El Borracho identified a lower-class member of the community who threatened the social order. The image of El Borracho, always a disheveled male, usually with a bottle, appeared outside a cantina or staggering down the street. This common figure in the game set, after the turn of the twentieth century, seems modeled on the 1901 drawing El Borracho by Jesús Martínez Cerrion, one of his series of images of city residents.[64] The satirical representation of the drunk reflected the aristocratic and bourgeois opposition to alcoholic beverages for the lower classes, and may also have alluded to the prejudicial attitude that drunkards in the cities were Indians. Other cards in the game represent a wine cask or whiskey bottle, indicating, if nothing else, the prevalence of alcoholic beverages in the society.

Women, representing both the "*gente decente*" and the dangerous classes, appeared as well. The latter appeared as La Sirena, the mermaid, perhaps the most common image in Mexican folk art and popular culture, and the former as La Dama, and occasionally as La Muerte, death. These female representations contained religious features for those who sought them. For example, La Dama could allude to pride, one of the seven deadly sins, while La Sirena referred to another of these sins, adultery. Other players would identify the Homeric epics that featured La Sirena. Other game sets featured the folkloric China Poblana—these are late in the nineteenth century—but did not include any references to motherhood, not even the Virgin of Guadalupe. The self-censorship that newspaper reporters and caricaturists exercised during the twentieth century that had them avoid any sarcastic reference to the Virgin of Guadalupe may reach back to popular cultural views of the nineteenth century, even when the secular politics might have made it legally possible. Motherhood remained sacrosanct as well; making light of mothers even in the gentlest ways could result in a mother's curse.[65]

A more positive masculine image, El Valiente, the brave one, boasted regional provenance and brute strength, such as the Valiente of Guanajuato. Posada, for example, produced the Valiente de Guadalajara and the Valiente de Bajío. His images and broadsheets contained motifs that identified rural character, male posturing, and masculine roles. For Guadalajara, the image mentioned both basketry and leatherwork, well-known crafts of two of the city's neighborhoods. The valiente, of course, challenged any and all comers with taunts and boasts. His boasts given in slang language indicated a lower-class origin, marking the difference from his literary and folkloric ancestor the Spanish *valiente*, generally an hidalgo, who even without wealth had good lineage. In another example, El Valiente from the Bajío boasted that he could dominate big-city pool players, because he used his machete as a cue. He swore with oaths that he could outdrink any of them, by swigging down a quart of tequila and twelve glasses of beer. He warned that when he came to town for a wedding, he might carry off the bride and boasted he had the eyes of an eagle and the strength to subdue wild bulls.[66] In the cities, especially the capital, these valientes, for all their braggadocio, were identified by authorities as criminals.[67] The images of the valientes on the lotería cards reflected both the positive, rural community view and the urban vision of the vulgar, country criminal. The latter became more common toward the end of the century in the game sets produced by Jacques and others from the capital city.

Games as ritual satire, besides teaching proper behavior and socially acceptable activities, also confronted other threats to the community. Lottery images and broadsheets with crude stereotypes and rough corridos or other doggerel served the same purpose. Commonly the corridos and poems on the broadsheets appeared as *décimas*, ten-line stanzas that were often used in religious poems and publications for moral exhortations. For example, in the late nineteenth century, for many villagers the railroad represented a major threat, portending the loss of land and sustenance, at the same time that the locomotive provided the most powerful symbol of modernization. Jingles, drawings, and *calaveras* repeated this fear, while the lotería sets, in general, represented the railroad as a positive symbol of modernization.

Some images represented figures and events by combining signs rather than attempting a literal depiction, in a manner that perhaps reached back to prehispanic practices of using conceptual rather than only representational visual icons. In both prehispanic indigenous and Roman Catholic pictorial records, the arms and the hands of highly stylized humans often form especially expressive images. As Miguel de Unamuno once anatomized Madrid as "a stomach, not a brain"—consuming the wealth of the nation rather than providing Spain with intelligent leadership—these body parts became significant iconic representations. In the Codex Sierra, Mexico City is represented as a giant outstretched arm with the palm of the hand cupped upward, awaiting payment.[68] Lotería cards did this as well, with both religious and political references. An arm in European dress with the hand grasping a key represented St. Peter, because the key served as his advocation as the keeper of the heavenly gates. The tall army boot served as a possible symbol representing the missing lower leg of the nineteenth-century *caudillo* Antonio López de Santa Anna.

## Some Conclusions

Lotería and other games that emerged from the colonial period into the nineteenth century developed from Spanish models but after independence quickly took on a national character that increasingly became more pronounced as some Mexicans began manufacturing toys as well as importing them.[69] By 1852, for example, Mexico City and Puebla listed twelve shops producing dolls.[70] Games and toys often became expressive and mnemonic devices of national identity. Even if not especially intended as such, those who played with them gave them a local, Mexican character.

Lotería cards did not directly offer social commentary; nevertheless, because they pictured everyday society, the game offered players an opportunity for making social profiles and identifying stereotypes. No matter in how many different ways an individual chose to read the images, often they served as mnemonic devices in exactly the same way as the pictures used in *el arte de la memoria*, first developed by Italian philosophers. This Italian memory system, like so many other cultural manifestations, arrived in New Spain when Fray Diego Valadés popularized it by publishing *Rhetorica Christiana* (1579), with various images.[71] The objects displayed appeared much like those pictured on the lottery cards. Moreover, playing cards since the sixteenth century in both Spain and its colonies had been recognized as representations of society. Worse, in the eyes of the Inquisition, the deck of cards represented an anti-Bible of forty-eight pages that when shuffled intermingled persons from all social classes, just as gambling houses inappropriately mixed people of all social groups.[72] Reading cards as metaphors was a well-established practice, and, for some players, lotería provided a book of common religious icons in contrast to the deck of cards as the devil's picture book.[73]

In whatever ways the cards served as mnemonic devices or story icons, they most often provided entertainment that mocked social pretensions of different stereotypical individuals and promoted pleasurable pride about national geography, monuments, and emblems. The former related to the general humor about occupations that appeared in various forms. Lizardi, for example, offered the following humorous topology in promising to train his servant for a trade: " ... you won't come out of this a mere barber, you'll be a physician, a surgeon, a chemist, botanist, an alchemist, and if you please me and serve me well, you'll even get to be an astrologer and a necromancer."[74]

Whatever association an individual chose to make, if he or she made one at all, with the image on the card, it could be directed only somewhat by the caller of the images or the numbers. For example, the instructions for the Campeche version of the game had the caller sing out, "number 72," or "el arbol de la noche triste (the tree of the Sad Night)," certainly a reference to one of the dramatic events of the nation's history, but why and how remained for each player to decide. A multitude of possibilities existed: the cypress tree might bring to mind the Spanish conquest, and all that it included, such as the introduction of Spanish culture, including the Catholic faith. Or, for patriots, the tree could epitomize the Spanish colonial policies of economic exploitation. For those opposed to the Spaniards and holding some sympathies for the ancient Aztec Empire, the tree represented the major indigenous victory against the Europeans. For the religious-minded, the tree provided a metaphor for the cardinal sin of greed that resulted in many of the conquistadors dying in their effort to escape with loads of gold. Moreover, for others the tree represented geography—the capital city to those who lived outside it, or the neighborhood of Tacuba, where the tree still stood for capital residents.

Both pleasure and pride could be found in understanding the lotería cards as the identification of national geography, the demonstration of ethnic diversity, and the presentation of national symbols. Images served as representations for different regions and groups, such as el alacrán (the scorpion, the icon of the north, especially Durango) and la rana (the frog, the symbol for Guanajuato). Popo stood for the center and the capital of the country. Moreover, the Indian, the black, and the white individuals represented the ethnic diversity of the nation. The symbols of the nation included the republican eagle devouring the snake, perched on a nopal; the national flag; the red Fresian or liberty cap; the bell that rang for independence; and the soldier, usually in an early nineteenth-century uniform, who defended the national borders. Toy soldiers of lead or clay had been popular since the 1600s and had become increasingly common in the nineteenth century,[75] so the image of the soldier recalled childhood at the same time as it symbolized the nation.

Moreover, the use of satire through at least the first half of the nineteenth century was widely regarded as a more truthful expression of reality than other forms, such as praise and celebration of individuals who were known for their exaggeration to curry favor and to give honor. At the same time, satire brought to the minds of listeners, viewers, or readers specific or implied pairs. For example, satire made no sense without capturing the binary behaviors of "sin and redemption, wild abandon and censure, disorder and order" and the ultimate repentance that led to rehabilitation.[76]

Some observers found in public humiliation the thrill of vicariously experiencing the transgression of the public code, either for the first time by having the episode brought to the public's attention or subsequent times seeing confirmation of public reports and rumors. This revealed the darker side of ostensibly ethical, or at least proper, civic behavior, in which the straitlaced civic moralist indicted improper activity by putting it on display and witnessing it. This comes across in the old saw that alleged the Puritans in colonial New England banned bear-baiting not so much because of the inhumane treatment of the bear but because of the enjoyment it seemed to bring the spectators. Much about visual satire in the lotería game offered the same pleasure.

As the images and gossipy local histories of almanacs and lotería both demonstrate, the culture popular among ordinary Mexicans appeared in a variety of forms. Perhaps this was best illustrated with the proposal for a new monument, suggested by José Guadalupe Posada. His "Project for a monument to the People" reused the classical motif of the figure of Laocoön. His drawing featured three figures: on the left, an Indian representing "the indigenous race"; on the right, a man wearing a cap, representing "the proletariat"; and in the center, "the people," a man who looks like a peasant but is wearing black trousers rather than the white trousers worn by campesinos. Of course, this monument was never built (nor was the one proposed for Díaz), but it served as a satire of the official statue-mania of the regime and shows the range of forms of popular responses.[77]

Finally, it should be repeated that in lotería and other similar games, whether they came from abroad or from the capital city, and whether or not the images represented local characters and stories, the players masterfully accommodated them to local interests. The dealer called out riddles and references known in the region, the prizes reflected local or family premiums, and the images were related to the individuals, heroic accounts, Bible stories, and old fables that made up the common knowledge of the community. In this way, games such as *lotería de figuras* had ties to everyday life and both reflected and taught local values.[78] Both the almanacs and board games contributed to a growing sense among common Mexicans of who they and their fellow citizens were and of the physical dimensions and character of their country—the essence of national identity.

## CHAPTER 3

# Independence Celebrations and Representations of the Nation

*Never to be forgotten, immune from judgement or regret.*
—Michael Dibdin[1]

*The strong do what they can*
*and the weak suffer what they must.*

—Thucydides[2]

Independence had to be invented by the new government administrators, and they turned to its celebration, among other things, to explain it.[3] Through the creation of the holiday, they projected the understanding of independence they wanted the public to accept. This evolved over the nineteenth century, so that witnessing the celebration shows the changing nature of what the nation meant to government officials. This preliminary analysis examines several independence celebrations during the nineteenth century to find the common elements and efforts to build a national community. This chapter discusses these episodes, examines in more detail their evolution from the administrative perspective, and then continues with an effort to appreciate the equivocal character of these celebrations. The evaluation focuses on the continuity and change in patriotic holidays.

## The First Celebrations of Independence

Both national and local leaders had to decide when to celebrate independence, and this required that they determine what exactly to celebrate. Leaders wanted to organize the individual, often narrow, even odd views of the past into an appropriate national history. Officials tried to accomplish their aims by dismissing contradictory and individualistic accounts as heresy, treason, folklore, or foolishness.[4] Leaders, both clergy and clerisy, proposed models of actions. To reach the people during the nineteenth century, they relied on the most pervasive popular medium, the public spectacle that formed part of religious ceremonies and civic festivals. In both cases, they attempted to give the spectacle a didactic purpose, relying on mnemonic devices that recreated specific accounts of the past. Sacred and secular ceremonies posed as behavioral templates. Leaders used processions, allegorical floats, instructions in the form of sermons or orations, and displays of relics and icons, especially of the parish folk saint or patriotic local martyr. Each resulted in a tableau vivant, a sensory assemblage that took the form of eloquent metaphors that represented the conscious campaign to establish amended memories and to ignore what they regarded as inappropriate silent innuendos.

The role of individuals, not just material images and ephemeral constructions, made the visible, direct, and personal tie between the present (the acquaintance in the procession) and all the previous yesterdays (the person whom the acquaintance represented). Abstractions acquired physical dimensions and personality as individuals participated or watched acquaintances participate as the reincarnation of images of the divine or the historic, the past or the future. Less melodramatic, but just as real and meaningful as spirit possession of individuals in Santería, or evangelical Protestantism, this collective low-grade social possession came with community celebrations and provided release, explanation, and intensity of experience from which one derived pleasure, dread, or wonder. These intense feelings helped community leaders as they attempted to build a political consensus. These festivals allowed for constant revision of events into the teleological calculus that justified the present.

Independence celebrations of the nineteenth century reveal much about the society: its politics and values, what Mexicans thought Mexico was, and what they wanted it to become. This examination of Independence Day celebrations represents an initial speculation on the meaning of this holiday for those who organized it: the meaning for the organizers and the meaning the organizers wanted to provide through dramatic didactic visual expressions to the general public. The participants and the audience could choose to draw a variety of meanings from these independence festivals. Certainly their responses varied greatly during the nineteenth century. Above all, it was the performance, not the text, that made independence a living memory.[5]

Independence was achieved in 1821 after a decade of sporadic, and at times extremely bloody, conflict. The first celebration occurred when Agustín de Iturbide led the Army of Three Guarantees into Mexico City, September 27, 1821, thus completing the victory over Spanish troops and marking the achievement of independence.[6] This military victory in 1821 resulted in a new regime, the empire of Iturbide, crowned Agustín I. His constituent assembly quickly reshaped the new nation's cycle of major celebrations. First, the delegates confirmed the continuation of religious holidays without change, and second, they devised a new list of civic holidays, including a celebration of independence.[7] The deputies intended to present dramatic statements of virtue, order, and civility through the public performance of rituals.

Emperor Agustin I issued a revised list of state holidays that combined the colonial list, after paring away the most representative Bourbon celebrations, with commemorations of the struggle for independence and its heroes. The holiday calendar made clear that the imperial regime found its historical roots in the Spanish conquest of the Aztec Empire. San Hipólito Day, August 19, remained on the calendar as the celebration of the conquest of Tenochtitlán, and the colors of the city's banner, made of green, white, and red cloth, displayed on the holiday, were soon adopted as the national flag as well. The organizers intended this celebration—a cavalcade from the national cathedral to the city hall—as a demonstration of the heroic action of a small group of Spanish crusaders and a display of the elite members of society. By honoring San Hipólito by parading his banner from cathedral to city hall, the emperor and his regime emphasized the continuation of the close relationship between the church and state.

This ritual had an equivocal nature. Republicans found in it the clear demonstration not of an independent regime celebrating its Hispanic origins but of a monarchy trumpeting its continuation of the colonial regime in every respect except the person of the ruler. For the lower orders, the fiesta marked again the rigid stratification of society, and for the indigenous peoples, it commemorated their humiliating defeat to Europeans and their horses. The polysemic nature of this celebration appeared as well in the other holidays that occurred during the short-lived empire.

The congress and the emperor also recognized as important holidays February 24, the Plan de Iguala; March 2, the establishment of the constituent assembly, the congress that had proclaimed Iturbide emperor; and September 16, the Grito de Dolores. As the origin of the new nation, that is, Independence Day, congress initially chose to celebrate September 27, the day Iturbide's army entered Mexico City.[8] The delegates thus identified as the foundation symbol the successful completion of the struggle for independence. They chose to celebrate the day Mexico, under Iturbide's direction, achieved its independence.

The imperial government honored those who achieved the victory over Spain with financial rewards and military promotions. Thirteen patriots who had given their lives in the struggle were named *benemérito de la nación* and had their names inscribed on the walls of the congress. Moreover, the imperial government called for the transfer of their bodily remains to the capital city. Commemorating where each of the thirteen had given his life, the emperor ordered that local officials locate the spot, plant trees, construct a pyramid with the name of the hero, and enclose the simple memorial with a fence.[9]

The empire survived only ten months. After Iturbide had been overthrown as emperor, the new republican congress revised the Independence Day celebration in 1823 to downplay the significance of the deposed emperor and thus shifted the holiday to September 16, to commemorate Padre Miguel Hidalgo's predawn *grito de independencia*, his call for independence, that launched the movement for national liberation. This change represents much more than merely a different day. The celebration of Hidalgo's initiation of the independence movement forms part of the same pattern of celebrations as those in France, with July 14, Bastille Day, as the beginning of the French Revolution, and in the United States, with July 4 as the beginning of the American revolution for independence. This subtle but significant change from the day independence was won to the day the struggle began represents a different attitude toward "independence" (or in the case of the French, the Revolution; and in Mexico, on November 20, the Revolution as well). The shift to the day it began incorporates the idea of an ongoing process, one that must be constantly protected as it evolves into the infinite future. Moreover, it carries with it the idea that the nation was born with the step toward independence. Earlier events (such as the colonial period) were dismissed as prelude, as patriotic leaders proclaimed themselves the descendants, not of the earlier Indian civilizations or the Spanish empire, but of Father Miguel Hidalgo.[10] The patriots in 1823 celebrated the beginning of the independence struggle and the patriotic invention of the nation in which the citizens needed to be vigilant that independence be constantly renewed and revitalized.

## Independence Day Celebrations until 1869

Although the first Independence Day celebrated on September 16 came in 1823, it was rather a minor event. Certainly, the clear association at this time between insurgency and religiosity, the divine approval for independence, received confirmation by the selection of the shrine to Guadalupe as the site to honor the remains of the patriotic heroes. The remains of José María Morelos arrived at the shrine on September 16 a little after noon, accompanied by Indian musicians playing cheerful tunes celebrating the hero.[11] The holiday also nearly resulted in a riot against the Spaniards still resident in the capital city. In the interest of maintaining order, the following year there were no major celebrations of the anti-Spanish struggle for independence. Of great consequence was the festival of September 16, 1825.[12]

The 1825 celebration became a major holiday. José María Tornel, President Guadalupe Victoria's private secretary, inspired the formation of a patriotic-minded committee called the Civic Committee of Patriots (La Junta Cívica de Patriótas) that organized and financed the Independence Day commemoration. The editor of the newspaper *El águila mexicano* seconded the idea and argued that it should be adopted throughout the country. He called on every town in the republic to establish a patriotic junta that would erect a triumphal arch to remind the people of the benefits of national independence. This indeed became the general pattern for organizing, financing, and administering Independence Day celebrations throughout the republic.

The Mexico City committee devoted its efforts to the celebration of September 16 and Hidalgo's call for independence.[13] The 1825 organizing committee, chaired by General Anastasio Bustamante, scheduled fireworks on the holiday's eve and for the festival organized events that made flamboyant acoustical and visual appeals to the audience: a grand procession, patriotic orations, a slave emancipation, orchestral music, dancing, and patriotic allegories performed in the Alameda and the city's theaters.[14] Of these events, the emancipation of slaves and the allegorical dances deserve special consideration.

First, the slave emancipation. The organizers decided to use some of the funds they had raised to pay for the liberation of several slaves. News of the proposal prompted more donations and offers to manumit several slaves by their owners. In this way, the committee provided a stirring, real character to the rituals of independence. The practice continued until slavery was abolished in 1829, and President Vicente Guerrero announced the new legislation on Independence Day.[15]

Performance of some aspect of the meaning of independence became habitual. Even after the national abolition of slavery, typically the organizing committee demonstrated the meaning of independence through acts of charity to fellow Mexicans in difficult or dependent circumstances. The junta collected donations to give cash allotments to disabled or destitute veterans or to the survivors of those who died in the independence struggle. The organizers also, on occasion, provided a special meal for prisoners in the jail and, more commonly, supplied clothing for poor children on Independence Day.

Second, in 1825 the patriotic committee sponsored a special performance called the *baile alegórico*. The title, the performance, and the dancing indicated the popular character of the celebration. Dancing had popular, secular, often confrontational, characteristics.

During the waning days of New Spain, dancing in the street had become rather common, and inquisitors had attempted to prevent what they considered lewd songs and dances, especially those performed in the street.[16] Moreover, attitudes favorable to independence in the late eighteenth and early nineteenth centuries found expression in music, especially dancing various *jarabes*, often by couples dressed in *charro* and China Poblana costumes or singing verses and jingles that ridiculed Europeans, especially Napoleon and Spaniards.[17]

In the Independence Day allegorical performance, which was typical of the independence period,[18] characters danced out the independence struggle. The costumed dancers appeared as Greek and Roman mythological personages and ideological inventions that served as idealizations of values and institutions. Thus, dancers represented "Liberty," "Despotism," "Mars," "Apollo," and "El Pueblo." The dance culminated in a grand finale with the coronation of the national eagle. Thus, the allegorical dance presented a depersonalized event in which the eagle, the symbol of the imperial Aztec Empire, not the people (El Pueblo), emerged as the ultimate victor. The reification of the regime at this ceremony created a clear and definite divide between the government and the people, who only witnessed the achievement of independence as the coronation of a new institution.

Conservative politicians, many of whom can be clearly identified with the monarchist party,[19] struggled during the next three decades until the 1860s to replace September 16 (commemorating Hidalgo) with September 27 (memorializing Iturbide), as they opposed the beginning of a popular struggle and the military imposition of a liberal authority. Despite their efforts, no regime ever replaced September 16. Rather, a few leaders tinkered with independence holidays by adding other celebrations, especially September 27, until 1863. For example, Mexico City's patriotic junta in 1837 incorporated September 27 into its holiday responsibilities. Lucas Alamán, the most prominent of the conservative politicians, refused to have dealings at all with the junta planning the independence holidays.

The patriotic junta established a regular pattern for the celebration of independence that endured until the Wars of Reform (1858–1861). Subcommittees arranged for decorating the streets, erecting a speaker's platform in the Alameda, commissioning the fireworks, hiring musical and theatrical performances, and selecting the principal orator. Occasionally other subcommittees organized competitions for plays, poems, essays, or portraits based on the theme of the independence struggle or individual patriots. From the mid-1830s onward, women's committees sought donations and, on occasion, arranged for schoolchildren to line the parade route. By far, most members served the patriotic committee as fund-raisers.[20]

During the period 1832 to 1855, Antonio López de Santa Anna relied on celebrations, often sponsored in conjunction with the church leaders, and patriotic reburials of independence heroes and, in 1842, his own severed leg to help promote his popular following. He celebrated September 11, the date he had defeated an invading Spanish army at Tampico in 1829, as the completion of the struggle for independence. Santa Anna generally engaged church officials in his celebrations, including a high mass as part of the day's festivities.[21] The reburial of heroes of the independence movement renewed popular interest in patriotic festivities, perhaps none more than the 1838 transfer of the remains of the man who achieved independence, the one-time emperor Iturbide, from Padilla, Tamaulipas, to enter Mexico City along the ceremonial route from Guadalupe to the central plaza, escorted by both religious and secular authorities. The remains arrived in the capital on September 27, the same day his army had captured the city in 1821, and after lying in state for slightly over a month, the remains were reburied in the national cathedral, in one of the major celebrations of the 1830s.[22]

Patriotic holidays had a different character during periods of civil war and foreign intervention that followed the final overthrow of Antonio Lopez de Santa Anna. Benito Juárez had opposed the September 27 holiday, but ironically it was the French puppet emperor Maximilian who permanently eliminated this celebration of Iturbide's triumph from the civic calendar. His action added one more disappointing decision to the growing list being kept by disenchanted conservatives. Maximilian even went to the village of Dolores to celebrate Padre Hidalgo's call for independence on September 16. He and his wife, Carlota, also funded the construction of an independence

monument in Mexico City that incorporated statues of the major patriots. Among the fathers of the nation, José María Morelos received
special attention from the emperor. Besides this Independence Day
holiday on September 16, the royal couple brought new enthusiasm
to the celebration of both Corpus Christi and Virgin of Guadalupe
Day.[23] Certainly, Maximilian, the second and last emperor, wanted to
put as much distance as possible between himself and Iturbide's failed
empire, whose image was summoned by the September 27 celebration. Consequently, Maximilian and his regime ignored this holiday.
These early celebrations of independence marked out the patterns
and established habitual performances that continued throughout the
century, even though the date itself was not completely resolved until
the 1860s.

## New Features of Independence Day Celebrations

The independence celebration in 1869 incorporated striking new
features with customary habits. Ignacio Manuel Altamirano wrote a
chronicle of these events. He began his account by repeating what
he said was the widespread complaint against the patriotic celebrations of independence. He reported the general hostility to what
had become over the previous two decades the stale, dreary festival
of independence. This hackneyed celebration resulted, he explained,
because the membership of the patriotic committee had remained
the same, and these "immortals" would not die, neither would they
change the celebration. The independence celebration from 1849
to 1869 had declined in people's esteem, at least as measured by the
concomitant declining participation. Each year's celebration had so
faithfully replicated the previous one, according to Altamirano, that
if the dead returned, the only difference they would notice would
be the widespread use of the formal coat with tails and the dancing
of waltzes. Moreover, the celebration had lost any genuine popular
participation.[24]

Dramatic, innovative revival of the independence holiday came
in 1869 with the focus on the completion of the railroad line between
Mexico City and Puebla.[25] Inauguration of the completed rail link

occurred on September 16 as the major part of the day's celebration. Following the twenty-one-cannon salute at dawn, the national congress officially opened, and Guillermo Prieto gave the traditional discourse in the Alameda. At this point, national leaders and their guests rushed to the Buenavista station for the 10:30 departure of the inaugural passenger train to Puebla.

The locomotive and its open coaches provided bystanders along the route the opportunity to observe a steam-powered procession that reflected the hierarchical views of the liberal regime.[26] Immediately behind the locomotive came the coach with the official police guard, followed by the coach for guests and family members of government officials, the coach for deputies of the congress, and the coach for judges of the supreme court, and in the last car rode the presidential cabinet members and the chief executive, Benito Juárez. As this train chugged through the states of Mexico, Tlaxcala, and Puebla, the only official delegations to meet the travelers before their arrival in Puebla City were the local militia units from several towns in Tlaxcala and Puebla that came to attention along the tracks to salute the president.

Despite heavy rains when the train arrived in Puebla, there was a tremendous reception that followed the Mexico City pattern of patriotic speeches and in the evening a grand dinner and dance in the Teatro Guerrero. The evening's patriotic celebrations included guests representing all the political factions—not because of a sense of national unity but because the host of the entertainment was the railroad company. Railroad officials ignored politics and invited every person of influence, including churchmen, in the community. The evening featured patriotic speeches and toasts to the defeat of the French and the restoration of national integrity and greatness. The highlight of the evening was the music, which reached a climax with the performance of a new composition by the Puebla musician Melesio Morales.[27] He had especially written "La Locomotiva" for the occasion and had invented new instruments to recreate the sound of the steam engine, its blaring whistle, and the click-clack of coaches on the track. The piece proved so popular that it was repeated in the early morning before the dance ended. The following day, September 17, President Juárez went to one of the main plazas, where he placed the first stone in a monument to be dedicated to General Ignacio Zaragoza, the victorious commander on the fateful Cinco de Mayo, when patriotic troops loyal to Juárez defeated the French invaders. The travelers returned to Mexico City the following day.

This 1869 celebration captured the essence of the republic restored after the expulsion of the French. National progress was given a real dimension with the steam excursion from the capital city to Puebla. The journey back and forth took just a few hours, with the only inconvenience caused by the rainstorm. This official excursion linked progress based on steam and steel to the restored, authentic Mexican regime that had deposed the European imperial imposter. Moreover, the railroad (at least the railroad company) united political factions, bringing them together for the Independence Day dinner and dance. Modern technology and enterprise thus could achieve what individuals had not been able to do before, even during the darkest days of foreign intervention.

But there is something more here. This celebration vividly states Benito Juárez's iron-willed commitment to civilian rule of Mexico. His belief in Cincinnatus—the patriot who became a warrior in times of crisis and then returned to civilian life, with no demand beyond the chance to serve his nation when he was needed—received clear expression. Guarding the presidential party was a traveling police unit, not a regiment of regular soldiers of the line. The official party did not include officers in a military capacity, although officers serving as deputies or cabinet ministers attended in that role. Officers in their official capacity did not receive invitations to the official dinner and dance to celebrate independence. Some attended as notable men, not as soldiers, of Puebla. Where the official delegation was received along the tracks, it was met by local militia units—the Cincinnati in the flesh. And these militiamen received reinforcement in their commitment to militia service and their attitudes about what has been called popular liberalism.[28] Finally, we should note that Juárez laid the cornerstone for a monument to a dead soldier.

Zaragoza's career also provided evidence for the liberal myth. Zaragoza had entered military service through the militia, which Juárez could trumpet, and later during the crisis created by the French intervention, he had resigned his cabinet post to return to the command of troops. The tribute to Zaragoza also brilliantly displays what Benedict Anderson calls "collective amnesia," the purposeful forgetting of contrary, negative, or unfortunate facts. Here, for example, the portrait of Zaragosa as a civilian soldier ignores the fact that he was secretary of war, so he was still a soldier while serving the government. Moreover, the creation of Zaragosa as hero ignored the fact that he had been born in Texas, the lost continent of Mexico.[29] Moreover, it should be noted that Juárez linked the struggle for independence from Spain (celebrated on September 15–16) with his own generation's struggle to maintain independence from France (symbolized in Cinco de Mayo). The president's participation in laying the first stone in the monument to Zaragosa dramatically made this connection.

For the sculptor of the representation of Zaragosa, state officials chose Jesús Contreras, who became as close to an official sculptor as the nation had. Contreras did the plaster of paris death masks of all the prominent, powerful politicians, including those of the Porfiriato (1876–1911), such as Manuel Romero Rubio. He eventually earned an international reputation for his bronze bas-reliefs of Cuauhtémoc, and statues of Ramón Corona in Guadalajara, Juárez in Chihuahua City, and González Ortega in Zacatecas. He was director of the Fundición Artística Mexicana, the company that the federal government contracted to construct all of the statues along the Paseo de la Reforma. (Díaz was honorary president of the company.) In the 1880s, the federal government sent him to Europe, where he studied sculpture in Paris and Italy in preparation for his work on the Palacio Mexicano at the Paris Exposition of 1889. On display were his sculptures of Cuauhtémoc, Cuitláhuac, Cacama, Netzahualcoytl, Itzcóatl, and the King of Tacuba. His most famous marble sculpture, *Malgré-Tout*, won the first prize at the Universal Exhibition of Paris in 1889.[30]

Finally, the music had a special place in the celebration (fig. 2). In Mexico City, the widely played holiday tunes were waltzes, and in Puebla, during dinner guests heard dance music, with the exception of the special composition to celebrate the locomotive. These festive dances offered the opportunity for audience participation, unlike the martial airs and rousing sounds of the National Hymn or marches that created

**2.** Musicians played a critical role in independence and other holiday celebrations. Their music served as an essential part of the collective memory that included a sense of national identity. Papier-mâché musicians from the Champion Folk Art Collection, Tucson, Arizona. Photograph by Cheryle Champion.

a watchful audience and uniformed marionettes stepping together. The marching troops represented unified hierarchy, and the dancers the individual freedom of liberalism. The nature of independence celebrations at the time of the restored republic focused on the expressions of material progress, the unity of social and economic elites, and the decision to downplay the military, taking no account of veterans, men who combined patriotic zeal with wartime camaraderie.

## Independence Day Celebrations during the Porfirian Years

The celebration of holidays during the Porfirian era, 1876–1911, had several innovations, but they built on the long-standing practice of using fiestas as dramatic statements of the dominant culture. Porfirian ritual celebrations provided an indisputable expression of governance. "Order and Progress," the slogan and the ideal of the nation's Comtian positivists, animated administrative policies and inspired governmental displays during the years of the Porfirian government. Civic celebrations assumed special importance as affirmations of the regime's anticlerical politics and modernistic drive toward secularization. These government-sponsored holidays revealed the values that the president and his fellow travelers in the full coach (as the public called his administration) hoped to promote, and they expressed the Porfirian understanding of what national virtue should be.

A new direction in the celebration of independence came September 16, 1883, along with many other changes in the economy and politics that have been labeled the Porfiriato. Many of the changes associated with Porfirio Díaz occurred during the blistering pace of development and reforms of the presidency, 1880–1884, of Manuel González. Independence Day in 1883 became the first civil holiday attended as a tourist event. This happened because some 1,200 miles of the track had been completed for the new railroads. Provincial Mexicans for the first time had the opportunity to become spectators at the capital city's independence fete, just as many of them, no doubt, had at one time been pilgrims—that is, religious tourists who find glory in the difficulty of travel—to the celebrations at the shrines at Tepeyac and Chalma.[31] In 1883, these first-time civic pilgrims included veterans of the Reform Wars, survivors of the fight against the French occupation troops, and the first products of the new secular schools. They were, in fact, the heirs of Benito Juárez and liberalism as it was popularly understood—although he had ignored many of them. For this September 16 holiday, more than 30,000 Mexicans came to the capital city, where they overwhelmed the city's meager hotel and restaurant facilities. Nevertheless, they arrived to celebrate the independence of their country, and they were not disappointed. The spectators witnessed a grand cavalcade of official history.

The Independence Day parade on September 16 featured fourteen floats designed to present the mnemonics of the national, liberal heritage. These memory devices were intended to educate spectators with the appropriate knowledge of the national legacy, reminding those spectators casually acquainted with their past of its proper sequence. The independence floats represented a new feature in civic holiday events. But floats, or *carros alegóricos*, had long been included in religious processions, including the Corpus Christi parades in Spain and New Spain that featured Tarascas representing the seven deadly sins.[32] The floats utilized symbols that were quickly and easily recognized by the spectators. These allegorical representations had a nimble character, as they moved from formal, academic art, to popular lithographs, to general references recognized by the people's common knowledge.

Appropriately from the Eurocentric tradition, the first float, called The Discovery of America, featured Christopher Columbus arriving in the New World. Aboard his caravel Columbus stood, dressed in the short black jacket, hat, and tights of a Castilian nobleman. On deck with him gathered two Spanish sailors and several Spanish soldiers. The latter wore helmets, breastplates, and uniforms of red and yellow, the colors of Castile. Outside the vessel, on the representation of the New World's shore, sat several maidens dressed in skimpy tunics and feathered headdresses, and carrying quivers full of arrows. The float recalled the narrative of male conquerors and female subordinates, implying the creation of a society based on the joining of these men and women as the major result of the discovery of Mexico.

The second float, named Allegory of Independence, featured two images of the world, labeled Europe and Mexico, with a broken chain between them. The centerpiece presented a woman identified as America, dressed in a white tunic with a red cloak and wearing a grand crown of feathers, pearls, and gold. This figure had been used since the colonial era as an allegory for America in general, and for New Spain or Mexico in particular. The most common representations featured her with the tunic tied above her waist with a sash, carrying a plumed staff, arrows, or short spears, and usually wearing a headdress of feathers. After independence, Mexico's tricolor often appeared on the headdress, sash, or staff. A widely known and popular expression of this image appeared in the painting *Allegory of the Constitution* of 1857. Petronilo Monroy entered this painting in the Academy of San Carlos's 1869 exhibition.[33] He painted the female figure in a wind-blown tunic, wearing a crown and carrying the classical laurel wreath of immortality in one upraised hand and in the other a stone tablet engraved with the words, "Constitution of 1857." The painting made the image appear as an angel or herald. This was an extremely popular and highly praised painting housed today in the Palacio Nacional.[34] For many, then, the float carrying the allegory of America inspired thoughts that the image heralded a progressive nation under the reforms of the 1857 constitution.

At the feet of America lay a large alligator. This image had served the Aztecs as the symbol of the earth. Above America presided the Mexican eagle, also drawn from Aztec symbolism. Thus, America, particularly Mexico, towers over the rest of the world in this representation. This float was sponsored by the Gran Círculo de Obreros, the mutualist worker organization.

The other allegorical coaches in the parade, in order, had the following titles: The Apotheosis of Hidalgo; The Republic; The Arms of Mexico City; Charity; The Fountain (the float of the water carriers); Commerce; Fortune; Water; Aurora; Minerva–Public Instruction; Float of the Carriage Drivers; Progress–Industry and Peace. Here as an assemblage, Mexicans brought together many of their concerns, such as potable water, civil order, secular education, and successful business, along with the chronology of the arrival of the Spaniards, victory of the independence patriots, and preservation of the republic, all the result of force of arms.

The float sponsored by the commission on public instruction featured Minerva, the goddess of wisdom, technical skill, and invention. This was clearly an appropriate allegory for education for many with even a hazy recollection of Roman mythology, but for some spectators the image had additional, more specific and significant allusions. This same icon served as the focal point in the mural at the top of the main staircase landing of the National Preparatory School, the center of positivism. Juan Cordero intended his work, called *Knowledge and Labor Triumph over Sloth and Ignorance,* to be a pictorial affirmation of Comtian themes. He unveiled his painting in tempera on November 29, 1874, to great fanfare. This allegory pictures Minerva enthroned with two figures representing steam and electricity below her. In the background, the mural includes sailors unloading a boat in front of a Parthenon-like structure, Clio writing, Envy fleeing, and in the distance a railroad train.[35] Seeing this float, anyone associated with the national preparatory school—faculty, alumni, students, and visitors—recognized that Minerva represented the values of Comte and the lessons of positivism for national *cientificismo.*

The last of the floats in the moving panorama was called Progress, and carried the slogan "Industry and Peace." Sponsored by the railroads of the Federal District, this float had gold and silver wheels as well as a gold and silver pedestal on which a carved wooden statue stood. The allegory presented "industry" and "progress" crowned by "Peace" embodied in the carving of a beautiful woman, reaching out to crown a railroad locomotive emerging from a tunnel. The float also had railroad items such as rails, wheels, sledge hammers, and so forth. At the front of the car appeared the image of the eagle, with its wings unfolded as in flight, holding chains in its claws as though pulling the float. Six black draft horses, each adorned with black cloth bordered in gold and with tricolor plumes, pulled the float. Three riders, dressed in the eighteenth-century Spanish style of three-cornered black felt hats with white plumes, red and blue velvet jackets with silver and gold trim, knee-length breeches, low shoes, silk stockings, and gloves, guided the horses.

The steam locomotive, here emerging into the sunlight from the darkness of the tunnel, served as the international symbol of industry. The railroad, with its speed and power and its smoke and noise, meant Mexico had arrived at modernity. The float, drawn by horses, clearly linked animal transportation and the old Spanish colonial society, while the national eagle soared with its connection to steel rails and steam locomotion. Lady Liberty, who crowned this symbol of progress, made a connection between modernization and the national liberals who held authority and who had made economic growth and national development a reality. No wonder this float was acclaimed the most popular in the celebration.[36]

An intriguing comparison to this celebration can be made with the Independence Day festivities in Guanajuato. Here the municipal authorities organized a September 16 daytime parade in 1884 that featured six elaborate allegorical floats, each of which included symbols of major themes and values of the local provincial community and the broader national culture.

The reconnaissance patrol of the Guanajuato First Squadron, a state militia unit, led the parade. Immediately following came The Discovery of America, a three-part float pulled by four spirited all-black draft horses, accompanied by four grooms, dressed in the clothing of the conquistadors. The front of the float featured the bow of a Spanish caravel, on whose deck stood Christopher Columbus, a friar, and two sailors. The next section represented the sea, leading to the Island of Guanamí, covered with exuberant tropical foliage of cacti, palms, and sycamores. Indians in this tropical forest seemed both amazed and yet prepared to defend their lands. The Guanajuatense-Zacatecana Mint Company and the city's agriculturalists paid for the float, designed by the prominent city residents Antonio Cuyás and Lorenzo Salgado. In striking comparison to the Mexico City float with the same name, this representation had both a presence and an absence that changed the visual narrative. Here a friar, a missionary, stood with Columbus, and the Castilian soldiers of the Mexico City parade do not appear. The emphasis in Guanajuato stressed the Spanish arrival as the bringing of Catholicism and culture, rather than as military conquest.

Next in the parade came miners and other employees of the mining industry, divided by company. Workers carried expensive silk standards with the name of their mine embroidered in gold and silver thread (each cost at least 300 pesos). These escorts led the float dedicated to mining, paid for by the owners of the local mines and smelters. The prow of their float had a coat of arms featuring mining tools placed above a canopy of national flags bearing the names of the principal mines. Covering the float was a green velvet cloth, gathered into waves by a dozen silver chains and marked at intervals with shields bearing the names of famous local miners. The float's front section recreated a mountain of the Sierra Madre, covered with plants and punctuated near its base with the mouth of the mine. The sign above the shaft read "San Nicolás," the patron saint of mining. On the backside of the mountain, a small ore car, with a rich load of minerals, emerged on narrow rails from the mouth of a tunnel into the middle of the float, which featured the representation of the mine's patio, on which were artistically strewn miners' tools and equipment. Two posed miners in work clothes, one doing a mercury test and the other examining ore, completed the patio scene. At the foot of the mountain, an engineer with his theodolite, the surveyor's instrument used to measure horizontal and vertical angles, took a visual sighting. Crowning the summit, as the symbol of the mining industry, a beautiful girl, richly dressed and bejeweled, holding a miner's hat, sat on a chunk of gold ore with the slogan "omnia vincit labor," that is, "work conquers all." The final part of the float featured a large canopy of national flags on whose upper edge in gold letters were the names of the smelters and processing companies of the district. Rising above the center of the canopy was the city's seal, the coat of arms of Santa Fe and Real de Minas de Guanajuato.

The float carried multiple references. The audience familiar with the regular series of holiday parades probably equated the mining company standards carried by the workers with the *cofradía* and parish banners carried in religious parades and likely made by the same seamstresses. The national flags with the names of the mines made an obvious equation between the nation and industry, between the miners and citizens. The elaborate expressions on the float combine two crucial values of liberal Porfirian society, the importance of technology and the significance of work as the keys to success. They also feature a statement of the salient contribution of women. Common in many of these mobile scenes, a woman provides the inspiration, in this case seemingly the prize along with the ore to be earned, so that financial success and domestic harmony were the results of hard work and appropriate technology.

Next in review came Independence and Liberty. This float consisted of a platform covered in velvet of the national colors, and tightly pleated satin in the national colors also covered each of the four wheels, fastened by flower wreaths. Dominating the float was the figure of Hidalgo, with his hands breaking the chain between the Old and New Worlds. At his side stood Allende and Aldama. Liberty appeared on the float as a luxuriously dressed young girl, who lighted the way for the heroes. The float's two designers rode in comfortable gondola seats. State and municipal workers from the city of Guanajuato financed this float. The role of Liberty personified as a young woman again provided the inspiration for the heroes of the independence movement, although curiously only three are identified.

A group of merchants marched next behind a blue standard with various nautical insignias and the slogan "Per ardua surgo" (I rise through difficulties). They preceded their float Commerce, one of the most elegant in the parade. The builders had symbolically represented trade as a Phoenician boat that featured a golden hull, decorated with gold and white reliefs, notably a griffin on the bowsprit, and masts with elegant unfurled sails. Crewing the ship were the Spirit of Commerce, a beautiful girl who held the helm in her right hand, and in her left a gold and silver caduceus, and a group of sailors dressed in what the organizers judged as Phoenician costumes. The float symbolically made it evident that commerce was not a local endeavor but one with reach beyond Guanajuato to the world.

Workers from various industries carrying their standard led their float Trabajo (Work) as a Roman chariot, artistically covered in blue painted cloth with garlands of silver flowers placed at intervals. At the front of the float, on a low, square, Tuscan base appeared the image of Peace, and at his feet the subdued figure of Discord. In the center of the float, a group of blacksmiths who tempered their tools on a heavy anvil represented Work. Presiding over and encouraging them, on silver clouds, the image of Abundance scattered gifts on everyone. This artistically conceived scene boldly expressed Porfirian liberal values, the national ties to the world of classic Rome, the values of work and peace as the requirements for abundance, a restatement of the dictum "Order and Progress." The image of Peace subduing Discord refashioned the common religious image of San Miguel defeating the devil, giving this civic value more transcendent meaning.

Delegations of students and teachers from the public and private schools and from the "Free School of Medicine" and the "State High School" led their float, entitled The Sciences. A garnet-colored canvas covered the base of the float. White shields with the names of eminent philosophers and scholars written in gold decorated the canvas. The float featured a stuccoed composite temple in which reclined Minerva. At her feet and on the temple stairs were all sorts of tools, instruments, and small machines representing science. At the front of the float stood representations of sculpture, music, and painting. The local community's ties to European cultural traditions came across clearly in this float as one of the attributes of education. The references also make clear that reading was not the only way individuals learned the names and traditions of the culture.

Following this last float marched the official party led by the governor, with delegations from the state supreme court, the state legislature, the city council, the senior employees of state and national agencies, and invited guests that included prominent members of the clergy and representatives of foreign communities. The parade ended with a military column. The parade passed through the major plazas of town on September 16, and on Friday, September 19, it made a second march through town, using a different route.[37]

Comparing the two parades, one of fourteen and the other of six floats, four floats match exactly. Both parades featured "discovery," "commerce," "independence," and education, in one parade called "Sciences" and in the other called "Minerva–Public Instruction." Guanajuato's sponsors had a float dedicated to mining, reflecting the major industry of the town, and another float representing work. Large draft horses drew the floats through the streets of both towns. Young women, that is, unmarried women presumably without family obligations, had a major role in both parades as the living symbols of liberty, commerce, and Minerva, and as the inspiration to male workers, heroes, and tradesmen. Significant differences, beyond mere size, appeared between the capital and provincial parades. Most dramatically, the provincial display included both the church and the military, both missing in the capital city parade. The role of the religion from the arrival of Columbus (as portrayed on the float) to Porfirian times (with churchmen in the official delegation) had a visible presence. The military symbolically protected the celebration with delegations that led and closed the parade, and the occasion provided an opportunity to display the military as both militia and regular troops, while the *rurales*, the constabulary, were excluded. The capital city celebration expressed the liberal ideas of a secular, civilian society, and the provincial one represented actual society. The provincial celebration was also all-inclusive, taking two days to reach all the town's neighborhoods, while the parade in Mexico City never departed from the ceremonial avenue. Gradually, the Porfirian government would invoke standard holiday practices throughout the nation, including by 1905 the ringing of replicas of the bell from Dolores Hidalgo in each municipality, and eliminating local variations such as those in Guanajuato.

The emphasis on parades moved the celebration to the daylight hours, with the idea of reducing disorders that occurred after dark. This effort formed part of the general campaign initiated in 1881 in Guanajuato, when the *jefe político*, Miguel T. Barron, tried to limit public disorders by prohibiting disguises in public, especially those in which individuals carried arms or clubs or wore priestly garb. He also prohibited jokes or actions during celebrations that made fun of the reputations of public or religious officials. Later, in 1887, municipal ordinances prohibited the unlicensed shooting of rockets and other fireworks within the city and in public parks.[38]

National holidays as celebrated in Mexico City and Guanajuato had different and often more revealing twists than in other provincial cities, even state capitals. Perhaps more typical was the 1885 Independence Day festival in Colima. Here the holiday began on the evening of September 15 with a special performance by the Lira Orchestra in the Santa Cruz Theater for an audience restricted to invited men and women of the community. Besides the music, a young medical student offered a discussion of independence, followed by readings by two poets. The governor, to conclude the evening, went onstage, held up the national flag, and offered the call, "¡Viva la independencia!" and "¡Viva Mexico!" to which the audience responded.

The following morning, as was the tradition in the Federal District, the new state congress took its seats. This was followed by a civic procession that represented the town. It featured members of the various guilds of artisans, students from the schools, merchants, employees of the city government, members of the militia, and, last, the members of the city council joined by invited private individuals. The procession moved from the government building through the blocked-off streets to the Núñez Garden, Principal Garden, and Plaza de Armas, ending at the Santa Cruz Theater. The theater was filled with members of the public, and several young women identified as the most beautiful señoritas of the community. Once again the medical student offered an oration on independence, the poets offered their poems to the nation, and the orchestra played to conclude the morning's festivities.

In the afternoon, many of the townspeople went to the Llano de Santa Juana (the park) to picnic and to participate in target-shooting contests. The holiday ended with a concert in the Principal Garden in the evening, which concluded with a fireworks display of Bengal lights, colored rockets, and hot air balloons that carried elaborate pyrotechnical images high in the air before they exploded.[39]

Still a somewhat different pattern developed in Jalisco. Guadalajara's city council in the 1870s and 1880s worked with Jalisco's state governors in the selection of the patriotic society, the committee of private citizens and public officials charged with the organization of civil celebrations. Using funds from both the city and the state and contributions from guilds, occupational groups, and government workers, this committee, like the national capital's organization, devoted its greatest efforts to Independence Day but also sponsored celebrations on May 5 (Cinco de Mayo) and Constitution Day.[40]

Until the mid-1890s, the patriotic committee collected funds to augment its small budget provided by the city council and usually matched with funds from the state treasury. The committee's president designated fund-raisers and assigned them groups to solicit. These contribution lists indicated the community members who were expected to participate in the celebration, and made apparent public perception of wealth and social standing. For example, the committee directing the 1877 Independence Day celebration raised the requisite monies by combining its allocation of 412.38 pesos from the treasury with donations of 226.71 pesos. Physicians led the list of contributors, although some doctors identified by name gave nothing. Additional contributions came from shopkeepers and local, federal, state, and municipal bureaucrats.[41] Soliciting contributions continued as the way of financing the celebrations of Independence Day and Cinco de Mayo during the 1880s, although the committee swung an ever-widening net for the collection of donations. The list of prospective donors in 1882 included federal and state bureaucrats, city employees, policemen, military officers and common soldiers, shopkeepers, and businessmen.[42] A decade later, the committee became a larger and more specialized group with the appointment of solicitors who raised monies from the Spanish, French, American, German, Italian, and Scandinavian colonies (totaling 315.00 pesos), dry goods and general shopkeepers (30.00 pesos), the jefe político and the police (57.01 pesos), grocers (13.50 pesos), artisans (88.23 pesos), clergy (27.30 pesos), government employees (45.00 pesos), lawyers (18.75 pesos), doctors (25.00 pesos), deputies of the legislature (12.00 pesos), judicial employees (23.00 pesos), and the entrepreneurs, especially landowners, agriculturalists, and industrialists, (68.50 pesos). Altogether, the committee in 1892 collected over 1,500 pesos in donations.[43]

The archbishop and the church in Guadalajara stand out by their absence before 1890. This serves as further confirmation of the timing of the rapprochement between Catholic and civil leaders and the disregard for liberals' efforts to keep the church out of public life during the high years of the Porfirian regime. In 1892, the archbishop and his cathedral chapter both made contributions to the funds to celebrate both independence and Cinco de Mayo.

Changes took place in 1895 in Guadalajara. The Junta Patriótica became an official committee of city council, and the celebrations underwent dramatic changes. Independence Day fiestas had taken place traditionally in the Plaza de Armas and the Plaza Constitución, located within a block of each other, and had featured serenades, dramas, and awards presentations to outstanding students, and, in the evening, a torchlight parade meandered through town before ending in one plaza or the other for a fireworks display and a public dance. Beginning in 1895, councilmen replaced the evening torchlight procession with afternoon parades of floats and decorated carriages in the city's five precincts. Torchlight parades throughout the nineteenth century had a close association with liberty, patriotism, and often the unrestrained Jacobinism of radicals. The city councilors seemed intent on restricting all symbolic emblems of values that might challenge their authority (especially as authority came to represent less politics, more administration[44]) and closer mimicry of European culture. The police captain in each of the precincts, rather than a voluntary civic committee, organized the holiday events. The establishment of de-centralized celebrations and the elimination of the torchlight parade made easier the maintenance of social order. An additional motive for the change to an afternoon parade was the desire to adopt the European holiday style, such as the grand bicycle and float parades of contemporary Germany, which in an ironic twist was the celebration of German socialist workers.[45]

The afternoon parades of coaches and floats offered the opportunity for members of the city's smart set to express their social prestige and political authority as they appeared before the former paraders, now turned spectators. In this way, the parades provide an intriguing view of the Tapatío (the nickname for residents of Jalisco) elites. The afternoon's grand promenades were followed by citywide bicycle races, organized by the Club Atlético Jaliscense in the Alameda, as the two-wheelers provided the expression of mechanized progress. Another revealing addition to the program was the collection of funds, clothing, and toys for distribution to poor children and families in each precinct. The city council committee directed school principals to submit lists of the poorest children in their schools to receive the holiday presents. This policy promoted participation through community charity rather than civil involvement in the previous patriotic committee and torchlight parade. Moreover, volunteerism now became the public activity of women, as society ladies got together to organize donations for the less fortunate and to sponsor medical and self-help programs for the poor.

Civic committee members no longer solicited funds for the celebration; rather, the city council sent either lawyers or bureaucrats as representatives to community groups with directives on what floats to build for the afternoon parades held in their precincts. Generally, the floats became commercial messages. The guilds no longer marched as artisans with skills and prestige important to the community; rather, after 1895 their floats had general marketing messages, announcing products that Guadalajara had available for the general Mexican and even international markets. Artisans participated only through their association with the commodities. The parades in this way reduced one-time celebrants to accomplices of production. Guild members continued to build floats until the end of the century, but the parade had become a peripatetic trade fair. The committee intended the public display of products to make visible the city's industry and commerce to spectators.[46]

In other communities, leaders had been making similar changes. Even earlier, for example, state officials had organized the events in the capital city with what they called a Patriotic Jubilee on the evening of September 15, and a more promotional celebration on September 16, 1883, which featured the inauguration of electric lighting and other new electricity-powered services.[47] The members of the Mexican and Mexican American community in Tucson, Arizona, organized a related procession. The fiesta became a celebration of middle-class values and a vehicle with which to praise Mexico and its progress. Women were made into idealized representations of virtue, and floats presented evidence of capitalist progress in Porfirian Mexico and among Mexican Americans.[48] The celebration revealed how fiestas can present and represent a number of ideals and points of view at the same time.

The changes in Mexico City, Guadalajara, Guanajuato, and other cities, even across the border in Arizona, embodied major alterations. The independence celebration became the cultural equivalent of what Hanna Pitkin calls "descriptive representation." Before, the constituent groups in the community actually had presented themselves, rather than abstract symbols, for public view so that the celebration displayed the urban population in all its diversity, forming a detailed, descriptive portrait of society.[49] Now socioeconomic groups appeared as abstractions, as the actual members of ethnic and economic groups in disfavor became spectators, and the celebrations displayed symbols of wealth and prestige for the local representatives of the national smart set.

The changing celebration of independence and other holidays came to represent the official view of nationalism and national identity, yet the spectators took away from the parades what they selected as part of their collective memory of the affair.

## Porfirio Díaz's Birthday and Independence Celebrations

During the 1890s, the celebration of independence took on a new, blended character as it was fused with Porfirio Diaz's birthday and at the same time became a more elitist display. It became one of the most important, that is, most lavish celebrations for the capital's high society. The Porfirians used national holidays to make presentations of their modern, progressive ideas and of the symbols that expressed modernity to them. The 1883 Independence Day celebration demonstrated clearly their effort to promote this image. During the 1890s, the effort became more dramatic—perhaps *melodramatic* would be a better word—as dinners usually given on September 15 to celebrate the president's birthday became an expression of the new progressive nation celebrating its independence. This episode created an opportunity to connect the triumph of Porfirian liberalism to the victory in the independence struggle, and offered a stage on which elite behavior could be used to set a model for the rest of the population.

As the heirs of Juárez's brand of liberalism, the Porfirians paraded their commitment to municipal autonomy, community defense, and, especially, individualism. For these leaders, individualism created a self-serving feeling of community responsibility, the sense of performing before an audience, appreciative or not, that needed an example of modern life. Conspicuous consumption provided one method of community display; it not only satisfied the consumer's ego but also served as a goal, they assumed, for the aspirations of the less fortunate. The president himself led this social parade, under the direction of his wife, Carmen Romero Rubio. Her influence, described at the time as the "bleaching" of the mestizo Porfirio, substituted table manners, fashionable haberdashery, and chic celebrations of birthdays and anniversaries for the crude, vulgar behavior of the barracks.[50]

Government leaders in the 1890s, encouraged by their resolution of crucial international debt questions and their settlement of severe internal disturbances, sought opportunities to celebrate the new national identity and cosmopolitan standing. The critical financial action came in the renegotiation of the external debt. This was the debt on which Benito Juárez had suspended payments, leading to the French intervention from 1862 to 1867, and Porfirio Diaz himself had suspended payments again in 1884. The Dublan Convention in 1888 refinanced all of the foreign debt with a new bond issue, over half of which was purchased by German bankers.[51] The internal disruptions had involved Apache, Yaqui, and Mayo resistance in the north, agrarian disturbances in the Bajío, political opposition in the west, and endemic and pervasive banditry. The reorganized army and enlarged rural constabulary, armed for the most part with newly imported mausers, suppressed the internal challenges to the regime.

Capital city elites felt the time had arrived for another celebration. They chose Díaz's birthday, which quickly became one of the most lavish celebrations for the capital's high society. Earlier, Díaz had celebrated his christening date rather than his actual day of birth.[52] Honoring the president's birthday in 1891, the leading Porfirians mounted a special fete. The organizing committee of twenty-eight comprised the nation's most important government and business leaders and was led by Carlos Pacheco.[53] This committee, which subsumed the Gran Circulo de Amigos del General Díaz, which had been involved in the 1888 presidential election campaign, represented Mexico City's political, military, business, and intellectual leadership. This junta did not move quickly enough to reserve the day of September 15, the president's birthday, for the celebration, so for this first dinner they decided to host a banquet on September 21.[54] Henceforth, the dinner would be held on September 15, Independence Day eve, merging the two events.

The committee invited the jefes políticos of all the nation's major municipalities. On the one hand, these invitations restored a personal touch to relationships with the president that had become rather distant, formal, and routine.[55] On the other hand, the invitation also had the character of ordering local officials to Mexico City to pay homage to the president, in the clear display of successful national centralization. The invitations offered free rail or ship transportation for the guests. Several prominent politicians added the offer to pay all expenses for guests from their home states. Vice President Ramón Corral made this offer to the jefes políticos of Sonora, for example. The guest list also included Mexico City's leading politicians, army officers, foreign and domestic businessmen, the diplomatic corps, and members of the Jockey Club who were not otherwise invited.

The celebration began with a grand military review, on September 14, clearly indicating the unbreakable ties between the army and the government officials, including President Díaz. The military parade saluted the officials of the government and reaffirmed Díaz's military origins and the bonds of camaraderie forged through the Wars of Reform, the French and Austrian intervention, and other domestic campaigns. It was the death rattle of these veterans in government, who were dying off.[56]

The independence celebration also featured the decoration of the major streets between the Zócalo and the Caballito, today's historic district. The displays featured flower adornment of columns and window facades on various business and public buildings, including the national palace. Banners and colorful decorations stretched across streets. The centerpiece was a grand floral arch resting on two quadrangular columns, covered with flowers and spanning Plateros Street.[57] This arch provided a clear, visual connection to the triumphal arches used to welcome the viceroys. It offered a literary echo to the arch that Carlos de Sigüenza y Góngora used to describe what he regarded as the characteristics of successful leaders in his version of *The Prince*, written in the eighteenth century. It also foreshadowed the triumphal arches built to honor Díaz in 1899.[58]

The first official activity for the invited municipal delegates came at the offices of the *ayuntamiento*, where Mexico City's councilmen hosted them. Following this reception, the jefes políticos were received at the presidential palace, where each individual met President Díaz and quite likely received his *carta de visita*, featuring his photograph, as a souvenir.[59] Throughout their stay in the capital, the jefes políticos attended the inauguration of several public buildings and public works.

The celebration climaxed with the opportunity to dine with the president. The organizers held the birthday dinner at the National Theatre on September 21. The guests numbered 588, seated at thirteen tables arranged into a head table and six additional seating groups. President Díaz occupied the center seat, flanked on his right by the minister from England, Sir Spenser St. John; Manuel Romero Rubio, *secretario de gobernación* and Díaz's father-in-law; and Thomas Ryan, minister from the United States. On his left were Baron Federico Daeloman, minister from Belgium; Manuel González Cosío, secretary of communications; General Pedro Hinojosa, secretary of war.

The dinner proceeded, according to the menu printed in French, in the English pattern of soup to nuts or, better said, soup to fruits, with eight wines that concluded with cognac.

The meal followed closely the banquets given in the celebrated restaurants of Paris, such as the Café de la Paix at the Grand Hotel or the Foyot.[60] The menu:

*Potages*
Potage á l'espagnole

*Hors-d'oeuvres*
Huauchinango á la princesse
Vol-au-vent truffé

*Salades*
Asperges au naturel

*Sorbets au kirsch*

*Entrées*
Poularde á la mexicaine
Filet de boeuf á la valencienne
Galantine á la parisienne
Dindonneaux rotis

*Desserts*
Gateaux assortis
Fruits divers

*Café, Thé, Vins*
Jerez

Medoc
Château Margaux
Sauternes
Bourgogne
Champagne Clicquot
Roederer
Cognac Martell

The banquet offered a metaphor of the goals of the Porfirian regime in which the preparation, the outer form of the repast, had a French inspiration, quite possibly the 1889 meal served to 1,800 French mayors at the Palais de l'Industrie.[61] The menu, including the wines, followed closely this French dinner, but some of the ingredients and some courses (the sorbet, for example) came from Mexican, even pre-columbian sources.[62] The menu projected the elite's confidence in its international character.

The wine list made the dinner a cosmopolitan event. Several of the wines had been recognized since 1855 (at the exhibition of that year) as outstanding French products. The Château Margaux remains among the first-growth elite of the Bordeaux region, the Medoc is still an outstanding wine, and the Sauternes was, as it would be today, a stunning selection. Champagne, the drink of monarchs since the previous century, had already developed a folkloric reputation for its taste and the luxury it represented, in large part due to the efforts of Nicole-Barbe Clicquot-Ponsardin, known simply as The Widow. When her husband died when she was twenty-seven, and with a child, Clicquot turned to improving the production, marketing, and promotion of her champagne to make it the preferred wine for celebrations with the European royalty. She succeeded, making Clicquot the premier champagne, although it was closely followed by bottles of Roederer.[63]

The wine list in general reflected the cosmopolitan pretensions of the Porfirian elite, if not the president himself. The circle of advisers and admirers, typified by José Limantour, had begun making imported wines one of the measures of social standing. They replaced no domestic industry, because national wineries produced bulk wine drunk in a few areas such as Parras de las Colonias, Coahuila, incorporated in communion services, or used as the base in brandy production. Mexicans made no fine wines. Díaz had made an effort, when he contracted with an Irish American winemaker, James Concannon, from Livermore, California, to introduce higher-quality vines into Querétaro, but the effort came to nothing.[64] Elites imported wines. As this social group in the capital city moved to the newly developed suburbs of the city, such as Colonia Roma, where they built neoclassical mansions, many had their architects include wine cellars. They filled their *cavas* with imported French wines, and occasional bottles of Italian or Spanish wine to complement what they held. Some individuals, such as Limantour, made periodic trips to France, both to visit Paris and to restock their wine cellars. Two prominent Porfirians with well-stocked cellars were Ignacio de la Torre y Mier, the husband of Amada Díaz, daughter of the president, and Antonio de Landa y Escandón, governor of the Federal District.[65]

The birthday meal of course concluded with a round of toasts: General Sostenes Rocha spoke on behalf of the Junta Central Porfirista, followed by Manuel Contreras as the representative of the jefes políticos, and the president offered the last toast in gratitude.

The official guests at the dinner included men only. Wives and other female family members of the guests were invited to observe the proceedings from the theater's boxes, making the event political theater. Only in these circumstances could women, in line with the moral literature reaching back to the sixteenth century, attend, observe men, and sit in theater boxes that architecturally had the appearance of windows. Their seating placement in the boxes, no doubt, moved them away from being visible but still allowed them to watch the proceedings. Thus away from the windowlike front, they were sheltered by the boxes in the same way the walls of their homes acted as the architectural equivalent of the chaperon, protecting the modesty of women and yet making them part of the performance.[66]

These boxes were also assigned through strict hierarchy. The ones on the second level were occupied by the president's wife, Carmen, and family, and the families of the cabinet ministers and diplomatic representatives. Following the banquet, President Díaz and the other members of the head table went up to the boxes that surrounded the floor to join their spouses for the concert performed by the Sieni Italian Company. The musicians performed a series of operatic favorites, largely Italian arias by Rossini. Following the concert, the hall was cleared for dancing. Díaz and Carmen joined in the festivities until 3:00 a.m., then left, but other guests danced on until dawn.[67]

After this initial celebration, the dictator's dinner party was moved to September 15. Thus, the Porfirians identified national independence, nationalism, and the dictator in one powerful image. Their action resulted in the significant conflation of independence, personalism, continuity of authority, centralism, and the military's prominence in national life.

The conflation of the national holiday and the personal birthday provided an opportunity for others to take advantage of the national attention focused on the president. In 1904, Ralph Cabañas, the representative in Mexico for the National Phonograph Company (Thomas A. Edison's phonographic enterprise), held a press conference to announce that the company would mark the Independence Day celebration and the president's birthday on September 15 by presenting a gold-plated phonograph to Díaz. Of course, Cabañas counted on the attendant publicity generated during the patriotic holiday to provide grand advertising for National phonographs and their musical cylinders. Phonographs and sound recordings, whether or not due to this publicity effort, quickly became popular. Walter Stevens, National Phonograph Company's foreign manager, evaluated the Mexican market as "one of the best talking-machine countries there is."[68]

This identification of Díaz with independence proved so successful and inviting that the Porfirians tried to make a similar connection between the celebration of Cinco de Mayo and Diaz's daughter. This effort did not succeed. The dinners and the association of independence with Díaz continued up to and through the centennial celebration of independence in 1910. Then revolutionaries drove Díaz from power and from the country, but the practice of celebrating September 15–16 as the official holiday continues to the present day. The dinners with the president served as a powerful image-building occasion that succeeded beyond the regime.

## Promoting Mexico Abroad

President Díaz and his advisers, who believed they had provided a new pride in the nation, turned to the difficult task of creating a new, modern, progressive, prosperous image as the symbol of national identity. They planned to project this image both at home and abroad.[69] Their efforts included enthusiastic participation in World's Fairs and expositions,[70] hosting promotional excursions on the newly completed railroads for potential investors, prominent politicians, and influential journalists,[71] erecting didactic monuments to represent a glorious past,[72] and offering attention-catching displays, especially holiday celebrations,[73] before both domestic and foreign audiences.

State and regional expositions provided opportunities to display new technology and successful production, just as the county fairs and expositions did in the other countries of North America. Offering examples of progress and modernization in the area, the exhibit halls and exhibits themselves often were put to use to promote these ideas. For example, the building constructed for the first Veracruzana Exhibition became in 1883 the Free College of Agriculture, Commerce, Arts and Trades of Orizaba, continuing the productive utilization of natural resources that had been exhibited there.[74] The school offered both theoretical and practical courses in agriculture and industry.

Participation in the 1889 Universal Exposition in Paris centered on the national pavilion—the first effort by the regime to present a national architecture. This building combined the regularity and symmetry of European designs with decorative motifs from Aztec culture. As a dramatic gesture indicating their reentry into the community of nations—that is, renewing diplomacy and trade with western Europe—the Mexicans used the pavilion to articulate two seemingly contradictory images, "a pre-industrial imperial antiquity and a technologically sophisticated present." The overall goal of the pavilion was to suggest the nation's latent potential for development.[75]

At the 1893 World's Columbian Exposition in Chicago, Mexican officials presented forty-two displays of photographs intended to inform visitors to the fair about the nation and to illustrate its resources. The exhibits trumpeted national natural wealth. At the anthropology venue, Mexico was represented with facsimile models of the ruins at Uxmal and Labná and casts from facades at Chichén Itzá. This displayed the country's exotic and sophisticated ancient heritage. The Bureau of American Republics presented 183 Mexican items, chiefly photographs, the largest number in the exhibit. The display in the Manufacturers and Liberal Arts Building included promotional photographs provided by the states of Oaxaca, Yucatán, Zacatecas, Puebla, Durango, and Querétaro, and by several government agencies, the War Department, and the Commission for Geological Exploration and Railways, for example.[76] These photographs demonstrated the nation's geographic size and variety, prosperity, and transportation infrastructure. In the agricultural building, Mexican officials presented a glass case of chiles of all sizes, shapes, and colors, chocolate in bean and processed forms, sugar, silk, vanilla, wines, and mescal.[77] These exhibitions indicated the agricultural diversity and capacity to produce tropical and unusual commercial crops. Thus, at the World's Fair, official exhibitors projected a nation rich in natural resources, with a culture reaching back to an advanced, exotic civilization and, in 1893, with the population and area size, agricultural variety, mineral wealth, and modern transportation to emerge as a major world state.

## The Crowning of the Virgin

Independence holidays and participation in international exhibitions provided opportunities to demonstrate Porfirian development as a liberal, progressive nation. In another way, a religious occasion allowed the Porfirians to offer a critical example of modernization, the separation of church and state. The government and its leaders remained outside of the celebration created to honor the nation's patron saint, the Virgin of Guadalupe, with the crowning of the Virgin. This event has received little attention, yet it deserves close analysis for the social and cultural messages that were encoded for Mexicans, visitors, and North American audiences to receive as demonstrations of the new Mexico.

First Lady Carmen Romero Rubio played a crucial role. She and her circle of elite society women became extremely active with charities and devotions, especially those associated with great expenditure. These allowed public performances by these ladies in imported European fashions. These prominent women had adapted Parisian fashions for themselves and encouraged their husbands to follow their lead in wearing French and English clothes, dancing the minuet, listening to French and Italian operas, and serving English and French, rather than Mexican, cuisine.[78]

Of all these efforts to create a new image, nothing rivaled the fund-raising efforts of doña Carmen, which finally climaxed in the crowning of the Virgin of Guadalupe in 1895. The circle around the first lady inaugurated a number of charitable and devotional activities besides the crowning of the Virgin, all of it so that the wives could perform for their husbands, to quote Thorstein Veblen's inimitable prose, "such an amount of vicarious consumption of time and sustenance as is demanded by the standard of pecuniary decency."[79] Devout female socialites helped restore the church to prominence after the liberal reforms, civil war, French intervention, and liberal reprisals. This pattern, it should be noted, is the same as that used after the Revolution by old Porfirians to regain positions of influence in the 1920s. Porfirian wives used social clubs and volunteer activities to restore the old social order.[80] The church, bold from its new rapprochement with the Porfirian government in the 1880s, and inspired by the papal exhortations in *Rerum novarum*, acted in coincident ways with the new and expanded civic celebrations. The church expanded its festivities as well. The church's new vigor appeared in a campaign of reevangelization, the creation of new dioceses in Tabasco, Colima, Sinaloa, Cuernavaca, Chihuahua, Saltillo, Tehuantepec, Tepic, Campeche, Aguascalientes, and Huajuapan de Leon (Mixteca),[81] and in the increased number of Jesuit fathers (39 in 1876 to 338 in 1910) in the country.[82] The renewal of church festivals was not as great in practice as it appeared. Even during the most violent years of the Reform, when the government limited the church's opportunity for public displays, the public often ignored the laws to celebrate the feast days on the religious calendar.

The church's reemergence appeared most clearly in the campaign to crown the Virgin of Guadalupe that succeeded in 1895. Coronation of an image of the virgin requires the permission of the pope, who theoretically performs it. This first step had been taken in the colonial period, when the Jesuit priest Juan Francisco López had obtained papal confirmation in 1751 of the Virgin of Guadalupe as Mexico's special patron and for a special mass on her feast day, December 12. Efforts to crown the image of Guadalupe began immediately but had no success until the archbishops of Mexico, Michoacán, and Guadalajara made a concerted effort in 1886. Pope Leo XIII approved their request in 1887 and granted additional offices in 1894. The Porfirian churchmen scheduled the coronation for October 1895.

Carmen Romero Rubio de Díaz, the president's wife, led a fundraising campaign for the crown. She and eleven other women of the most prominent families contributed 35,000 pesos for its purchase. Their next effort was to provide the appropriate apparel—in this case bejeweled accessories for the image of the Virgin. Parisian jeweler Edward Morgan crafted the crown according to the ideas of Rómulo Escudero y Pérez Gallardo and the design of painter Salomé Pina. Morgan produced a ponderous thirty-pound object of silver, gold, and enamel worked into a maze of angels in relief, stars, ecclesiastical symbols, synodal arms, state shields, and bishops' names. It is covered with rubies and other precious stones, including fifty-two diamonds in its base. Diener Bras, Jewelers, produced a copy of this crown in gold for daily use.

Crowning the Virgin made Mexico the center of attention throughout the Catholic world in 1895. The pope authorized indulgences with the purchase of medals and rosaries of the Virgin sold in the sanctuary. The bishops of Zacatecas, Durango, Yucatán, San Luis Potosí, and Querétaro contributed to the celebration by donating 4,000 pesos each for the painting of five murals, 9 × 7 m in size, in the sanctuary by the artists Ibarrán and Pina y Parra. Bishop Antonio Plancarte y Labastida of Mexico City sponsored a contest for a hymn in the Virgin's honor. From fifty-seven entries, he selected "Himno cantado en la solemne coronación de la Virgin de Guadalupe, el 12 de Octubre de 1895," with words by Luis Mendizabel y Zubialdea and music by Francisco de P. Andros.[83]

The events provided another day for religious adoration. Henceforth,

October 12 was celebrated both as El Día de la Raza (that is, Columbus Day) and as the Virgin's coronation day. The day had hardly become associated with Columbus. The first Día de la Raza celebration had occurred in 1884 and had not received much attention until 1892. The celebration combined support for the Spanish-speaking world and a reference to the importance of the bringing of Spanish civilization and religion to the Americas.[84] The fund-raising committee and other ladies of the capital continued their association with the event by forming Las Hermanas de Guadalupe, the Sisters of Guadalupe, an elite devotional society. The coronation attracted bishops from throughout North America and the first families from across Mexico. Indians—obviously this meant those dressed as Indians—and others not properly attired for the occasion were not permitted to enter the basilica grounds on the day of the coronation but were made to wait until the following day to offer their devotions to the Virgin. For the lower segments of the society, Antonio Vanegas Arroyo printed a prayer sheet devoted to Guadalupe's crown, which sold on the streets for five centavos the day of the coronation.[85]

Thus, in less than a century, the Virgin of Guadalupe changed in the popular mind from the terrifying emblem of Padre Miguel Hidalgo's insurrection, and the patron of downtrodden, rebellious Mexicans, to the patron saint of the dictatorship's elite. This seems not to have been simply a reversal in the representation of the Virgin, but rather a renewed emphasis on another of the colonial advocations made by the symbol of Our Lady of Immaculate Conception. In this more muted (at least as portrayed by recent scholars) voice, the Virgin spoke as an instrument of the hierarchy and as an affirmation of authority. As the intercessor between the people and the Lord, as William Taylor argues, "the Virgin was a model of acceptance and legitimation of … authority." Thus, in 1895 the Virgin's authority again confirmed the regime as it apparently had done until the end of the colonial period,[86] with an emphasis on patience, forbearance, hierarchy, and unqualified trust in authority. Porfirians could not have invented a more serviceable emblem. Moreover, the crowning of the Virgin redoubled the regime's reconstructed history, with echoes of noble Aztecs, colonial glories, and miraculous apparitions.

Observing the anticlerical niceties of the Liberal party program from Valentín Gómez Farías through Benito Juárez, President Díaz attended none of the official activities associated with the crowning of the Virgin. This also reflected his government's official mourning following the funeral ceremony the week before for Díaz's cabinet minister and father-in-law, Manuel Romero Rubio, who died on October 3 and was laid to rest on October 4, 1895. The funeral proceeded with the assistance of a solitary priest, who appeared only at the family vault in the French cemetery.[87] Of course, President Díaz exchanged pleasantries at several of the receptions and informal gatherings arranged for the visiting prelates by his wife.

Moreover, Porfirio created a bridge between the coronation and his efforts to create new national images. He developed policies that not only pounded out elite distinctiveness but also emphasized an image of nationalism that merged Díaz himself, the Virgin of Guadalupe, and the army as the heir of the patriots of the independence era and other defenders of the nation.

The historical episode that made this identification possible came from the actions of Padre Miguel Hidalgo, father of the struggle for independence in 1810. After ringing the parish bell to mobilize the villagers of Dolores, Guanajuato, Padre Hidalgo seized a banner of the Virgin of Guadalupe to serve as the standard of his revolutionary army. Díaz and his fellow liberal veterans traced their military service back to Hidalgo's patriotic army with its Guadalupine flag. This connection received careful and specific identification during the Porfirian years with the erection of monuments to Hidalgo and widespread incorporation of his actions into Independence Day celebrations. Moreover, in 1895 in the same month as the Virgin's crowning, the Díaz government ordered that all relics, especially battle flags, be submitted to the national government for preservation in the artillery museum at the national armory. The Department of War assigned Jefe Político Eduardo Velásquez to bring the Guadalupe banner from the Virgin's shrine to the museum. Velásquez, over the protests of church officials, collected and stored the banner for transfer to the museum.

The banner promptly disappeared. Greatly embarrassed, the courier had to solve this theft of a national treasure. Government investigators quickly traced the Virgin's insignia to the house of the archbishop, who confessed that he and a group of conspiring priests had reclaimed this most significant relic. Velásquez, with government orders, redeemed himself by recovering the flag from the archbishop's residence and presenting it to the minister de gobernación, General Manuel González de Cosío. The minister authenticated the celebrated flag. The public presentation of this banner occurred the month after the Virgin of Guadalupe's coronation, and it remained on display in the position of honor in the Artillery Museum.[88] Díaz had converted a popular religious symbol of the Virgin into a nationalistic image for his regime, one that simultaneously identified the president, the arch-patriot Miguel Hidalgo, and national independence.

Crowning the Virgin not only gave Mexicans a new religious holiday but also prompted an expanded celebration of December 12, the Virgin's feast day. In addition to the customary pilgrimages and devotions, such as village journeys to the shrine and penitents crawling on their knees for blocks to reach the basilica, new ways of celebrating the holy day appeared. The capital's well-to-do followed the example of the governor of the Federal District, Pedro Rincón Gallardo, who decorated his home with electric lights that he burned through the night of December 12. His neighbors, the Escandón family, and other Porfirians in the fashionable new neighborhoods adopted the practice. Soon they added a variety of decorations to the electric illumination. Nearly every household had a dinner to honor a family member who bore the name Guadalupe, and the custom became firmly established that this dinner required a meal of turkey mole. This meal combined a pre-columbian meat with a colonial mestizo sauce, whose creation is attributed to nuns in Puebla. Visitors to the shrine regularly purchased *gorditas de la villa*, small sweetened tortillas, usually wrapped in brightly colored paper.[89]

Both dining with the dictator on his birthday on the eve of Independence Day and crowning the Virgin had been constructed by the male and female leaders of elite society as part of a campaign to forge new images of the nation for both domestic and international audiences. Manuel Gamio's call for forging nationalism and progress suggested the workshop's forge, but in its nuances it also referred to production of counterfeit products.[90] Certainly the regime and society expressed in the dinner with the dictator and the crowning of the Virgin were bogus inclusive national displays of what were, in reality, celebrations of elite exclusivity.

## Defining Society and Exclusive Nationalism

The campaign to reestablish some distance between the elite and the hoi polloi seemed especially necessary to members of high society in the 1890s because of the burgeoning population of the capital city. As the city grew from 230,000 (1877) to 329,774 (1895),[91] it increased the rubbing of shoulders with ordinary Mexicans, who demanded recognition as veterans of the struggle against the French and as fellow speakers of the liberal idiom. This conceit of the masses created uncomfortable feelings among the Porfirian bon-ton society. They responded by establishing social and physical space between themselves and the lower groups. They moved to newly created neighborhoods in the city's southwest and west, along the prolongation of Reforma Avenue. Homeowners in the new neighborhoods often obtained designs and blueprints from Europe, so that the neoclassical homes resembled sections of Paris or Brussels. These homes were financed by U.S. banks and construction firms, with huge profits for the initial investors.[92]

Middle-class residents of the capital, made desperate by the city's chronic and worsening housing shortage, turned to residential hotels and walk-up apartments built by U.S. contractors. Creating great attention was the capital's first modern apartment building, built by T. S. Gore, and the additional building projects of R. A. Pigeon, who built a new apartment complex every year from 1904 to 1907 in what today is the Zona Rosa. By the end of the regime, U.S. housing designs for multifamily dwellings dominated the city. Deliberate business expansion forced working-class families out of the center of town into cheap housing to the east of the central plaza. Other worker residences were rushed into existence near new factories. Thus, Colonia Romero Rubio, a light industry zone, also had a neighborhood of ramshackle dwellings.[93] This urban pattern was repeated in Hermosillo, Sonora; Parral, Chihuahua; and Mérida, Yucatán.[94]

The exigencies of urban growth and residential social patterns demanded some coordinated urban plan. Between 1901 and 1903, such a program emerged under the direction of Roberto Gayol y Soto and Miguel Angel de Quevedo, professional engineers, who focused on public health, potable water, drainage, and parks for the city.[95]

More important even than physical space was the desire to create social distance between the elite and the masses. This resulted in the creation of new social customs and institutions exclusively for the elite. Porfirians acted in the same way as their social equals in Boston and Buenos Aires. The elites in Boston, Massachusetts, felt threatened by the rising tide of immigrants (especially Irish) in the city. They responded by creating exclusive institutions, such as the Boston Symphony Orchestra and Boston Museum of Fine Arts, in which they could isolate themselves. In Buenos Aires, the elites who felt they were being submerged in a tide of Italian immigrants undertook the construction of several institutions, most notably the Colon Opera Theater and the Jockey Club, as social citadels.[96]

Moreover, in the newly created or expanded social spaces, high-society leaders established ways of giving performative utterance, that is, enacting their membership in the cosmopolitan elite culture that they defined as respectability. New York City's elites constructed their class identity and drew social boundaries through promenading.[97] Upper- and middle-class citizens also turned to tourism, especially to areas with a nostalgic character such as Nantucket, Massachusetts, and another rural town that appeared to be a "living history museum." This escape from the multiethnicity, congestion, and cultural mishmash of the city included a new interest in handicrafts, primitive cultures, colonial revival furniture, colonial silverware patterns, and historical novels.[98]

Mexican society's middle and upper segments developed similar interests and practices with decisive steps. They created an expanded, formal museum of anthropology and history to host the Eleventh International Congress of Americanists in 1895. On that occasion, Díaz inaugurated the monoliths wing at the national museum,[99] and the theater of fine arts. The social leaders also organized several elite social organizations, including the Jockey Club. Leaders of high society in Guadalajara initiated similar changes in the social locations created by celebrations in Mexico's second city as well.[100]

Not every effort worked as intended. The elite also created the National Conservatory of Music to encourage composers and to train musicians. Rather than becoming a center for transposing European orchestral music, the directors focused their efforts on a style of national romantic music that paralleled the costumbrista movement, which focused on distinctive Mexican traditions, in literature and appealed most to aspiring middle-class Mexicans. This difference in attitudes between the elite with international connections and pretensions and the middle sector with its more national concerns appeared clearly in the music selections at the presidential birthday in 1891, when the arias of Rossini and other Italians—not those of Juventino Rosas, who wrote the internationally famous waltz "Sobre las Olas,"[101] or some other Mexican—filled the theater.

During this period, different social groups invented or defined themselves by creating class identities. For example, both the working and middle classes hammered out social characteristics, often in response to each other. In the case of the middle groups, their moral and self-discipline reform campaigns became the forge of their self-definition.[102] But for the elites, nothing defined their identity and created the social distance from their poor, rural, and indigenous countrymen as well as dining with Díaz and participating in major events such as crowning the Virgin. The political expression of these capital city elites came in the domination of offices, which also brought economic opportunities. To the provincial elites, denied these preferments, the coach of government seemed to be filled; hence, they referred to this pattern as the full car.

## The Centennial of Independence

The climax of a century of independence celebrations came in the centennial festivals of 1910. The commemoration used all the available media, the traditional—lectures, books, iconography, painting, sculpture, scenography, music, parades, and popular fiestas—and the modern—newspapers, photography, cinema, civic ceremonies, and the museum—to broadcast a multiplicity of symbols and messages of nationalism.[103] These events stretched across several weeks and included a variety of events, international gatherings, dedications of statues and buildings, and dramatic cavalcades through the streets. On September 15, 1910, the spectators witnessed the History Parade, which offered them tableaux of the past in motion. This parade featured several sections, beginning with the "Epoch of the Conquest," which focused on the meeting of Moctezuma and Cortés and required a cast of 839 people (most of them as Aztecs, with historically accurate costumes). The principal organizers of the celebration, José Casarín and Guillermo de Landa y Escandón, decided to bring more than two hundred indigenous persons from the Huasteca of San Luis Potosí to represent diverse peoples at the Aztec emperor's court.[104]

The second section, representing the "Epoch of Spanish Domination," focused on the Promenade of the Pennant of San Hipólito, marking the August 13, 1521, Spanish conquest of Tenochtitlán. This section incorporated 288 people in the parade.

Most interesting was the third section, the "Epoch of Independence and the Present," which had seven floats. The first paid tribute to the father of independence, Padre Miguel Hidalgo, and was sponsored by the Hidalgo state government; the second float featured Padre José María Morelos, sponsored by the state of Michoacán. The third element was a group of horsemen representing the entrance into Mexico City of the Army of Three Guarantees under the command of General Agustín de Iturbide, accompanied by Generals Vicente Guerrero, Manuel Mier y Terán, Guadalupe Victoria, and Anastasio Bustamante, as well as riders representing the major military units. The fourth float, presented by the State of Veracruz, honored the cadets who defended Chapultepec and Mexico City against the U.S. invaders during the U.S.–Mexican War. The remaining two floats represented the states of Tabasco and Colima.[105] Thus, the panoramic historical cavalcade featured nothing more contemporary than the Colima float, featuring a state first created in the 1857 constitution, which also served as a vague reference to this liberal document and its personification, Benito Juárez. Altogether, the historical procession certainly skirted individuals such as Juárez, who might inspire unfortunate comparisons with Díaz and direct references to the liberals and the 1857 constitution that had by and large been discarded, at least in political terms.

The United States, during the centennial celebration, honored with a marble obelisk the Boy Heroes, those six cadets who had heroically defended Chapultepec in 1847. Díaz and the U.S. representative attended. The U.S. spokesman said: "Just as Rome had its Augustus, England had its Elizabeth and Victoria, Mexico has Porfirio Díaz. Everything is well in Mexico. Under Porfirio Diaz has been created a nation."[106]

Frederick Starr, an anthropologist from the University of Chicago and one of the delegates to the Congress of the Americanists held in conjunction with the Centennial of Independence, observed all of the festivities that focused on elite and foreign perceptions of the nation. Afterward, he reflected on the centennial celebration that had been estimated to cost about one peso per capita of the population (some 15,000,000 pesos). He wrote, "If the celebration embodied appreciation of the principles for which the fathers fought, if it emphasized the blessings of freedom, if it increased respect for the national constitution and kindled sound patriotism—it was cheap at that price. But if it was simply the opportunity to make a grand display, to give gay pleasure and enjoyment to a rich few, it was a grievous burden."[107] His observation of the centennial festival serves as a measure for all Independence Day celebrations. Certainly the Porfirian definition of nationalism and national identity had moved away from the inclusive collective memories and national attitudes of the majority of the people as expressed in almanacs and board games, and especially as it appeared in popular performances aimed at the general population. The popular sense of national identity continued to find expression in popular performances, including puppet theater.

## CHAPTER 4

# Itinerant Puppet Theater and National Identity

*Even legend and rumor usually have some basis in reality.*
—Michael Connelly[1]

Itinerant puppet theater, during the nineteenth century, helped create popular memories of history, geography, society, and culture that together constituted national identity. Puppet companies offered scenes, sketches, and plays that provided a way for ordinary people to make an identification with other Mexicans and with their nation. Puppeteers had no overt didactic ambitions, neither was the puppet company simply an entertainment enterprise. It provided employment for the puppeteers and for the rest of the company. At stake was their livelihood. Puppeteers had an urgent need to attract spectators, entertain them, and bring them back. They had a desperate need to identify the interests of the audience and appeal to them, or they would face empty seats at the next performance.

Moreover, puppeteers often competed for centavos with other entertainments. Beyond saint-day fairs, in any given season these might include balloon ascensions, organ grinders, accordion players, displays of monkeys and bears, raffles of dishes or household goods, optical devices to show scenes of historical significance and foreign lands, and carnival performances such as "The Beautiful Emma Banamichi, the Queen of the Jungle, with her Troupe of Poisonous Reptiles" and "Señora Adelaida Guzmán and the Demons in the Body," as well as theater, circuses, and opera companies, and even other puppet companies.[2] Theaters in the provincial capitals, such as the Teatro de la Paz in San Luis Potosí, featured dramatic and musical performers from Mexico City and even Europe. The self-proclaimed first lady of the theater, doña Inocencia Navarro de Espinosa, for example, entertained Potosinos when she starred in *Los lazos de la familia*.[3] Colima, capital of the state with the same name, had a succession of musical performers, cockfights, merry-go-rounds, plays in the Teatro Santa Cruz, pastorelas during the Christmas holidays, acrobats, and the occasional circus, and once had the opportunity to see a performance by a strongman called Hercules.[4] Even the smaller towns, such as Dolores Hidalgo, had a succession of itinerant entertainers, among others, acrobats, magicians, lecturers, wild animals, and someone who displayed something called a bioscope.[5]

Nevertheless, the availability of entertainments should not be overstated. In the provincial towns, only a few of these performances took place each month, often with a concert in the central plaza on Sunday evenings. In towns such as Colima, entertainments halted during the rainy season and periodic yellow-fever epidemics. Additional problems included the absence of available sheet music, so that the Lira Colimense Orchestra in Colima had a first-run season followed by a repeat of the same musical numbers in a second season.[6] This is all to say, when puppeteers came to a provincial town, they attracted a good deal of attention.

For puppeteers, the audience provided the final and only judgment. Consequently, they knew that the performance—not just the performers, the stringed actors—mattered. Creating and meeting popular interest remained the constant challenge.

## Puppets in the Colonial Era

Puppets had played prominent evangelical and entertainment roles during the colonial era. This puppet theater reflected the older Iberian peninsular patterns of performances. Scholars, in some instances, have traced puppetry back to Cro-Magnon peoples who craved tiny human figures; later peoples added movable limbs.[7] Four interpretations explain the origin of this Iberian heritage. One hypothesis finds the invention of puppets in ancient India and traces their migration to the Mediterranean societies of classic Greece and Rome and from there to Spain. Another account of the origin of puppets credits the Greek hero Daedalus, who, according to accounts, liberated sculptured figures when he separated the arms and legs from blocks of wood and stone, and opened their eyes. He soon began making statues that could move. These automata were called Neuropasta.[8] Another explanation repeats a rather romantic tale of a lay Capuchin brother who wandered the Spanish kingdoms preaching Christianity, and who discovered that shadow images helped hold the attention of his audience. From this experience he soon began to make shadow puppet figures to illustrate his sermons.[9]

The final explanation argues that the Indian heritage was lost and that the Spanish medieval puppet theater had Italian origins, taken from Italy to France, and then to Spain in 1116 by *juglares*, who performed puppet jousts. The Italian puppeteers apparently drew on the Roman tradition of street-corner puppets called *farsas atelanas*, and they became quite popular in the eleventh century. Records indicate that in 1086 at Cluny, in the preeminent Christian monastery, the Benedictine friars manipulated stringed puppets to tell the passion of Christ. These representations of the holy mysteries included a bleeding Christ on the cross, a weeping Mary, and a Jesus ascending to heaven.[10] Little angels, often called Little Marys, or Mariettes, featured in the presentations provided the presumed origin of the word *marionettes*. Puppets in Venice in the same period gave secular performances in public squares, and even crossed the street from the square to stage plays throughout the city.[11] Other records contain reports of puppets, jugglers, and acrobats in Spain during the reign of Alfonso X of Castile and León, including a performance called *Declarato del senhor Rey N'anfós de Castelo*.

Other entertainments came directly from Italy to Spain in 1582 and were popularized by Alberto Naceri de Ganassa, the author of commedia dell'arte. Little information about performances and puppeteers exists before the seventeenth century; then increasing evidence becomes available, especially through the records of the Cofradía de la Novena in Madrid. Established in 1631, this cofradía soon had a monopoly over theatrical productions, because all performers were required to become members. Sketchy information on a few plays appears in descriptions from 1698, when Francisco Londoño presented twenty-six puppet comedies in a marionette theater. Earlier, puppeteers also had told religious stories with their stringed actors, and this practice was strengthened at the Synod of Orihuela in 1600, which reiterated the ban on theater performances during Lent but allowed puppet performances dealing with the life of Christ, the Virgin, and the saints.[12]

Puppets, perhaps because of the shortage of missionaries, or the Synod of Orihuela, or both, were widely used in the evangelization of New Spain. The *Capture of Jerusalem* first given in Tlaxacala in 1538 became the prototypical performance across the colony, acting out the battle between the Christians and the Moors. It offered the Spanish verison of the struggle between good and evil, Christians and infidels, and God and the devil that justified the conquest of Mexico. The missionaries organized analogous dances that reproduced the same struggles, called the Santiguaros, after Santiago, or Moros y Cristianos, or Danza de la Pluma.[13] In the puppet plays, the moral of each told the audience that the miraculous interventions demonstrated that the new religion had more power than the old.[14] Performances of the Christmas story and the Holy Week passion of Christ had large followings, but the most popular sketch showed the arrival of the three kings (El Auto de los Reyes Magos). Colonial elites also sponsored satirical and burlesque marionette performances of dances, cockfights, and bullfights, accompanied by guitar music, in their homes.[15]

The secular puppet performances dated to Hernán Cortés on his initial 1519 expedition, which included two conquistadors, Pedro López and Manuel Rodríguez, who were also puppeteers. One of them joined the ill-fated 1524 expedition from Mexico to Honduras that incorporated two other entertainers, a musician and an acrobat. These Spanish puppeteers perhaps built on an existing tradition in the New World. Articulated figures of some form used in public rituals or entertainments, dating from 700 BC, have been identified by archaeologists.[16]

During the colonial era, one of the important, and perhaps typical, centers of puppet performances was the Teatro Coliseo Principal (today the Teatro Francisco Xavier Clavijero) in Veracruz, where puppeteers, probably from the local monastery of San Agustín El Viejo, offered evangelical dramas. The theater also hosted itinerant groups. In 1780, María Josefa Dávila Galindo performed with the puppets she had taken across much of the colony.[17] As a result of the evangelization and entertainment efforts represented in these and other puppet shows, popular dramas such as the pastorelas (tales of the shepherds on the way to Bethlehem) and printed images, by the end of the colonial era, had created a constellation of symbols, metaphors, and iconic figures that became part of the culture. These included Adam and Eve, the apple tree and the serpent, the Three Wise Men, the angels and the demons, the shepherds coming to Bethlehem, God the Father, the Christ Child, Jesus, the Virgin Mary, the patron saints, and the Moors and Christians. Representations appeared in the churches as well as in popular devotions such as handicrafts, dances, celebrations, and puppet shows.[18]

## Puppets in the Early Republic: Don Folías and El Negrito

Independence at first did not represent a major break in this performance culture. In eighteenth-century Antequera, as Oaxaca City was known at the time, puppet performances had become common. After independence, one troupe of marionettes became increasingly popular. Soon this group came under the direction of Chato Bado, and it remained his company into the 1880s. The public developed a high regard for his puppet personalities, which included Tata Chepe, Nana Catarina, Pascualillo, Colás the Fool, and the wily sheriff. The plays often featured El Tata Chepe with his heterogeneous extended family of old folks, Indians, dancers, animals, and ghosts who became popular in Oaxaca City. The audiences usually consisted of children and maids, but these plays even drew the social elites. The puppets even became popular in the villages across the state. Common knowledge reported that there was not a fair or fiesta anywhere in Oaxaca, no matter how remote, that Bado, traveling by mule with his puppets, did not attend. The performances featured amusing stories, ones that nevertheless represented national culture, with both its positive and negative features.[19] Tata Chepe, Nana Catarina, and the rest of the family were as well applauded after each display of their wit, according to one local historian, as Harlequin and Polichinela of centuries past in Italy, as Guignol and Pierrot in France, and as Punch and Judy in England.[20]

In the rest of the country, following the Wars of Independence, puppets became clearly related to political events, popular culture, and the people in general. The plays recounted the struggle for independence and its meaning for the people. A small volume, *Función estraordinario de títeres magicos en el Callejón del Vinagre*, published in 1828, described the "magic puppets" of Ambrosio Prunela and his dramas about independence. The ode to Café Aguila Mexicano provided a patriotic discussion of puppetry. In one performance, the curtain went up on a high-society café with puppets playing and watching chess games. After one checkmate, another puppet arrived with a peepshow called "The Scottish New World," an apparent reference to the Scottish Rite Masons and their involvement in national politics. The puppets peeked into the box and saw the Scottish figures writing editorials and managing politics, and as part of their disguises, each had its forehead marked with "FP" (*fingido patriota*), fake patriot. These Masons had plans to open the Pandora's box of politics in the Mexican republic.[21]

Besides this political satire, the first well-known puppet, don Folías, "El Orgulloso" (don Folías the Proud), appeared. The first permanent puppet theater in independent Mexico City was established in the former cockpit, and consequently was known as the Teatro de los Gallos. Spectators became familiar with the popular puppet ensemble that featured don Folías, whose name combined references to a popular dance of Portuguese origin and to the clowns in women's clothing at Portuguese bullfights who lured the bull away from the men placing banderillas. Other stock characters included his wife, Mariquita, and his nemesis, El Negrito, with his woman, Procopia. These puppets made up the regular cast. Often their plays included the narrator, Juan el Panadero, who appeared outside the stage to provide the moral of the story. These characters appeared in numerous sketches about the struggles between men and women, and, of course, the devil's temptations. El Negrito had a great following because in virtually every play he told don Folías that his wife had cuckolded him. Don Folías immediately became livid, causing both his neck to stretch out and his nose to extend to great lengths. This sent El Negrito into a foot-stomping dance that the audience members encouraged by stomping their feet and pounding on the railings. In fact, often the audience would call for El Negrito to appear in the play, to tell his tale, or to welcome him onstage with the same foot stomping and pounding rhythm. Welcoming actors, alive or stringed, with applause was common at the time.[22]

These domestic plays offered short melodramas in the pattern of the commedia dell'arte, with its formula known as the "imbroglio," with stock characters and common experiences. The puppets represented archetypes by exaggerating one personality or sociological characteristic that often repeated the common knowledge. Some examples included the sly fox, the crafty devil, the generous nobleman, the stupid policeman, and the beautiful lady. Because the brief performances had no time to develop complex personalities, the puppets used exaggerated metaphors to tell their stories. Moreover, the narrative often took second place to actions that caused surprise, followed by either disappointment or ecstasy for one of the puppets. Most of the members of the audience had become familiar with this type of dramatic presentation from the use of exempla to illustrate a lesson during sermons. The Jesuits perfected this manner of preaching, but others, including parish priests, used it as well.[23]

This essential characteristic of puppet theater, Pilar Amorós and Paco Paricio conclude, creates complicity with the audience. Rather than constant changes of scenery, costume, and location, the puppets must rely on austerity, that is, less to express more. They rely on the metaphor, the symbol, and the synthesis.[24] They must bring together the drama and experience, through, in the words of Alberto Manguel, "a link of coincidences."[25] Compare two types of actors: humans use their performances to communicate emotions to the spectators, and puppets use their actions to motivate the audiences to recall and reproduce their emotions, or as Joaquim Maria Macho de Assis would have it, the audience must "recognize the phantoms of their own thoughts and passions about related experiences."[26] The human actor's credibility depends on his or her expressive ability; the puppet's credibility depends on its invocation of the audience's sensibilities, making the spectators accomplices in the performance.

In this way, the puppets offered performances that different members of the audience could understand in different ways. Incidents of the drama could be interpreted differently by different spectators depending on their age, class, gender, ethnicity, and individual experience. At the same time, the laughter at certain points must have made everyone who did not get the joke or the humor of the incident wonder why not. In this sense, the puppets inspired a common understanding of their melodramas.

The puppets had to create situations that were analogous to real or imagined experiences of the audiences. The leitmotif of El Negrito telling don Folías that his wife had put horns on him, that is, that she had committed adultery, demonstrated how the complicity with the audience worked. Puppet theater made suggestions, and the audience completed the drama based on its imagination of events and common knowledge of community values.[27] Of course, El Negrito caused trouble in these dramas. The prevailing assumption of the audience finds that he reported on the adulterous behavior of Mariquita to her husband, don Folías, because he was a friend, or a gossip, or a meddlesome acquaintance. But nothing in the plays, beyond the macho confidence or the male hope of female susceptibility to seduction, confirmed that she in fact cuckolded him. Just as persuasive is the interpretation that El Negrito knew how to cause trouble among racial and economic elites, and he was doing just that.

Don Folías attempted to reverse events in a later play, *Celos del Negro con D. Folías*. Antonio Vanegas Arroyo published this melodrama in the 1880s in the series of chapbooks called *Galería del teatro infantil. Colleción para niños y títeres*. In it, don Folías attempts to seduce La Negra (known in other plays by her name, Procopia) at her window. El Negrito, suspecting that they have committed adultery, spies on them and, once La Negra leaves the window, confronts don

Folías. The latter leaves, returns with a pistol, and shoots at but misses El Negrito, and El Negrito then stabs don Folías several times, eventually killing him. El Negrito also murders a gendarme who arrives to stop the brawl, confronts Procopia, and then murders her as well. The play concludes with the statement, "I killed Folías and La Negra, and the public night owl [the gendarme], and now El Negrito only waits for a round of applause."[28]

The denouement not only brought the play to a conclusion, but also served as the most ideological portion of the drama as the resolution relied on the expression of society's values. It made evident the prevailing view of life. Both through its form (poetic, naturalistic, expressionistic, or symbolic) and the action (murder, in this case, but also marriage, death, betrayal, or reunion), the cultural values received explicit display. Here the audience witnessed a battle over respect and reputation. Honor, in fact, appeared in some way in all the puppet stories, especially when they involved public perceptions of a man's relationship to his wife or another woman. Civil authorities could do little to restrain popular forms of dueling, such as that between don Folías and El Negrito. These were not the stylized aristocratic duels, because class and ethnic differences prevented it.[29] The play showed the familiar weapons of each class, with El Negrito armed with the knife common to the popular classes and don Folías using the upper-class pistol, and it showed the general hostility toward any intervention by law enforcement officers. Because men fought each other over a woman, whose explanations and actions were ignored, these plays dramatically combined all the elements of daily life. In this story, El Negrito had defended his honor, and he had punished the adulterers. According to the traditional laws, the charge and punishment of adultery had to be made against both persons, and strong suspicions provided enough evidence for action. He could well ask for a round of applause. In this case, El Negrito forced the audience to reveal its point of view about murder above dishonor, the appearance of deception, hints of adultery, seduction of females, marital rights of husbands, interference by legal authorities, and, of course, relationships between ethnic groups, if spectators applauded El Negrito.[30]

Another popular form of puppet performance appeared by the mid-nineteenth century. Puppeteer Juan de la Colina established a theater that regularly commented on political events and politicians' behavior. This became known as the Live Theater. Because some marionettes offered political commentaries, the puppet theater became especially popular in the capital city, during the 1860s (during the French intervention, for example; see the introduction) and during the 1880s and 1890s (when the Porfirian regime reached its apogee). This tradition of having the puppets comment on politics and social happenings continued throughout the century. The puppets and their political commentaries achieved their greatest successes in the capital city.[31]

Throughout the Live Theater, and puppet performances in general, the puppets had latitude not available to live actors. Mocking political, religious, and social authorities has always been the stock in trade of these performers. They have been compared to court jesters, who have license to make sarcastic comments, because like the jesters they have been considered inconsequential. Authorities generally ignored their activities.[32]

The nation's most prominent puppet company developed in Huamantla, Tlaxcala. Several members of the Aranda family, who earned a meager living working in the local textile factory and selling fodder for horses to the coachmen traveling the principal road from Veracruz to Mexico City, were always looking for ways to supplement their income. According to the family story, the local priest asked two of the brothers to build a manger scene. Creating the figures for this Nativity tableau inspired the family's interest in puppet figures. The sisters made the clothing, and the brothers made the clay heads that could be used in crèches and pastorelas. Soon, local *hacendados* began to call on them to perform with their figures, and they even began to travel to Orizaba, Xalapa, and other towns. In 1830 an Italian immigrant, Margarito Aquino, arrived in town and taught them how to make and manipulate marionettes.[33] The family members Julián, Hermenegildo, Ventura, and Maria de la Luz Aranda expanded their repertoire and their performances.[34] Their success, or perhaps their impending failure, as local audiences demanded new material—

because many of the local audience spoke only Nahuatl, so did not understand the dialogue,[35] and they wanted at least different forms of action—resulted in travel to other communities with new audiences. The family began to make trips to Puebla (where they performed in a stall at the side of the cathedral)[36], Hidalgo, and Mexico City. In the Federal District, they performed in a theater in San Agustin de Las Cavas, later known as Tlalpán, and famous for its fair and weekend entertainments. There, Maria de la Luz met and, after a long engagement, married another Italian immigrant, Antonio Rosete. The new husband and the family in 1850 formed the Rosete Aranda Company. The puppeteers gained popular attention when General Antonio López de Santa Anna invited them to perform in the presidential palace. They received national acclaim a few years later when President Benito Juárez invited them to return to the presidential palace. Later they received another presidential invitation, from Porfirio Díaz, to give a performance at Chapultepec Castle as part of the Independence Day celebration, September 16, 1891. For Díaz, they reenacted Padre Miguel Hidalgo's *grito*, using over 500 puppets.[37]

After Rosete married into the company, the family members initiated formal programs on a full-time basis, in 1850, and shortly afterward began to make yearly tours of the republic. Their annual travels reached from Mexico City north through the Bajío, with stops at the major towns, to Zacatecas, and sometimes farther to Ciudad Juárez, or, more frequently, east to Monterrey; the company members then doubled back, down the Pacific coast to Oaxaca, and returned through Tehuacán and Puebla to their home in Huamantla. In 1883, the company toured in the United States.[38] The majority of their performances took place in Mexico City, where they eventually had a theater, and where they spent as many as three or four months a year.[39] Officially organized in 1880 as the Compañía Nacional de Autómatas Hermanos Rosete Aranda, the company became the best-known group of puppeteers in the nineteenth century. Columnist Juvenal (Enrique Chávarri) wrote, in *El monitor republicano*, that they had justly become famous for the perfection of the performances, in which the puppets performed so naturally that he thought actors must envy them.[40] Today the National Puppet Museum is located in Huamantla,

Tlaxcala, as a tribute to the founders of this company and its development of popular art and entertainment.⁴¹ The puppet troupe, at least
the name, survived until the 1950s.

When the Rosete Aranda Company began, the puppeteers performed dramas that included don Folías, "El Orgulloso," El Negrito,
and Juan el Panadero.⁴² Later, the puppeteers invented marionettes
of their own, who became famous. Encarnación or Carnación, better
known by his stage name, Vale Coyote, represented a campesino who
spoke for the desires and sentiments of the people. He performed as a
kind of organic intellectual and trickster, recognizable as Harlequin,
the wily peasant who left Bergamo to seek his fortune in the city of
Venice.⁴³ Vale's name may have drawn on the newspaper *El Coyote*,
which satirically battered the opponents of Manuel González's successful presidential candidacy in 1880.⁴⁴ Apparently, Vale Coyote first appeared as an opening act before the performance of *El cometa del '82*.⁴⁵

The repertory of the Rosete Aranda family evolved from 1850 to
the 1880s. By the latter date, each performance included the discourse
of Vale Coyote, the "Coplas de don Simón" by doña Pascarroncita,
and a mixture of musical and dramatic performances called the
*"género chico mexicano,"* after the Spanish variety shows, the *"género
chico español"* that had first appeared in Madrid in 1807.⁴⁶ The difference between the género chico and the similar zarzuela was the
music that accompanied the former, and, after the social upheavals
in Spain during the 1860s, these one-hour performances included
an emphasis on costumbrista themes.⁴⁷ The costumbrista emphasis
characterized the puppet program, as it usually included traditional
stories, a calendar of twelve major religious and civic holiday scenes
that ranged from Holy Week, to the Nativity, to independence, to
other feast days, and the presentation of typical scenes—the promenade on La Viga and Bucareli streets, bullfights, cockfights,⁴⁸ and
historical events. The puppets presented episodes of national history,
from the Spanish Conquest to the Porfirian presidency. They paraded
in a panorama of historical figures such as Cortés, Cuauhtémoc,
Hidalgo, Allende, and others, including Díaz, and popular folkloric
and fictional characters, such as Chucho El Roto, the genial bandit,
and don Juan Tenorio, the classic rake. The performances, of course,

included some scenes intended only to draw laughs or elicit awe from audiences. These included sketches such as "Manicomio de cuerdos," that is, "The Madhouse of Sane People," and the representation of "the Crystal Palace."[49]

The performances included, and often concluded, with a parade of folktypes, including the China Poblana and the Tehuana, from across the republic. The performances made audiences familiar with the cultural diversity of their national society. Moreover, the puppets promenaded a series of gender expectations: for example, the China Poblana, according to various commentators, projected traditional values, Catholic morality, and demure submissiveness, or epitomized lower-class brashness and flirtatious charm, or both. A measure of the widespread acceptance of the China Poblana as a symbol appeared in the publication of chapbooks about her by Antonio Venegas Arroyo with engravings by Guadalupe Posada. In one typical publication, their pamphlet "La Poblanita: Cuarta colección de canciones para el presente año" featured a striking image of the Poblana on the cover. Amado Nervo in an 1890s poem connected her to the Cinco de Mayo battle of Puebla, the cradle of the Porfiriato. So the puppets helped make this figure recognized across the nation.[50]

The Tehuana also emerged in the second half of the nineteenth century as a folktype. No doubt this reflected the international interest in the Isthmus of Tehuantepec as a crossing between the Gulf of Mexico and the Pacific Ocean, and as an area of interest to Porfirio Díaz, with his longtime lover, Juana Cata of Juchitán. The number of foreign travelers and scientific expeditions to the isthmus helped popularize the Tehuanas. By the end of the century, the Tehuana dress had become popular at Porfirian carnivals and costume balls. The puppets, during the last three decades of the century, paraded in the famous skirts often dyed with indigo or cochineal, huipiles trimmed in gold, and another *huipil* used as a headdress.[51] Altamirano praised the puppets for their performance of a tableau of customs, which he said highlighted an "accultured" indigenous person and the simple and gracious little fiestas of the indigenous mountain villages.[52]

The puppets also performed music popular in Mexico City and offered operas, including *Aïda* shortly after it debuted with an Italian troupe in the capital city.[53] Following the 1884 founding of the first *orquesta típica* with musicians in charro costumes,[54] the puppets quickly followed the model, and the marionette version became a regular and popular feature of the performances. Overall, the puppeteers took domestic and neighborhood anecdotes and combined them with national developments to create their variety program.

## Vale Coyote's Independence Day Speech

Once the family had created them, Vale Coyote and doña Pascarroncita became the stars of the program (fig. 3). Their performances deserve close attention and analysis. In cities up and down and across the republic, Vale Coyote would deliver a discourse to the public.[55] This performance entertained audiences at the same time that it offered a lesson in the development of individual responsibility, national history, and civic duties that constituted national identity. In giving his speech, he utilized the customary and widely recognized techniques of rhetoric used by priests and other orators. He also managed to incorporate all of the rhetorical strategies of distortion, exaggeration, antithesis, and exempla.[56]

The oration had a narrative structure, with the introduction, the main body, and the conclusion based on priests' homilies from the mass and sermons given on fiesta days, although the Coyote's speech, of course, had comedic purposes. In the introduction, Vale, one of the nineteenth-century words for *guy, pal*, or *friend*, called on his "fellow share-croppers and trusted friends" to hold off applauding him until he had completed the "speechification of his well-scrubbed oration." He then continued his introduction in rhyme,

> Attention, with your fingertips to your lips,
> Because I am going to pronounce
> The oration that is my turn to give,
> This trusted friend does not belittle you
> Upon finding that he needs your help
> Respectable audience;
> With the pardon of his excellency

**3.** The Rosete Aranda family created two widely known puppets, doña Pascarroncita and Vale Coyote. Guanajuato artisan Mauricio Hernández Colmenero made the *calavera* and the two famous marionettes. Papier-mâché *calavera* and figures from the Champion Folk Art Collection, Tucson, Arizona. Photograph by Cheryle Champion.

I am going to let fly my "espiche"
Full of salt and lye
Pardon any impropriety.
I have never been a deputy
Nor do I have the practice of a gossip,
But if I sparkle
In what they call
The higher squash flower society,
I'll be displeased in getting there;
This shit causes me care,
But if I give you pleasure,
Applaud, don't scare
Poor Vale Coyote.

Following these self-deprecating and self-serving remarks, the Coyote began the main body of his speech:

FELLOW SWEAT-IZENS:

What significance does this meeting have? Already I see, preceded by the chief of our town, I see the servile authorities and the military, those who ordered public destruction and the well-behaved youth of this same town, and last I see the sweat-izens, all classes of society, from the poor minister to the rich proletariat.

Why have you all come to this performance of a theatrical spectacle? Is it to use your time evaluating the speaker's learning? … No sweat-izens; you have come to fulfill your debt as a sweat-izen to celebrate the great and eloquent day of our beloved independence won with the forceful injections of blood.

And who am I, who climbed up to the divine tribune to address you about the instantaneous holocaust of the terrible birth of our dear independence, when other times chosen engineers [chosen men with titles] have spoken about it with such mastery that it has left nothing to be desired in my commentaries?

I will do it with the support granted to me by the señor priest, my godfather, and the rest of my friends who have made me someone with a title, my good intentions satisfying in this manner the beautiful [prior] oratories.

FRIENDS:

There was a time in which the Europeans believed themselves completely virtuous and for this very reason they took what was not theirs, subjugating us to their holy will. How unfortunate! But that's the way it happened. The King and Inquisition put back our loose screw and, God bless me! They did not even listen to us in public meetings; they only governed, the public body never was better than they, so therefore when some little Mexican thought out something completely, Bam! They burned him up completely, making him a crackling in the Holy Inquisition.

Orphans in our own home, we didn't have the freedom even to laugh, and in such monstrous misery we did not need anything, but only wanted the grave.

You there form more of an opinion that it is, like the one well said by an author whose name I don't remember at this moment because it has fled the top of head, that the people want to be free. Now, for example, I say that in the year 1810 in a small town there was an ancient gentleman Priest named Sr. Costilla, whose venerated gray hair is still worthy of total general respect.

This Señor never mixed in anyone else's business, but nevertheless the insurgents, who had been walking in the dark, had faith in his cause when one night, alas, around midnight, Lord of my Soul, this chief got angry and threw out a cry so strong that he made the entire earth tremble, and at the same time he ordered the bells repeatedly rung, calling together the common people and some generals who were grazing their horses in the field of Mars. And, he said, "Upward, boys! Take off your cloaks! No more your idolatrous love for a woman!" And, full of holy enthusiasm, he launched the war with a fistful of men who were more than double he-men! And, don't you believe they were armed with Colt pistols, nor Remingtons, nor carbines, minuets, nor coffee with *aguardiente*. No, fellow sweat-izens, with slings, wooden clubs, machetes, and wooden lances, the never "most sincerely thought of and publicized" Hidalgo charged blindly ahead, and here is the beginning of the insurgent war that lasted several centuries. As if by magic, many common men sprang up from the earth who also said: Long live liberty and independence! And ... they drank wine and ate more tamales!

It was said, after all, that the people who want to be free are, of them we have the patent deeds done by the Anglo-Americans who made themselves free from England when don Washington said: "Get out Englishmen, Russians, Turks, Chinese, Everyone. Where have they flourished but in the shadow of Liberty?"

And if not, let's put before our eyes the very great works of Alejandro Dimas, Eugenio José, Fraymarión; the eminent orations of Chato Briones, of Juan Jacobo Rosiao, and from them, you can pick the moral fruit of liberty.

If Cesar Angosto, Carlos Mago, Julio Verde, Cesar Cantor, and other illustrious men were great, according to what Victor Lugo says, it was because they proclaimed the independence of their people, shouting: Long Live Liberty and Independence!

Here I should end my badly forged allocution, but I need to punish your virginal ears for another minute, giving you the story of some domestic affairs, with respect to our current reality.

GREAT FRIENDS!:

Those familiar men who want to make themselves rich at any cost are almost on top of us. And we have filibusters on the border of our territory, and, finally Gentlemen, we are so accustomed [to this] and so without legal protection, that if God doesn't fix it, in the coming year, there will be no civic performance of duty, only well-combed hair; therefore, I invite you upon finishing my poorly combed oration that we join together, not as grains of sand, but as a rock in the social edifice, [and] hope that the blast hurls the boat of Aqueronte across the River Styx.

MEXICANOS:

Today let's give each other kisses of peace, let's pull the guts out of the discord between us, and let's shout like Chato Catarino: Long Live Peace! Long Live the Faith, Long Live Your Mercy and Doctrine! Long Live September 36, 1814! Long Live all the Herods of the country and Long Live me!

FELLOW SWEAT-IZENS:
Long Live the Country,
That according to what they say
Is very skinny,
Because its sons
Suck and suckle
What is a pleasure,
What is a bargain.
Long Live the Memory
Of the brave Aldama,
Of the Priest Hidalgo
And of the other lower-class people
Who helped him
In the campaign.
Don't become afraid of
The foolish fathers
Of our cousins [the Americans]
Who bark so much.
Independence
Cost a great deal,
Don't lose it,
Protect it;
And today
With such glory,
We all swear
That we will furiously defend our country.
God grant that there be peace,
Friends of my soul;
God grant that it not be said
That the country of Anáhuac
Is a poor nation
Of pure cowards....
Long Live the Free!
Long Live the Mother Land!
And, with your permission, I will leave the squabble.
Carnación, alias "Vale Coyote"
The servant of all you dear people.

In his oration, the Coyote began with an apology for his lack of experience as a deputy and as a speaker. His comment made it evident that members of the audience had some knowledge of the political system and that some level of civil society existed where the puppets appeared. The obvious and, in many ways, the most significant statement made in this independence "espiche" came when Vale Coyote identified citizenship with those who work, especially those who do hard, manual labor, including his "fellow share-croppers." The near pun on the word *citizen* with "sweat-izen" in Spanish even more nearly forms a homonym. This expressed the view that hard work brought political entitlement, a perfect example of the moral economy that helped shape popular liberalism characteristic of the nineteenth century.[57] Citizenship also entailed responsibilities, as the Coyote made clear, reminding his audience to "fulfill your debt as a sweat-izen to celebrate the great and eloquent day of our beloved independence." This celebration commemorated those who had given their lives, including Aldama, Hidalgo, and other lower-class people, in the struggle "won with the forceful injections of blood" that he calls the "instantaneous holocaust of the terrible birth of our dear independence." Near the end of his oration, he reminds his listeners that "independence cost a great deal." Civic and political rights and responsibilities thus were based firmly on hard, decent work and on patriotic military service that could require a costly payment in blood.[58] This insistence that ordinary Mexicans had paid with "rivers of blood" for independence, and therefore had rights as citizens and must never concede their liberty without a fight to the death, formed regular themes in independence speeches.[59]

Explaining citizenship, the speaker made clear that its definition must include freedom, therefore requiring that the citizens must "furiously defend our country." This contrasts, he explained, with the reputation as a nation in which Mexicans have only looked for easy ways to perform their duties as citizens. This reputation emerged metaphorically in the oration in the discussion of sons who sought nourishment only when it was a pleasure or when it was bargain; that is, when it cost little effort, as a result they produced a "very skinny" rather than a robust nation. This image reveals the orator's origin from the region of greater Puebla. The civic language used in Puebla and its

sphere of influence, which stretched to Veracruz, relied on the metaphor of the family, with the martyrs of independence as the father,
the country as the mother, and the citizens as the often ungrateful or
unworthy sons.[60] The description of the struggle for independence
emphasizes the sacrifice made by the independence heroes.

The focus on sacrifice brought the account of independence into the
ubiquitous Catholic narrative cycle of sin, sacrifice, and redemption.
This popular understanding required actual sacrifice with an emphasis on blood, no doubt drawing on biblical accounts of Christ's blood,
the blood of the Lamb, and Most Precious Blood to achieve redemption. This sanguinary side of everyday religion provided a framework
without which the notoriety, if not the apotheosis, of Santa Anna's leg,
Obregon's arm, and Cuauhtémoc's bones would appear as rather aber-
rant behavior by ordinary people. It also united the insurgents with the
saints through stories of blood and relics.[61] The Coyote's speech refers
to sacrifice in terms of blood as only one of his religious themes.

Vernacular Catholicism served as one of the most prevalent dimensions of the framework of the community's common knowledge.
Despite the widespread belief of Western liberalism that civil society
flourished best with the separation of church and state, secularism did
not eliminate religious images, practices, and contexts of local communities. The mid-nineteenth-century victory of Benito Juárez and
the liberals, expressed as the constitution of 1857, restricted the influence of high church officials, but not that of local religion. Former
practices lingered. Most telling in this regard was the Coyote's statement near the beginning of his speech, in which he begged the indul-
gence of officials for his speech by saying, "Respectable audience, with
the pardon of his excellency." *Excellency* never referred to republican
political leaders; rather, it indicated respect for high churchmen or
royalty. Since it appears that only the local priest and municipal officials were in the audience, the use of *excellency* exaggerated their
positions and mocked their pretensions at the same time. Throughout
the oration, Vale made additional references, generally courteous, if
not completely respectful. He generally called the local pastor señor
Cura, or Reverend Father, and reserved his caustic comments for the
Spanish church of the colonial era, especially the Holy Inquisition.

Throughout the oration, the Coyote made numerous references and allusions to religious practices. The ideas of the origins of human beings drew on the biblical stories of creation, and the names of biblical figures appeared throughout local discussions and in the names of individuals. In another undated play, *Discurso patriótico por Juan Pico de Oro*, the main character, Juan el Borracho, referred to the creation, undoubtedly drawing laughs with his confusion about the time "Our Mother Ebria [for Eve; Drunk] and Our Father Adrian [for Adam] ate the apple."[62] Religious references had ubiquitous places in political speeches and everyday conversations. The critical political organization, the Masonic lodges, to which most of the national politicians belonged also relied on the basic Christian symbolism and narratives. The Masons probably served as a bridge between secular politics and clerical society, and certainly as the tie between individuals who composed the political interest groups, called *camarillas*.[63]

One of the most interesting references in the speech is that of Chato Catarino, because it conflates issues of popular religion, gender, and political opinions. Here Vale Coyote seems to refer to Santa Catarina, Saint Catherine of Alexandria, martyred c. 305, whose day falls on March 24 or on November 25 in the Mexican cycle of saints.[64] How she became Chato Catarino reflected nineteenth-century social patterns and Vale Coyote's sense of humor. The explanation begins with the widespread practice in the nineteenth century of using *Catarina* for *Catalina*, igniting a debate among several experts, who each weighed in on the proper form. The Mexican view, as opposed to the Castilian argument in favor of *Catalina*, was that *Catarina* is correctly derived from the Latin *Catharina*, and specifically refers to the martyred saint of Alexandria as opposed to the other Saint Catherines of Siena and Ricci. In Alexandria, Saint Catherine was to be broken on a spiked wheel (later popularly commemorated with the *rueda de Catarina*, a popular carnival ride), which she survived, only to be beheaded. She became an extremely popular saint, formally referred to as Santa Catarina Virgin y Mártir and more colloquially as "The Rose of Alexandria" during the colonial period. Cortés's first wife had her name, and one of the important Spanish parishes created in the capital city in 1568 was named for her. Many in the audience, especially at performances in Mexico City, knew that the parish church through-out the colonial era had retained the right of ecclesiastical asylum for criminals (civil authorities could not enter the church or its grounds to arrest anyone) but that Pope Clement XIV had removed this sanc-tity from all the parishes but this one. Santa Catarina was also known as the patron of the university, with popular processions of faculty and students on her saint day, and of philosophers and intellectu-als.[65] Nevertheless, in and around Puebla, including Huamantla, the reference to Catarina might well have brought to mind the famous painting *Santa Catalina de Sena jugando a los dados con el Niño Jesús* by Francisco Martínez.[66]

Others in the areas surrounding Puebla (Huamantla is about thirty kilometers away) might easily have recognized a reference to the pop-ular local saint, Catarina de San Juan, an Indian girl brought through Manila as a slave to Puebla, where her piety and alleged miracles at-tracted a following that the Inquisition attempted to halt by declaring them false visions and prohibiting the circulation of images of her. She is generally regarded as the model for the China Poblana.[67]

Vale masculinized the saint's name, perhaps like Rosario, and then gave it the endearment Chato. Used as an adjective, Chato can be translated as "pug-nosed," but more often it was used without any physical reference as an endearing term for the youngest or smallest child, something like "little sister." Here the puppet demonstrated the essence of popular Catholicism, the insistence on a personal relation-ship between individuals and their saints, whom they often address in personal, including diminutive, terms such as this.[68] Moreover, in dra-matic style, he gave voice to Santa Catarina on the wheel, "Long Live Peace! Long Live the Faith! Long Live Your Mercy and Doctrine!"

Other allusions to religious practices include what appears to be a reference to the mass and is certainly a biblical reference, when Vale said, "Today let's give each other kisses of peace, let's pull the guts out of the discord between us." The phrase referred to the way the mass ends with the handshake of peace, that often friends and relatives turn into a kiss or a hug of peace, and certainly it refers to the biblical story of the kiss of peace.

Additional biblical references appeared when he called "Long Live all the Herods of the country"—referring to those leaders whose decisions led to the death of the nation's sons, dragged into combat by those politicians and churchmen who led the country into military coups and civil wars, or as he recognized in another place, "those who ordered public destruction." The Coyote made a special effort to link the crown and church of the repressive colonial era in his statement that no native-born person could think freely, with the statement, "When some little Mexican thought out something completely, bam!, they burned him up completely, making him a crackling in the Holy Inquisition." This description captures an interpretation of the colonial experience and the relationship between the Spanish crown and church, and it reveals Mexican culture and language, with the reference to a crackling, the cleaned and cooked pig skin.

Other religious inflected forms of behavior were so typical of everyday life they nearly escape detection. For example, when the Coyote explained how he dared to give this speech, he mentioned the support that he had received from "the señor priest, my godfather, and the rest of my friends." Here the references to the priest and his friends displayed the role of local authorities (the priest) and of community approval (his friends), and, from the perspective of vernacular religion, the critical validation that came from the support of his godfather. The system of fictive parents served each critical life passage (christening, first communion, marriage, and death), and other major events requiring psychological or financial support. His godfather's encouragement indicated the significance of giving the Independence Day oration and demonstrated the continuation of the religiously inspired social network. Communities, no matter how large or small, represented webs of social interaction based on the family and the fictive family created by the *compadrazco* system that established the ties of both patron–client and mutual exchange relationships.

Similarly, in recounting the poor equipment of Hidalgo's small force of men who initiated the struggle for independence, as the first of their improvised weapons the Coyote listed the sling. This made an immediate equation between the struggle between Hidalgo's ill-prepared insurgents and the Spanish Imperial Army and the biblical account of the fight between David and Goliath. The audience might have liberal political views, but the frame of this discussion of the birth of the nation remained one of vernacular Catholicism.

Finally, and most significant in the way religious beliefs and practices remained ingrained in the political practices of the nineteenth century, was the importance of the word. Vale Coyote's recitation of the struggle for independence stated, "It was said, after all, that the people who want to be free are," and he cited the example of deeds of the Anglo-Americans, "who made themselves free from England when don Washington said: 'Get Out Englishmen, Russians, Turks, Chinese, Everyone.' Where have they flourished but in the shadow of Liberty?"

The popular religion embedded in the oration clearly was the Catholic faith of the Renaissance, not the medieval, church. That is to say, the oration used a reference to Greek mythology through the lens of Dante's *Inferno* that bridged medieval and Renaissance literature. The Coyote finished the main body of his speech with the "hope that the blast hurls the boat of Aqueronte across the River Styx," referring to the mythical Charon with his boat, often called *la barca de Aqueronte*, filled with the dead crossing the River Styx. This also has Catholic references in it, because Charon would transport only those who were properly buried with a coin to pay him to cross the river to the underworld. The others had to wander the shore of the river for a hundred years before they would be taken across.[69] So the Coyote encouraged his listeners to form a solid part of society (a rock, not a grain of sand, in the social edifice) and, at death, hope the winds would push the boat across the river to the underworld.

Both *La barca de Aqueronte* and *La Laguna Estigia* had received a good deal of publicity in the last two decades of the nineteenth century as a result of two major paintings with these names, by the Philippine painter Felix Resurrección Hidalgo. This painter studied in Madrid and then opened a gallery in Paris. He received widespread recognition in the Spanish-speaking world for his paintings that he exhibited at the Exposición Nacional de Bellas Artes (1884), the Exposición General de las Filipinas (Madrid, 1887), the World's Fairs in Paris (1889) and Chicago (1893), and San Diego's Panama-Pacific Exposition (1915).

Beyond religious references, orators and citizens celebrating independence did more than demonstrate their commitment to the nation and remember those who had died for Mexico. The audience reaffirmed the story of independence as they listened to the retelling of the struggle, in which the orator offered an example of the sacrifice required of the nation's citizens—not just its politicians and generals, but its common people. Vale Coyote delivered his Independence Day speech, even though he identified the day as September 36, 1814, in the same way as other public officials and local priests who celebrated the day of Hidalgo's grito across the country.[70]

The pattern of oral, public politics, greatly expanded in the Spanish Constitution of 1812 and given strength during the decade of the independence struggle, comes out clearly in the oration. Civic duty required citizens to attend public gatherings that featured either orations or the reading aloud of documents and news. Such events, beginning in the colonial era with the proclamation of the king's coronation, death, or birthday, required public oaths, as did later readings of national constitutions. The public swearing of loyalty took place on such major holidays as Independence Day, as shown here when Vale Coyote, after noting the glory of its patriots and their victory in the struggle for independence, calls on the audience to take the oath with him: "We all swear" to defend the country. He continued with the rhythmic chant of the mass: "God grant that there be peace, friends of my soul; God grant that it not be said that the country of Anáhuac is a poor nation of pure cowards. . . . " and then stated, in what appears to be the call and response of the mass, "Long Live the Free! Long Live the Mother Land!" This oral, civic culture centered on the plaza, the public square. The tribune, the public podium, from which the Coyote delivered his oration, drew its name from the Roman official charged with the protection of the plebes, thus reflecting a belief in civil behavior as the protection of the people.

The oration furthermore contains references to the significance of the public gatherings of citizens as the ultimate expression of the civic will. In the colonial era, these were called the *cabildo abierto*, which occurred during times of crisis, and, with the constitution of 1812, the creation of numerous *ayuntamientos*, these meetings became the political institution of urban life. Vale Coyote, as he listed the reasons for the uprising that led to independence, charged both crown and church with neglecting the popular will, as he said, "God Bless Me!, they did not even listen to us in public meetings; they only governed, the public body never was better than they." This expressed precisely the liberal and republican view of the will of the people, expressed through the sovereign gathering of the community's citizens. Revolutionaries in 1910 took up arms for several reasons, including the demand for the invigoration of the "*municipio libre*," by which they meant the assembled body of local citizens, exactly as described by Vale Coyote. The orator also discussed the spoken word as deed, in this instance in reference to independence.

Vale Coyote relied heavily throughout this oration on the technique of irony. This ploy allowed him to make sarcastic comparisons between what he said, which in turn called to mind what he did not say. His reference to poor priests and rich commoners, of course, inverts the usual circumstance. Irony requires an audience familiar with the actual or usual state of affairs (rich churchmen and poor commoners), otherwise the comparison and the humor disappear. Anyone attending the puppet show had to appreciate the common wisdom of the time to get the jokes by understanding the irony. In this sense, the Coyote's oration documented the local community expressed in its political and social attitudes in the public sphere.

The oration also exhibited the panoply of intellectuals and novelists who created the mix of Mexican republicanism and liberalism. The Coyote played with names and references in such a number of ways as to satisfy diverse audiences. "Alejandro Dimas" for many listeners referred to the novelist Alexandre Dumas, who so swiftly churned out a succession of cliffhangers and novels serialized in the newspapers that Coyote called him "Tell more" (*di más*). French newspapers had first adopted the strategy of using installment novels in 1836, and Dumas became one of the most successful novelists in this form.[71] Manuel Payno published the first Mexican example, *El fistol del diablo*, in episodes (*por entregas*),[72] and then combined the sections into a complete novel in 1859. For others the reference recalled San Dimas, the thief crucified next to Christ, with an allusion that political thieves whom he was satirizing could or should be crucified to be redeemed. Of course, Dumas's most famous novel, *The Count of Monte Cristo*, tells the story of a wrongly accused thief—according to experience and folklore, the experience of many working people with law enforcement officials and the cause for social banditry. Even more directly related to politics of the era, Dumas's novel *The Three Musketeers* offered the principal idea for extreme liberals and the few socialists, stated as "*Todos para uno, uno para todos*" (All for one, one for all). It certainly expressed republican views of citizenship, in contrast to the political hierarchy of the colonial and imperial regimes.[73]

The Coyote referred to other popular writers of serial fiction. The mention of Eugenio José referred to French writer Eugène Sue, known as the king of popular melodrama for his novels, widely read as serials in newspapers. He became the most widely read author in France—and perhaps in all of Europe—in the 1840s. His most popular novel, *Los misterios de Paris* (1849), in the fashion of Charles Dickens, with its heroine Fleur-de-Marie (perhaps the archetype for all the Mexican Marías from the novel *Santa* to the present), focused on the city's vagrancy, misery, and criminality, drew derogatory comments from Karl Marx, inspired the writing of Victor Hugo, and prompted his own socialist politics. Chateaubriand also achieved fame and some fortune through his fiction published in this form.[74]

The same playful approach served the other names as well. Fraymarión projected a multitude of references to the audience. Those who knew church and state issues might have recognized the compression of the church (fray, or friar) and the republic (Marión, Marianne) in Fraymarión. Other listeners might have heard a collapse of genders in the appeal to Brother Marianne, with the same gender inversion as took place with Chato Catarino, perhaps recalling the angry warrior singing "La Marseillaise" in the statue by François Rude.[75] Still others, with positivist or spiritualist interests, in the 1880s and 1890s, might have heard a reference to Camille Flammarion, the astronomer who served at the Paris Observatory and the Bureau of Longitudes until 1883 when he established a private observatory. He published popular studies, including the widely known *Popular Astronomy* (1880), *The Atmosphere* (1871), and *Death and Its Mystery* (1920–1921).[76] Late in the century, those with a literary bent found an additional association with French publications through the Flammarion Publishing House, established in 1875.[77] Of much greater political notoriety were the speeches of "Chato Briones" (François René Chateaubriand) and Juan Jacobo Rosiao (Rousseau). The political philosophy of both represented to many liberals the basic tenets of politics. Vale Coyote assured his listeners that the two offered the "fruit of liberty" that would make them free.

The speaker continued by identifying other men who had become illustrious because they had claimed for their people both independence and liberty. His list included Caesar Augustus, called "Skinny Cesar," Charlemagne as "Carlos Mago," Jules Verne as "Julio Verde," Nero as "Cesar Cantor," and others that he said were identified by "Victor Lugo," that is, Hugo. This is a remarkable series of references to European writers and politicians, one that might have made some audience members laugh just to hear the odd names, but would be hilarious only to those who knew the references. How interesting that Victor Hugo appeared as the arbiter of greatness, that Nero became Cesar Cantor, or the Singing Cesar, because of his musical ability, although some audience members might have identified this as a reference to Claudius as a joke on his tendency to stammer.[78] Jules Verne and his science fiction tales that set people free from everyday reality and gravity might inspire someone to break free from everyday moral codes. Humor also came in the wordplay involving his family name as given here in Spanish (Verde), because it refers to the risqué. His novel *Around the World in 80 Days*, published in 1873, had great popularity in Mexico, where many writers made comparisons between the characters in the novel and the nation's first international scientific expedition in 1874 that also circumnavigated the globe, with the chief objective of stopping in Japan to view the eclipse of the sun.[79] In his last novels, Verne turned his attention to republican issues, such as voting, for African peoples.[80] Thus, this part of the speech suggested that the audience knew some of the outstanding political writers and novelists of the time as well.

Hugo in particular had an affinity with Mexico. Mexicans knew he had left France for exile in opposition to the rise to power of Napoleon III and that he had spoken out against the French military adventure in Mexico. In his self-proclaimed role as international intellectual and statesman-at-large, he had addressed a public letter in 1867 to Benito Juárez, whom he celebrated for restoring the republic and whom he elevated to heroic status, standing with Liberty above the ruins of the French colonial regime in Mexico (he also unsuccessfully asked Juárez to pardon Maximilian).[81] Hugo attained a status among Mexicans as perhaps the world's greatest intellectual and writer. During Hugo's last illness in 1884, the newspaper *La Patria* proclaimed, "Homer is the combat, Aeschylus, the storm, Tyrtaeus, the Fatherland, Virgil, the Day, Dante, the Night, Shakespeare, the Heart, and Victor Hugo, the combat, storm, fatherland, day, night, and heart." Following Hugo's death, May 22, 1885, extensive obituaries appeared in newspapers across Mexico.[82]

The Coyote also described through irony, reference, and allusion the stratification of society and the historical explanation for independence, and reflected the general contempt for high government and church officials. He described his "respectable audience" that made up the citizens of the community. This assemblage included, of course, "his trusted friends and neighbors"; elite individuals that he called the "squash flower society," a likely adaptation of the common term *flor y nata* for elites, which he ironically declared he did not want to join; the chief of the town; the servile authorities, as a rather nifty description of bureaucrats; the military; the youth of town; and the "sweat-izens," who represented all classes of society from the minister to the proletariat. Later, he provided additional definition to the elites by referring to the Engineers, that is, men who held the title *Ingeniero*, who had previously delivered the oration, and he again mentioned the role of these degree holders (in this case, *Licenciados*) in society, when he said the priest, his godfather, and his friends had made him someone with a title. The urban community, that is, its civil culture, was formed by ties of class, family, religion, bureaucracy, and degree. And it was male.

In this society, word and dress encapsulated action and culture as civilized behavior that identified the individual. Thus, early in his oration, Vale Coyote asked rhetorically if the audience had come to judge his learning by evaluating his oration, then answered no, that they had come to celebrate independence. Referring to his oration as a "theatrical spectacle," he made clear that speaking served as one of the principal measures to judge the individual. The Coyote explained he lacked polish as a speaker, because he had never been a deputy, neither did he have the practice of speaking in public like local gossips. His preamble seemed disjointed, reflecting the faltering beginning of an inexperienced speaker, and once he even resorted to an inappropriate vulgar term in describing his nervousness. Nevertheless, throughout the oration, the Coyote talked about appearance, especially well-appointed appearance, as another major measure of the individual's standing in society, despite the warnings from many popular authors about the dangers of relying on appearance to judge the individual.[83] He began by referring to his "well-scrubbed oration" and told the audience that his speech included "salt and lye." This rural, domestic phrase referred to salt used as the basic condiment for beans and tortillas, and to lye (caliche or *cal*), which was used to give strength to adobe blocks and to separate the rough sheath from the corn kernels before grinding for tortilla dough. Thus, he planned that his speech would separate out the chaff, and that it would have strength and flavor.

Later, he adopted self-deprecating ways of describing his oration. For example, he seemed to be appealing for compliments as he talked about finishing his "badly forged allocution" and "poorly combed oration." Throughout the speech, he made numerous references to well-groomed individuals and events, such as the point that if God did not intervene against the threats that appear poised to overcome independence—filibusters and economic exploiters[84]—then the next year there would be nothing left of civic behavior except "well-combed hair." English, French, and American judges, gentlemen, and some general officers wore wigs (Mexicans after independence did not[85]) or appeared with trimmed, groomed hair. The use of hair as a metonym for the person appeared most clearly with the comment about Padre Hidalgo, when the Coyote began his discussion of the independence story, saying there was an extremely old priest named Castilla, that is, Miguel Hidalgo y Castilla, "whose venerated gray hair is still worthy of total general respect."[86] This reference made a tie between Hidalgo and the biblical injunction of Leviticus 19:32 to honor elders. Hair as the metonym for Hidalgo, who deserved respect, continues to the present as images of the father of independence commonly show him with long gray or white hair to indicate age, wisdom, virtue, and experience.[87]

The oration demonstrated a curious familiarity with and grudging respect for the American independence movement. He praised the Anglo-American Revolution, especially the role of George Washington, called "don Vasinjetón," who ordered out the "Englishmen, Russians, Turks, Chinese, Everyone." Then he told his fellow citizens not to be afraid of the noisy threats by Europeans. At least this seems to be the meaning of the comment, "Don't be afraid of the foolish fathers of our cousins who bark so much," in which "cousins" referred to the Americans, and their fathers would be the Europeans and their blustering demands for debt payment. On the other hand, he noted the rapacious nature of the contemporary Americans, those who wanted to "make themselves rich at any cost" and those "filibusters on the border." Against these invaders, Vale Coyote noted that Mexicans had become so accustomed to having no legal protection that only God could resolve the situation. In this comment, one hears an allusion to the well-known aphorism, "Poor Mexico, so near the United States, so far from God."

At the core of the speech, the Coyote identified the patriots who created an independent nation and had earned the right to participate in public life. He began by pointing out that Hidalgo, a man who "never mixed in anyone else's business," finally became so angry that he called on his fellows to give up their idolatrous love for women, take off their cloaks, and take up the challenge of independence. This description made clear that Hidalgo intended some self-sacrifice because of his well-known adultery with his housekeeper, which formed part of the popular biography of this patriot. At this point, Vale Coyote reminded the audience that when Hidalgo called together the insurgents, he rallied a few generals who were grazing their horses, and the common people. This fistful of men, whom he called more than super men, began a struggle even though they lacked the experiences of the trained Spanish officers (skilled at even the minuet), provisions of loyalist forces (such as coffee and aguardiente), and modern firearms of European armies. The rebels had to improvise with slings, clubs, and machetes, weapons they actually used; nevertheless, they undertook a struggle that the Coyote and popular imagination believed had "lasted several centuries." When these first men fell, magically, according to Vale Coyote in a kind of garbled allusion to Jason and the dragon's teeth, other common people sprang up from the earth who carried on the struggle for independence.

The puppeteers continued this version of the independence struggle, with a major addition. In the 1936 libretto entitled *Hidalgo*, J. J. Mario del Villar had the puppets emphasize that if the officials of the Holy Inquisition captured Hidalgo and insurgents, they would make *chicharrones* of them. Without weapons, the common people (the Juans and the Marías) had to use sticks and rocks in the battle. This version added a significant role for women: María at first planned to stay home, while Juan went to war with Hidalgo, but then she decided to march with the insurgents. She explained to Hidalgo that she intended to encourage Juan, provide his food and drink, and "clean the blood from his wounds." To which, Hidalgo responded: "Come to my arms, María, in you I recognize the self-effacing woman of the Mexican soldier."[88]

In the earlier description of the struggle for independence in particular, but throughout his speech, Vale Coyote identified the virtues of a citizenship that began with someone who minded his own business until circumstances forced him to military action. This allusion to Cincinnatus represented the basic character of the nineteenth-century revolutionary and civilian-military, romantic hero.[89] This was the man—one who could sacrifice personal romance, avoid gossip, struggle for years to maintain independence against all odds, and, if necessary, make the supreme sacrifice. Men who lived by this code had a role in public life and a claim on republican government. Juárez promoted this ideal among the liberals of mid-century.

The invocation of Hidalgo as the image of the insurgents who won independence for the nation became a seal in everyday life. Just as the symbol of the eagle and snake on the nopal cactus promised, and still does, the legitimacy of documents and testifies to their validity in the future, Hidalgo expressed nationalism, self-sacrifice, and faith in the religion of the Virgin. His name and likeness became the antonomasia of humility (the good priest opposed to the institutional church of wealth and hierarchy), authenticity (the spirit of Mexico, not of the distant crown), liberty (individual rights and responsibilities), and patriotism (the sentiment rooted in the community). Thus Hidalgo confirmed romantic nationalism, with its innate distinctiveness drawn from the land and the people, and sealed its probity for all time.[90] Hidalgo formed an essential sentiment within nationalism.

As another one of the ties of nationalism, Vale Coyote's speech and the other sketches of the puppet performances contributed to a more uniform language. The Coyote, like Cantinflas later, used rural accents, linguistic mistakes, and twisted syntax to compose his dialogue. His malapropisms became apparent and humorous only to those who knew proper Spanish. Hearing Vale Coyote's speech and then the laughter pushed members of the audience to learn proper Spanish to get the joke, or at least gave them the incentive to learn enough to avoid appearing ignorant because they did not understand it.

Vale Coyote called on each citizen, not as an individual "grain of sand," but united together as a "rock in the social edifice," as the key to national defense and to the nation's future. In this way, the Coyote identified the unity of men who had earned citizenship as essential for the construction of the public sphere in the nation's municipalities, especially the capital city.

Puppet performances proliferated during the century after independence, with an emphasis on Padre Hidalgo y Costilla and his call for independence, the Virgin of Guadalupe, and the colors of green, white, and red. The puppets performed Independence Day celebrations that featured other folk heroes, such as La Corregidora, the woman who escaped house arrest to warn the patriots that the Spanish planned to arrest them, and Ignacio Allende, who made the horseback ride to alert Padre Hidalgo that the Spanish had learned of their plans. For the public, the independence celebrations required dress (sarapes and sombreros), meals (such as chiles en nogada), and music that created a patriotic evening. Often puppets doubled the event, performing independence celebrations for spectators attending independence celebrations. These puppets often determined that part of their civic duties required commenting on political events and criticizing local officials by measuring them against the ideals of independence.[91]

## Doña Pascarroncita and Don Simón

The Rosete Aranda family also created doña Pascarroncita Mastuerzo de Verdegay Panza de Rez y Gallo Verde (or Pascarrona Mastuerzo de Berdegay Tenteahí Panza de Res y Gallo Verde), the snooty, high-society matron of eighty years who, once her daughters Glicerina and Bicicleta persuaded her, sang the famous "Coplas de don Simón."[92] The daughters' names gave a hilarious expression to the meaning of modernization, with the former referring to the basic ingredient in gunpowder and the latter to a major product of industrialization. Once she agreed to sing, her songs offered a political commentary that often tied the local audience to national and even international events. Doña Pascarroncita in an evening dress singing couplets that were often bawdy provided an amusing sight in itself. Moreover, the lyrics presented serious subjects in a humorous form. Once again, the subjects and the themes in the couplets required some knowledge of national politics and economic developments in order to enjoy them. She normally criticized doctors, politicians, and people of poor character.

In her first scene, doña Pascarroncita often would open by singing,

> Don Simón, I am eighty years old,
> strong and healthy by the grace of God
> and I am contemplating the enormous scandal
> of the evil, corrupted world.
>
> Don Simón, don Simón, recalling,
> in the years the Lord gave me
> never have I seen what I am seeing
> in the illustrated story.
> In the past, the people were good
> and showed their education,
> but the devil walks free today
> Ahhh, these times, don Simón![93]

In another example, she trilled:

> Today for a cold they call on them [doctors]
> They bring a saw, a dagger, and hoe
> to make mincemeat out of the sick,
> and ... [they charge] a peso each day, don Simón.[94]
> ...
> When I was young, a few foreigners
> came to our country.
> The journey was a long and inconvenient
> sea voyage for them.
> Today a multitude of Yankees
> arrive among us. Each train
> brings a million who [think they] have to flog us
> behind the store as a precaution, don Simón.[95]

These limericks expressed much of the popular dissatisfaction with the new Mexico of the Porfirians after 1876, which brought the hustle and bustle; the professionals, including doctors; and the foreigners, especially Americans, of the modern period to the country. The U.S. managers and workers who received double the pay of local employees doing the same job did both actually and metaphorically flog Mexican workers, whom one historian called outcasts in their own land.[96]

Another puppet singer, Casianito Redondo, also sang *coplas* such as:

> What beautiful bells
> the bell ringer rings
> what comfort it gives me
> that I played them first.
> Trees of the Alameda park
> have leaves at their tip
> that don't produce avocados
> to eat as a sweet [*cajeta*] from Celaya.[97]

This verse, like other references by the puppets, demonstrates the requirement of the audience's complicity. They had to be familiar with church bells, municipal parks (*alamedas*), and the famous sweet pastes of Celaya. The latter, in particular, meant knowledge of commodities, if not physical geography and perhaps the transportation system created by the railroad.

Other puppets besides Vale Coyote and doña Pascarroncita used in the Rosete Aranda family's performances included prominent political figures, such as Padre Miguel Hidalgo, Benito Juárez, and Porfirio Díaz. They also included well-known entertainers, such as the famous clown Ricardo Bell, and stereotypical figures in local communities such as el Pilluelo Dinamita, the scamp, who represented the neighborhood rascal. These puppets all appeared as versions of the stock characters in commedia dell'arte. Moreover, all the puppets had the ability to synthesize in form and language social inequities and complaints and to create universal metaphors and popular symbols with a spirit of criticism and a sense of humor. In fact, the puppets were archetypes.[98] These little melodramas, through everyday events that often went badly, taught behavior patterns and displayed the community standards that reflected the class and ethnic nature of the society.[99]

## The Rosete Aranda Tours

The annual tours during the second half of the nineteenth century had an impact on the shaping of national identity. The Rosete Aranda troupe traveled from Tlaxcala to Mexico City, then to the Bajío, north to San Luis Potosí, Zacatecas, and Durango. On occasion, the group would continue on to Chihuahua and across to Monterrey, especially to the popular barrio of San Luisito. Once the company completed its northern performances, it then doubled back to the south, eventually to Oaxaca, then to the resort at Tehuacán, Puebla, and home. A secondary winter circuit included the mining and textile zone of Pachuca, Real del Monte, and Xalapa. Wherever they traveled, the puppets had an impact on popular attitudes and recollections. The audience always remembered Vale Coyote, and often don Folías and El Negrito.[100] Two persons interviewed in the 1950s still remembered the puppets and their plays in Puebla in the 1890s, especially Vale Coyote, but also the imbroglio involving don Folías and El Negrito. A 1919 account reported that in Monterrey, everyone in the entire town knew Vale Coyote. He was described as "incomprehensible" and as a poet and a dipsomaniac journalist, who loved to drench himself in tequila in the lowest places in town. He was remembered along with other well-known figures, including Marquitos, the blind, hump-backed guitar player; and the stingy Guico, who even in the dead of winter dressed only in drill; and the Crazy Man of San Vicente.[101]

The Rosete Aranda company in 1880 had 1,300 marionettes, and by 1900 the number had increased to 5,104 figures.[102] The Rosete Aranda family traveled with hundreds of puppets, so they could create a sense of verisimilitude by using costumes, language, and music of the regions and celebrations of the parts of Mexico that they portrayed. They also used backdrops for their performances that created a sense of location. In subtle ways, these backdrops also revealed attitudes about the country's environment. These background scenes presented to audiences a visual expression of the regions of the nation and its physical diversity. These backdrops have largely disappeared, discarded as they became too tattered and worn out, repainted with new scenes, destroyed through travel, or put to a hundred other uses. Nevertheless, the surviving scenes show that the backdrops offered views of the national geography, its physical forms that created a sense of national uniqueness. They offered still another look at the architectural monuments regarded as most representative or most expressive by Mexicans. These scenes paralleled those presented in almanacs, in popular lithographs, and later in World's Fairs exhibitions.[103] A few examples of these backdrops exist today at the Rafael Cornel museum in Zacatecas.[104]

Besides presenting the plays to audiences in the towns they visited, the Rosete Aranda troupe incorporated some of the locals into their performances. The company at first traveled with musical instruments and sheet music. In each town, the director hired local musicians to perform with them and provided them with the scores. The importance of available sheet music cannot be overestimated in the provinces. As has been noted, the community orchestra in Colima played a repeat season of its weekly concerts because it lacked sheet music. The same no doubt held true in other parts of the country.[105] Local musicians learned, if they did not already know, national tunes and songs. Later, the company traveled with its own musicians; nevertheless, the puppets and puppeteers helped create a kind of audio or musical nationalism. They created a national familiarity, in the sense that the music came from across Mexico. The popular music called *canciones mexicanas* that consisted of the *son*, the corrido, and the *canción romántica*, described or fit into daily life and celebrations from different regions.[106] In a direct way, audiences learned about their national culture, which included regional versions of the *son* with different types of guitars supporting major instruments, especially the *son huasteco*, also called the *huapango* (played with the violin), the *son jarocho* (with the harp), the *son guerrerense* (using the *cajón*, a percussive instrument of African origin), the *son oaxaqueño* (performed by local bands with brass or marimbas), the *son michoacano* (using a large harp), and the *son jalisciense* (played by mariachis). No doubt the music became a part of the repertoire of local musicians that could be performed on later occasions. Recognition of these popular regional songs, such as "Son de la negra," "Jarabe tapatío," and the "Zacatecas march" resulted in well-known songs that created sentiments as strong as those associated with the national anthem. Alfonso Ríos Toledano compiled *Aires nacionales*, which identified all the songs associated with the nation's cultural regions. It included the songs listed above, as well as others, including "El sombrero ancho."[107] The visits by the Rosete Aranda troupe or some other itinerant puppeteers appear to have had a multiplier effect. These shows seemed to prompt imitation by local amateurs, who offered performances as the Rosete Aranda Company departed and visited the surrounding villages to present puppet shows based on the Rosete Aranda program, although in a reduced form and without much, if any, music. For example, after the Rosete Aranda puppets appeared in San Luis Potosí in 1891, Eleno Flores gave a puppet show in Meson de San Jose to capitalize on the public interest. In Guanajuato and Léon, locals Desideño Jarramillo, Marcelino Ramírez, and Ascención García obtained separate licenses to perform puppet plays in neighboring Dolores Hidalgo. It cannot be determined whether these local imitators used marionettes or the easier-to-manipulate hand puppets, to present derivative performances.[108] In some cases, aspiring puppeteers may have drawn on the

Rosete Aranda repertoire, copying their puppets and performances. That certainly appears to be the case in Monterrey, where imitators tried to reproduce Rosete Aranda marionettes and performances to benefit from the widespread popularity of the famed company from Tlaxaca. Critics used the Rosete Aranda marionettes as the standard, such as the Orizaba newspaper writer who reported that Sr. Zane's puppets gave a performance equal to any given in the town by the Rosete Aranda family. He added that the wonderful scene called "La danza macabra," set in a funeral home that featured a skeleton that fell into pieces and then reassembled, while leading the other puppet dancers, exceeded anything the Rosete Aranda had done.[109] Moreover, when the Rosete Aranda group began traveling with musicians, it likely inspired local players to try out music from different regions.[110]

## The Puppets in the Twentieth Century

The Rosete Aranda Company entered a second era after 1913, when portions of the company passed through several different hands. Francisco Rosete Aranda inherited the company in 1911 and became director. Apparently, he sold a large portion of the company (equipment and puppets) to Enrique Rosas, who became a pioneer moviemaker. Rosas soon resold the puppets to Carlos Espinal, who gave performances as "The Rosete Aranda Puppets, Carlos Espinal and Sons Enterprise."[111] Meanwhile, Francisco also continued with another part of the company's marionettes.

Puppets around the world faced increasing competition for audiences from variety shows in the vaudeville fashion (*carpa* theater), spectator sports, and movies.[112] In response, Francisco made the marionettes larger and had some new ones made by the well-known sculptor Max Ocampo, especially for religious scenes such as "Las cuarto apariciónes de la Virgin de Guadalupe," "La Pasión de Cristo," and "San Felipe de Jesús."[113] He also added to the repertory, including stories and personalities from the traditional tent variety shows, called the *carpas de variedades*. In 1925, he bought a carpa as part of his puppet theater.[114]

During the 1920s and 1930s, another genre of puppetry emerged, with the sponsorship of the department of public education and the program of Bellas Artes. This development used hand puppets to entertain children, teach literacy and hygiene, and explain national history and heroes. The first leaders of this program were German and Lola Cueto; the program had both rural itinerant programs and regular visits to kindergarten and primary school classes throughout the capital city.[115]

Carlos Espinal succeeded in having his puppets appear in movies but eventually, faced with increasing competition in the entertainment world, he sold the name, some puppets, and librettos. Television offered new entertainment opportunities and challenges. The first TV program was a 1952 broadcast of President Miguel Alemán delivering his annual report, and it was followed by a performance by the Rosete Aranda puppets, featuring don Ferruco, the creation of another puppeteer.[116] In 1958, the company gave its last performance, although the puppets have been used for special museum performances on occasion since then.[117] In 1978, Carlos and Emilio Espinal sold their father's puppets to the national government. This set off a public clamor, because the Rosete Aranda family claimed the government had not bought the Rosete Aranda puppets, but rather ones Espinal had constructed. Olga Rosete Aranda claimed both her family and the Espinals had sold the family's marionettes to private collectors and the puppet museum in Atlanta, Georgia.[118] The popularity of the Rosete Aranda puppets led to the decision to place the National Museum of the Puppet in the family's hometown of Huamantla, Tlaxacala, where the museum sponsors an annual International Puppet Festival that continues to the present.[119]

## Rival Puppet Companies

Other important puppet companies existed in the nineteenth century. Both large and small companies toured the republic, companies of marionettes and of hand puppets, called *guiñol*. The smaller companies with one or two puppeteers, usually using hand puppets, appeared at fiestas and fairs or on street corners; while the larger companies, often with a dozen or more puppeteers, usually using marionettes, performed in theaters.[120] The company called La Carpa de Don Heleno

Flores included puppets. The impresario, known as El Gracioso Enano Flores (the Dwarf Fool Flores), born in Irapuato in the 1880s, as a child with his brothers Lucia, Máximo, and Miguel, formed a group of itinerant puppeteers who traveled on mules from Sombrerete, Zacatecas, to Irapuato, giving performances at fairs and in public places. They both acted and manipulated the puppets they had made. They adapted local history and invented their own stories. By the first decade of the twentieth century, the company had a national reputation and had achieved success to the point they traveled with their own small orchestra. Their sketches included "El pastelero (the pastry baker)," "La casa robada" (the robbed house), "El circo" (the circus), "Las cuatro apariciones de la Virgen" (the four appearances of the Virgin [of Guadalupe]), "La corrida de toros" (the bullfight)," "La pelea de gallos" (the cockfight), and "Lucas Pérez de Guanajuato," probably written by Heleno Flores. This company continues to the present in Zacatecas.[121]

Even better known was the wandering puppeteer don Toribio; several companies tried to capitalize on his renown in the early twentieth century by appropriating his name. Don Toribio, an old man in the 1880s, traveled to fairs and fiestas on his Pacific coast circuit from the south of Colima to El Rosario in Sinaloa; nevertheless, his name became known across the country. Walking from town to town, he carried his makeshift stage and his reduced group of performers, don Folías, El Negrito, and his wife, Procopia. He tried to attract an audience by having don Folías perform on street corners, telling passersby that they would get a belly laugh from watching him make fun of the suspicious jealousies of El Negrito, a man who knocked himself down when he sneezed. Don Toribio's puppet don Folías had a long neck, rosy cheeks, and an enormous nose. The long neck, *pescuezo* in Spanish, was a visible expression of the figurative use of the word for the stiff-necked haughtiness and pride of the ne'er-do-well upper class. The puppet appeared as a dainty, vain, capricious practical joker and womanizing rogue. These negative characteristics notwithstanding, don Folías's little comedies, according to commentators, never became vulgar, but rather were ingenious and amusing.[122]

Three companies were extremely popular in Mexico City during the Porfirian era. The Omarini company gave performances called

"Marionetas italianas" in the Tívoli Park and the Principal Theater, and the José Soledad Aycardo group performed around the city at the Teatro del Reloj, the Alameda, and the Plaza de al Constitución (the Zócalo); and, of course, the Rosete Aranda Company.[123]

Other regional companies existed. Some, for example, the Carmona family troupe, acquired national reputations during the Porfirian era, and others had only provincial recognition. In Monterrey, newspapers reported the activities of various performances in the 1880s and 1890s.[124] Veracruz residents had been able to attend puppet performances since the colonial era, when puppetry done in harmony with African rhythms and dances had been banned both in Cuba and Veracruz. During the mid-nineteenth century, Veracruz had an itinerant puppeteer, who specialized in plays featuring Juan el Panadero, and, of course, any foreign companies arriving in the country would give performances in Veracruz. Other lively regional puppet traditions, including the large puppet figures, the *mojigangas* used in parades, existed in Puebla. No records have been found of puppet companies in the Yucatán peninsula before the Rosete Aranda family visited in 1893.[125]

Puppeteers wandered the country giving performances for a day or two in provincial towns. Little is known about such individuals as Justo Hinojosa, who offered marionette performers on two weekends in Colima in May 1880.[126] More than likely, he and others like him used the stock characters of don Folías and El Negrito. These two puppets appeared in other popular forms as well. For a brief time, a *Calendario de don Folías* existed. Agustín Orellana established a print shop that produced works for the puppet theater. None of the booklets for the Porfirian era and early Revolution have been located, but the ones printed from 1917 to 1924 varied in size from six to thirty-two pages and generally constructed their stories on the dichotomous, contentious relationships between student and teacher, buyer and seller, accuser and accused, doctor and patient, renter and landlord, boss and worker, husband and wife, or lovers, and between the stock characters don Folías and El Negrito.[127] Much better known is the work of the publisher and illustrator of popular themes Guadalupe Posada, and that of Antonio Venegas Arroyo, who produced chapbooks for children or puppet theater that featured the two characters.[128] Posada also produced a calavera for the Day of the Dead about the pair and their women, which included this doggerel account.

> Aquí están las calaveras de Don Folías
> (Here are the mock-skeletons of Don Folías)
> y El Negrito que irse a la parranda
> (and El Negrito going out on a spree)
> los metieron al cuartito
> (they got to the place)
> Don Folías y su mujer
> (Don Folías and his woman)
> se fueron para el panteón
> (left for the cemetery)
> a ver a las calaveras
> (to see the holiday skeletons)
> porque esta es su devoción.
> (because they are devoted to them.)
> Encontraron de repente
> (They quickly met)
> al Negrito y su mujer
> (El Negrito and his wife)
> y se fueron derechito
> (and they left right away)
> a la taberna á beber.
> (for the tavern to drink.)
>
> Sin tener respeto a nadie
> (without respect for anyone)
> sacó luego su cuchillo
> (then [el Negrito] pulled out his knife)
> Don Folías se levantó
> (Don Folías stood)
> con la Negra y su señora
> (with the Negra and his wife)
> y dirigiéndose al Negro
> (and threw himself at El Negro)
> le quebró la Chirimoyo.

(and bloodied his head.)
Los dos, se batieron fuerte
(The two fought fiercely)
rompiéndose los hocicos.
(pounding each other's faces.)
Los gendarmes se acercaron
(The police rushed to the scene)
y en el acto echaron pito.[129]
(as they blew their whistles.)

The violence between El Negrito and don Folías occurred in every play, and often it led to death or serious injury. It reflected both the violent life common among popular society at the time and how racial hostility bubbled just below the surface of daily behavior, even among friends. Violence touched the everyday lives of the popular classes as homicide and battery reached alarming levels, higher in their capital than in other contemporary cities. The puppet murders hardly seemed extraordinary because of the audience's experience with actual incidents and sensational news stories. They recognized that daily life involved the high-stakes game that the puppets as well as the audience's neighbors, friends, family, and they themselves played for honor. The indigent, the indigenous, the Afro-Mexican, the working poor, and the rural migrant, like the social elites, fought for respect, the essence of honor.[130] It proved particularly difficult to maintain a sense of honor because of the liberal insistence on the disposal of such markers as birth, fashion, and occupation and the preoccupation of Porfirian officials with the maintenance of social order.

Civil authorities talked about the criminal world and the underworld as often invisible but parallel realms to the city's acceptable society. Three knife murders on the puppet stage could not cause much reaction among the audience compared to the succession of sensational and brutal murders illustrated in the broadsheets of Guadalupe Posada and other engravers. Posada used titles such as "Terrible y Verdadera Noticia" (Terrible and True News), "¡Horrible y Espantosísimo Acontecimiento!" (Horrible and Shocking Event!), and "Sangriento Drama en la Carcel de Belem" (Bloody Drama in the Belem [sic] Jail).[131] Moreover, audiences that witnessed the puppet murders no doubt could place them within legal traditions. Many probably knew that under the 1871 penal code (the law until 1931), anyone who committed a murder or battery defending his or her honor could not be prosecuted for criminal charges. What looks like a senseless homicide today, the spectators recognized as a socially sanctioned battle over honor, a duel.

Moreover, the puppets often turned to violence because they could. The colonial religious dramas and their European predecessors presented the martyrdom of saints, and the violence and murder of early Christians used puppets because it was impossible to use human actors. In some cases, puppetry presented the violence of the Crusades, for example, the Sicilian epic *Orlando Furioso*, but often the violence was slapstick clobbering, typically by the puppet Punch, known in Spain as don Cristóbal. This latter character broke all laws and crossed all boundaries of behavior, and got away with it. In this way, he performed the ultimate fantasy fulfillment of every person hemmed in by the rules of life.[132] In this sense, puppets turned the world upside down with violence in the same way as carnival or other popular celebrations.

While the overall effect of itinerant puppet theater was to contribute to the formation of familiarity of Mexicans with Mexicans across the republic, Guadalupe Posada often chose to use the well-known figures to address other issues in the capital city. Here, in the calavera, he refers to the common relationship between drinking and violence. What made his calavera appealing was that the public knew the puppets as archetypes of their society. The well-known puppet characters continued to appear in various forms. Frida Kahlo, for example, included El Negrito in her film *Frida en naturaleza viva*. The recourse to violence surprised no one; rather, it added the touch of verisimilitude to the dramas.

## Puppets and Civil Society

Moreover, the puppets both reflected and promoted life in the public sphere. The nineteenth-century creation of civil society and partisan culture following independence in 1821 provided the dimensions of the public sphere, a synonym for the social interaction motivated by patriotism and politics of governance, responsibility, and entitlement. The expression of the individuals and issues that shaped the public sphere and participated in its urban, municipal institutions received recognition and criticism through various performances, including, among others, celebration of holidays, construction of monuments, entombment of heroes, and enactment of entertainments.[133] Ordinary people learned about the public sphere, urban life, and civic behavior through various popular sources that included the melodramas of itinerant puppet theater.

Among the puppets, Vale Coyote, like Harlequin of the commedia dell'arte, appeared as a stereotypical rural resident, and for those campesinos new to the capital and other cities he offered a model for coping with urban life. As an unlettered intellectual, he became the crafty adversary of urban elites and government officials. He outwitted his social and political betters by understanding and taking advantage of how their system worked. Stated differently, he understood the city, its civic society and political culture, and how the public sphere unintentionally allowed for individual maneuverability and unwittingly permitted criticism, based on irony and other humorous forms. The puppeteers understood that their marionettes had the freedom to say things that citizens, even actors, did not.

In particular, the puppets' speeches, even as they evolved, rested foremost on their use of rural accents, regional argot, malapropisms, linguistic twists, and double entendres. The orations also demonstrated knowledge of international, national, and local affairs, blended together in confusing and curious combinations. Nevertheless, the appearance and form of the speeches reproduced a familiar structure of popular events that represented the public sphere.

## Some Conclusions

The puppets and their little dramas told fundamental stories about Mexico, its history, and culture. Their performances, without intending to do so, offered an index to society, and the audiences saw that life was not an involuntary act.[134] There were no puppets named "the state," "the market," "the church," or "the people." Rather, the puppets represented men and women who made up the government, commerce, church, and community and who therefore could and should be held accountable for events. This served as a reminder that human beings, including every member of the audience—not invisible forces or great institutions—made history and culture. In this way, the puppets taught lessons of individualism and encouraged holding people responsible for their actions.

The puppet theater of the nineteenth century brought together local knowledge and linked it to the emerging national memory. The puppets offered stereotypes of each region, the major civic and church events in the calendar, and the heroes and heroic moments of the past. Moreover, as the puppets went about this formation of popular and collective memory, they incited, if not demanded, audience participation. This was especially the case with the *cócoras*, or hecklers, who formed a vital part of the live theater as they challenged the puppets to more artful performances.

The popular memory of national history as performed by the puppets in the nineteenth century revolved around the actions of men and women. To say that Hidalgo, Juárez, La Corregidora, and the Virgin of Guadalupe personified the heroic moments and tragic realities of the nation's past does not in the slightest discount the rest of the people, the pueblo. Only if one ignores the obvious or resorts to some dismissive theory of politics or overdetermined theater of life can one insist that this emphasis on men and women fails as a national history. Hidalgo, for example, in his role as the father of independence is not a solitary actor, nor is he a metaphor for a social class or a narrow elite. Rather, Hidalgo is a metonym for one large segment of Mexicans; he did form part of the same group with them, and his experience, his life's drama was to a large extent theirs. How odd that this truism came not from historians—not then and not now—but from puppets, who, moved by strings, pulled the strings of national memory and identity.

## CHAPTER 5

# The Plainsong of Nineteenth-Century National Identity

As Mexicans exercised their curiosity about the new nation and its peoples that emerged with the achievement of independence in 1821, they developed collective memories based on popular sources that stressed ethnic, cultural, and physical diversity. These came to represent popular national identity as it evolved across the nineteenth century. At the same time, the official campaign to create nationalism became increasingly focused on the more homogeneous, Europeanized population in the effort to give Mexico a modern, cosmopolitan appearance. Tension existed between these two conceptions of national identity that clashed in everyday life, often in the encounters between law enforcement and common behavior.

The collective national memories, that is, national identity, slowly emerged, and it needs to be emphasized again that they received their enduring promotion from persons reaching a broad audience for their goods and performances so that they could secure a livelihood. They responded to the curiosity that Mexicans had about themselves and their nation, and built on both literary and oral sources of information.

This discussion allows three final and more sweeping generalizations. First, public spectacles always included puppets broadly defined (masked figures, *mojigangas*, articulated figures on floats, Judases, and other puppets), and masked figures for such fiestas as Carnaval, Corpus Christi, dances, pastorelas, and Independence Day. These figures, with distinctive masks and clothing, moved through the streets and plazas. They represented historical, biblical, fictional, and mythological personages and creatures, and they reduced virtues, vices, and political abstractions to anthropomorphic figures. These representations used a visual language to bring political ideas, religious concepts, popular literature, fictional characters, and folkloric figures to the general, almost completely illiterate population. This visual instruction began in the colonial period.[1] For example, the masquerade in January 1621 included figures from the well-known and popular chivalric romances written by Amadis de Gaula and don Belianis de Grecia, and, even this early, don Quijote de la Mancha. These characters remained popular at costume parties and public celebrations throughout the nineteenth century.[2] Street and festival celebrations constituted one, perhaps the major, method of transmission of the cultural legacy. Moreover, songs, fashioned in the tradition of Spanish minstrelsy, in Mexico became *coplas* and corridos that popularized, reinterpreted, enriched, and celebrated the culture of literary protagonists, legendary episodes, expressive gossip, foundational moments, and national heroes. Literacy might have expanded this repertoire, but it also froze stories in place and had the potential to reduce community experience to the solitary activity of reading. Puppets and other popular forms used political, religious, and literary characters and expressions as they appeared before the general population. Although usually not part of some pedagogical campaign, the puppets nevertheless contributed to the ever-changing popular religion, civic culture, and national identity.

Second, puppeteers like the Rosete Aranda family, editors of almanacs, artisans who produced the ephemeral trappings of fiesta celebrations, from fireworks to holiday foods to traditional gifts, and printers and painters of lotería games created a popular sense of nationalism and national identity during the nineteenth century. Government officials at various times in the nineteenth century tried unsuccessfully to promote widespread nationalism, and the intellectuals, especially writers, devoted much of their efforts from 1821 to 1889 to creating a literature that reflected national attitudes.[3] The latter was somewhat successful, especially in costumbrista novels, but the purveyors of popular sources had a greater impact. This resulted not by design, but rather coincidentally, or perhaps accidentally is better said, as these individuals went about the business of making a living. These were the petite bourgeoisie, a rather surprising group to achieve this feat, but unintentionally they did it. They demonstrate the most ignored and perhaps only law of history, the law of the unintended consequences of the individual's actions.

Third, the petite bourgeoisie helped to create a national identity that recognized cultural, ethnic, rural–urban, and physical differences. El Negrito, Vale Coyote, and the other puppets helped formulate this nationalism that stressed, above all, cultural and physical diversity. They represented it through backdrops of the landscape and the cavalcade of regional figures and celebrations. This emphasis on regionalism contradicted the centralizing and standardizing programs of the national regimes, especially the Porfirian government that increasingly narrowed what ethnic and racial groups should be included in society. The continued representation of the more diverse society was not resistance on the part of these small entrepreneurs, attempting in subtle and indirect ways to challenge national centralization, but rather an effort in more accurate and entertaining ways to portray the nature of the country and its people and earn a living. For government officials, including its local representatives, the jefes políticos, El Negro and the other puppets represented a potentially troublesome sentiment, but what may have appeared to be resistance from the perspective of government officials was little more than a taxonomy of regional representatives and geographies aimed at entertaining through self-recognition the people in the audiences.

This national identity then built on the values, preconceptions, and behaviors that expressed deeply embedded attitudes about ethnicity, gender, and social hierarchy, at the same time it developed cultural and physical diversity. The puppets located this sense of national identity in the local community, with its emphasis on pueblo traditions. This created a romantic national identity that in literature and art has been labeled costumbrismo,[4] and which reflected many western European as well as Mexican liberal political and social views. The romantic artists produced picture books that presented images of local people and their occupations. The 1840s witnessed the appearance of many publications, including: *Heads of the People or Portrait of the English*

(London, 1840); *Les français peints par eux-mêmes* (illustrated by Caumier, Grandvile, Gavarni, and others, Paris, 1840); *Los españoles pintados por sí mismos* (Madrid, 1844); and *Los cubanos pintados por sí mismos* (Havana). A group of Mexican authors (Ignacio Ramírez, Hilarión Frías y Soto, Pantaleón Tovar, and Juan de Díos Arías) and illustrators (Hesiquio Iriarte and Andrés Campillo) published *Los mexicanos pintados por sí mismos* (Mexico, 1854).[5] Unlike foreigners, such as Claudio Linati, who portrayed Mexicans, especially the indigenous, as exotic beings, these illustrators and writers showed their fellow men and women as familiar, if little-known, members of their national community.[6] This liberalism that recognized the diversity of ethnic, social, and economic groups created a frame in which popular nationalism emerged. It did not inspire but ran parallel to the widespread sense of national identity that resulted from, among others, the itinerant puppeteers. This sense of national identity was barely in place before a second generation of Porfirians, that is, the generation of technocrats who replaced the veterans of the war against the French, took charge of the national regime beginning in the 1890s and denied this national diversity. They promoted the criollo culture along the lines suggested in the statistical tables of the 1830 Instituto Nacional de Geografía y Estadistica.[7] They defined rural, indigenous, African, Asian, and other different Mexicans as quaintly folkloric as represented in costumbrista illustrations or dangerously uncivilized as revealed in criminal statistics. The intellectuals, especially writers, who might have served as the national leaders of nationalism based on cultural and geographic diversity, had scattered after 1889, as many of them joined the antiromantic, anti-costumbrista literary movement called *modernismo*.[8] Thus, the government technocrats, scientific promoters, and literary intellectuals in the 1890s all spoke the same language of positivism and adopted the national goal of modernization, cast in the rhetoric of a local version of social Darwinism. The 1910 revolution, in many ways, was the consequence, certainly unintended, of their actions.

# APPENDIX

## El Discurso de Vale Coyote

Súplico a todos mis aparceros y valedores, que sí me queren palmi-
miar aguanten las ganas un ratón, no más mientras que yo acado de
vociferamentar mí restrengido descurso.

Atención y punto en boca;
Porque voy a prenunciar
El descurso que me toca,
Este valedor no apoca
Al que le sabe ayudar
Respeitable concurrencía;
Con perdón de su eíselencia
Voy a soltar un espíche
Lleno de sal y caliche
Perdonando la indeiciencía.
Nunca he sido deputado
Ni de hablador tengo tranza,
Pero sí que la he brillao
En la clase que han llamao
La flor de la calabaza,
Al venir siendo desgusto;
Me achícopala el cerote,
Sí consigo darte gusto,
Aplaude, no de un susto
Al prove "Vale Coyote."

CONSUDADANOS:

¿Qué sínifica esta runión? Ya lo veo pecedida por el jefe de nuestro
pueblo, veo a las utoridades serviles y melitares, a los que dijieron la
destruction pública y a la joventud adecuada de este mesmo pueblo, y
veo por último sudadanos, a toda la clase de socicieda, desde el probe
menistral hasta el rico proletario.

¿Para qué habéis venido a la representación de un espectáculo tia-
tral? ¿Es empliar el tiempo calificando la linternatura, del orador. . . .
No consudadanos: habéis venido a cumplir con el deber de sudadano

a celebrar el día más grande facundo de nuestra cara independiencia conquítada a fuerza de injuciones de sangre.

Y soy yo, quíen trepado a la trebuna deba dijeriros la palabra en holocauso fulminoso del fefasto nacimiento de nuestra cara independiencia, cuando ingenieros escojidos la han vociferamentado otras veses con tal maistría, que nada han dejao que desiar a mis cometientes. . . .

Lo hare por el favor que me dispensa el siñor cura mi compadre y todos los demás mis amigos que me han creído caletriao, saisfaciendo de esta manera las bellezas oradatorias con mis reitas intenciones.

CONCLAPACNES:

Hubo un tiempo en que los uropeos dialtiro se creyeron güenos y por lo mesmo pretendieron cogerse lo ageno soyugándonos a su santa voluntá. ¡Qué desgracia! Pero ansina sucedió. El rey y la inquisición, no pusieron el tornillo en su lugar, y ¡lálgame! Ni siguiera se nos escuchaba en audencia; solo ellos gobiernaban, el cuerpo político maiden era major quellos, pos cuando inventaba algún mexicanito alguna cosa ¡sas! Lo tatemaban y lo hacían chicharrón en la santa inquisición

Hierfanos en nuestra propia casa no teníamos libertá ni para rellieos, y a ten mostrosa desgracia no nos faltaba más quienes a la sepolitura.

Más cate usté allí, que como dice muy ben un aitor cuyo hombre no recuerdo en estos momentos porque se me ha ido de la cúspide de la guasmorra, que el pueblo que quere ser libre, lo es; por ejemplo, agora digo queen el año de 1810 había en un pueblo un anciano siñor Costilla, cuyas veneriadas canas son hasta la fecha dinas de todo respeuto general.

Este siñor que no se metia con naiden, pero no ostante todos los insurgents lo andaban tantiando; cuando una noche ¡ay! ¡siñor de mí alma! Como aquello de las doce, se enojó el Caudillo y pegó un grito tan juerte que hizo temblar toa la tierra y al mesmo tiempo mandó que arrepicaran las campanas y que arrejuntaran a toda la plebe y algunos Gerenales que andaban pastiando con sus caballos en el campo del Martes; y dijo ¡arriba muchachos! ¡ajera capas! ¡nomás tu amor mujer idolatrada! Y lleno de un santo entusiasmo, se lanzó a la Guerra con un puñado de hombres, eso sí, muy rete machos y no crean ustedes, que armadas con pistolas coles, i remegintones, ni carabinas, minués, ni de la fosefó; no consudadanos, con Hondas, garrotes, tranchetes, y garrochas, embistió esta impresa el nunca bien ponderado Hidalgo, y he aquí el prencipio de una Guerra insurgental que duró algúnos centurions. Como por encantamiento brotaron después de la tierra múchos hombres deslustrados, que dijeron también: ¡Viva la liberta y la independiencia! Y ... ¡echen vino y más tamales!

Decía, pues, que el publo que quere ser libre lo es, y de ellos tenemos patentosos hechos en los ángulos americanos que se hicieron libres de la Inglaterra a lora que don Vasinjetón dijo: ajera ¡Ingleses! Los Rusios, los Turcos, Los Chinos, todos ¿donde han florecido sinó a la sombra de la libertá?

Y sí no, poneos delane de vuestros ojos, las furibundas obras de Alejandro Dimas, Eugenio José, Fraymarión; los eminentes descursos del Chato Briones, de Juan Jacobo Rosiao, y de ellos, sacreís el fruto ático de la libertá.

Si jueron grandes César Angosto, Carlos Mago, Julio Verde, César Cantor y otros esclareficados hombres, según dice don Vitor Lugo, fué porque proclamaron la independiencia de sus pueblos, gritando ¡Viva la libertá y la independiencia!

Aquí debia terminar mí mal foarjada alocación, pero necesito castigar otro momento vuestros virginals güidos, dándoles cuenta de algunos suceisos interinos, respeuto de nuestra autural fotografía.

¡APARCEROS!:

Tenemos cuasi encima a esos siñores communes que queren hacerse ricos a costa de lo ageno, tenemos a los filibusteros en la frontera de nuestra comarca, y por ultimo siñores, tan sólidos y desamparados estamos, que si Dios no lo remienda, para el año quentra, no habrá funión cívica sino permanente, pore so es que yo os envido al concluir mí mal peinao discurso a que arrejuntemos, no nuestro grano de arena, sino una piedra, al edeficio social, que de la laguna estigia arroja el soplo la barca de Aqueronte.

MEXICANOS:

Démonos en este día ósculos de paz, destripemos la discorancia entre nosotros y esclamemos como el Chato Catarino: ¡Viva la paz! ¡Viva el trinta y seis de setiembre de mil ochocientos catorce! ¡Vivan todos los herodes de la patria y viva yo!

CONSUDADANOS:

Viva la patria,
Que asegún dicen

Está muy flaca,
Porque sus hijos
Chupan y maman
Que es un contento,
Qes una una ganga.
Viva el recuerdo
Del bravo Aldama,
Del cura Hidalgo
Y de los parcias
Que le ayudaron
En la campaña.
No nos arredre
Las necias papas
De nuestros primos
Que tanto ladrán.
La independiencia
Costó muy cara,
No hay que perderla
Hay que guardarla;
Y en este día
De Gloria tanta,
Juremos todos
Que a nuestra patria
Defenderemos
Hastga con rabia.
Que haya Concordia,
Vales de mí alma;
Que no se diga
Que el país de Anáhuac
Es probe pueblo
De puros mandrias. . . .
¡Vivan los libres!
¡Viva la patria!
Y, con permiso de ustedes me paso de la trifulca.
Carnación (alias) "Vale Coyote"
Un servidor de vuestras personitas.[1]

# NOTES

## Preface

1. José Zorrilla, *El drama del alma. Algo sobre México y Maximiliano. Poesía en dos partes con notas en prosa y comentarios de un loco* (Burgos: D. T. Arnaix, 1867), 28, 29.

2. Maurice Halbwachs, *On Collective Memory*, ed. and trans. Lewis A. Coser (Chicago: University of Chicago Press, 1992).

3. Patrick H. Hutton (*History as an Art of Memory* [Hanover: University of Vermont, 1993]) provides an excellent starting point for the study of how historians have examined the relationships between memory and history. He writes in detail about Halbwachs, Phillipe Ariès, and Pierre Nora.

4. Benedict Anderson, *Imagined Communities*, rev. ed. (New York: Verso, 1991).

5. Hutton, *Art of Memory*, 49–52.

6. For a persuasive argument for shifting analysis from text to performance, see Joseph Roach, *Cities of the Dead: Circum-Atlantic Performance* (New York: Columbia University Press, 1986).

7. For an introduction to the history of everyday life, see Pilar Gonzalbo Aizpuru, *Introducción a la historia de la vida cotidiana* (México: El Colegio de México, 2006).

8. James Sallis, in *Black Hornet* (New York: Avon Books, 1996), 178–79, attributes this quotation to Juan Goytisolo, *Realms of Strife: The Memoirs of Juan Goytisolo*, 1957–1982, trans. Peter Bush (San Francisco: North Point Press, 1990), 261, but it is a paraphrase of a statement by Walter Benjamin.

# Chapter 1

1. Alejandro Mendez Aquino, "El teatro del siglo XVI a la mitad del siglo XX," *Historia del arte de Oaxaca*, vol. 2: *Colonia y siglo XIX*, coord. Margarita Dalton and Verónica Loera y Chávez Castro (Oaxaca: Gobierno del Estado de Oaxaca, 1997), 370.

2. Miguel Ángel Fernández, *Coleccionismo en México* (Monterrey: Museo de Vidrio, 2000), 138.

3. See Juan José Barreiro and Mancela Guijosa, *Títeres mexicanos: Memoria y retrato de autómatas, fantoches y otros artistas ambulantes* (México: Grupo Roche Syntex de México, 1997), 71. See Zorrilla's memoirs about his time in Mexico, entitled *Memorias del tiempo mexicano* (Mexico: CONACULTA, 1998), ed. Pablo Mora, and *La drama del alma. Algo sobre México y Maximiliano* (Burgos: D. T. Arnaiz, 1867), an epic poem about Maximilian's experience and death in Mexico.

4. Daniel Moreno, "La época independiente entre la Independencia y la Reforma," *Artes de México* 18, no. 147 (1971): 227–33, 114; Eileen Blumenthal, *Puppetry: A World History* (New York: Harry N. Abrams, 2005), 167.

5. Colección LaFragua, La Universidad Nacional Autónoma de México.

6. This tradition of puppet satire has global examples. In the United States, Bread & Puppet Theater since 1961 has acted as a gadfly, protesting a variety of topics from the Vietnam War to government bureaucracy. As recently as the 2000 Republican Party Convention in Philadelphia, the police arrested Matthew Hart and other members of the Spiral Q company for planning protests using marionettes (Vincent Anthony, "A Snapshot of Puppeteers of the United States and Canada," and Lowell Swortzell, "A Short View of American Puppetry," in *American Puppetry: Collections, History and Performance*, ed. Phyllis T. Dircks [Jefferson, NC: McFarland, 2004]), 12, 30.

7. Guillermo Prieto, *Memorias de mis tiempos*, 5th ed. (México: Ediciones Patria, 1968),4:197–98; reprinted in Sonia Iglesias Cabrera and Guillermo Murray Prisant, *Piel de papel, manos de palo: Historia de los títeres en México* (México: Espasa-calpe Mexicana, 1995), 82.

8. Prieto, *Memorias*, 197.

9. On bitter humor especially in politics, see Teodoro Torres, *El humorismo y la sátira en México* (México: Editora Mexicana, 1943); and Moreno, Artes de México 18, no. 147 (1971) (the issue "El humorismo mexicano").

10. Moreno, "Epoca Independiente," 26, 113–14.

11. Blumenthal, *Puppetry*, 88, 93, 96–97.

12. For both the religious and governmental opposition to blasphemy as a threat to social order, see Javier Villa-Flores, *Dangerous Speech: A Social History of Blasphemy in Colonial America* (Tucson: University of Arizona Press, 2006).

13. Teodoro Torres, "El Negrito poeta," in *El humorismo y la sátira en México* (México: Editora Mexicana, 1943), 149–55; Daniel Moreno, "Mito y realidad del Negrito poeta," in *Artes de México* 18, no. 147 (1971): 9–18, and 109–10; Yolanda Jurado Rojas, *El teatro de títeres durante el porfiriato: Un estudio histórico y literario* (Puebla: Benemérita Universidad Autónoma de Puebla, 2004), 36; José Joaquín Fernández de Lizardi, *The Mangy Parrot: The Life and Times of Periquillo Sarniento, Written by Himself for His Children,* trans. David Frye (Indianapolis: Hackett, 2004), 223 and n. 4, 291–93, nn. 9 and 10; Nicolás León, *El Negrito poeta mexicano y sus populares versos* (México, 1912); Eduardo Montes Moctezuma, *El Negrito poeta mexicano y el dominicano: ¿Realidad o fantasía?* (México, 1982); Iglesias Cabrera and Murray Prisant, *Piel de papel,* 160–61.

14. Claudio Lomnitz discusses Juárez as one of Mexico's three totems along with the Virgin of Guadalupe and the playful *calavera,* or skeletal image, in *Death and the Idea of Mexico* (Brooklyn, NY: Zone Books, 2005), 1–5.

15. Scott Cutler Shershow, *Puppets and "Popular" Culture* (Ithaca, NY: Cornell University Press, 1995), 171.

16. Michel-Rolph Trouillot (*Silencing the Past: Power and the Production of History* [Boston: Beacon Press, 1995]) discusses the general pattern of dismissing the Haitian revolution in Western historiography.

17. Luis Reyes de la Maza, *El teatro en México entre la Reforma y el Imperio (1858–1861)*(México: Imprenta Universitaria, 1958), 189. This melodrama remained popular, and was performed in Tlalpán's Teatro Larrea in 1907. See Archivo Histórico del Distrito Federal (AHDF), El Archivo Histórico de Tlalpán (AHT), Licencias, caja 224, expediente 54, approving Compañía Dramática Mexicana's performances of *La cabaña de Tom, ó La esclavitud de los negros,* which included dances in the Cuban style. In the United States, *Uncle Tom's Cabin* was performed by the Afro-American Jubilee Singers and puppeteers using the Buffalo Historical Marionettes as part of the Federal Theater Project, 1935–1939. See Blumenthal, *Puppetry,* 177.

18. Ben Vinson III, *Bearing Arms for His Majesty : The Free-Colored Militia in Colonial Mexico* (Stanford, CA: Stanford University Press, 2001), 1, 25.

19. Patrick Frank, *Posada's Broadsheets: Mexican Popular Imagery, 1890–1910* (Albuquerque: University of New Mexico Press, 1998), chapter entitled "Folkloric Subjects and Rural Heroes," 70–85.

20. Catherine Bremer, "Defying U.S., Mexicans flock to buy 'Racist' stamps," Reuters, July 1, 2005.

21. Enrique Florescano, *Bandera mexicana: Breve historia de su formación y simbolismo* (México: Santilana, 2000).

22. The other five cadets were Juan de la Barrera, Fernando Montes de Oca, Vicente Suárez, Agustín Melgar, and Francisco Marquez. The Boy

Heroes are celebrated across the nation. For example, there is a painting of the six in the municipal offices of Ocotlán de Morelos, Oaxaca. For a history of this legendary event, see E. Plasencia de la Parra, "Conmemoración de la hazaña épica de los Niños Héroes: Su origen, desarrollo y simbolismos," *Historia mexicana* 45 (1995).

23. Cees Nooteboom, *Roads to Santiago: A Modern-Day Pilgrimage through Spain*, translated by Ina Rilke (New York: Harvest Books, 1992), 196–97.

24. Barreiro and Guijosa, *Títeres mexicanos*, 30.

25. Pilar Gonzalbo Aizpuru, *Historia de la vida cotidiana* (México: El Colegio de México, 2006), 21–22.

26. John M. Ingham, *Mary, Michael, and Lucifer: Folk Catholicism in Central Mexico* (Austin: University of Texas Press, 1986), 74–76. Ana Maria Alonso, *Thread of Blood: Colonialism, Revolution, and Gender on Mexico's Northern Frontier* (Tucson: University of Arizona Press, 1995).

27. This is the theme of James C. Scott, *Seeing like a State: How Certain Schemes to Improve the Human Condition Have Failed* (New Haven: Yale University Press, 1999). He calls this local knowledge *mētis*.

28. Carlos Illades, "La representación del pueblo en el segundo romanticismo mexicano," *Signos históricos* 10 (July–December 2003): 20.

29. Without debating the authors directly, this study reviews the arguments of, among others, Benedict Anderson in his book *Imagined Communities*, Eugen Weber in *Peasants into Frenchmen*, and, in different ways, the conclusions of James C. Scott in *Weapons of the Weak*, and of Enrique Florescano in several essays and books about the rise of Mexican nationalism.

30. See Luisa Fernanda Rico Mansard, *Exhibir para educar: Objetos, colecciones y museos de la ciudad de México (1790–1910)* (México: Ediciones Pomares, 2004).

31. Ricardo Pérez Montfort, *Estampas de nacionalismo popular mexicano: Diez ensayos sobre cultura popular y nacionalismo*, 2nd ed. (México: Centro de Estudios Superiores en Antropología Social, 2003).

32. Victor Manuel Villegas, *Arte popular de Guanajuato* (México: Banco Nacional de Fomento Cooperativo, 1964), 26. I have seen examples of these tortilla presses in museums and in photographs but have never been able to locate one in use. I thank Bill French for joining me on several chases to Vizarrón, Querétaro, and beyond in pursuit of the elusive *toquel*.

33. See for example the agenda for independence celebrations in Oaxaca since 1830 in the Archivo Histórico Municipal de la Ciudad de Oaxaca, Manuel R. Palacios, fondo "independencia," 7 boxes.

34. The only historical study of this topic is Isabel Quiñónez, *Mexicanos en su tinta: Calendarios* (México: Instituto Nacional de Antropología e Historia, 1994).

35. A good place to begin the study of these games is Ilán Semo, coord., *La rueda del azar; Juegos y jugadores en la historia de México* (México: Ediciones

Obraje, 2000), especially the essay by Álvaro Vázquez Mantecón, "La república Ludens," 93–126. In particular, the lottery cards used the symbols associated with the advocations of San Jerónimo. My thanks to Terry and Margarita Rugeley for helping me make this identification.

36. Barreiro and Guijosa, *Títeres mexicanos*, 14.

37. Elvia Mante and César Tavera, "Los titeres en el Norte de México" (Baúl Teatro A.C., Monterrey, Mexico, http://www.baulteatro.com), consulted July 1, 2004.

## Chapter 2

1. Walter Satterthwait, *Accustomed to the Dark* (Toronto: Worldwide, 1998), 163–64.

2. A convenient introduction to this work is Alexander von Humboldt, *Political Essay on the Kingdom of New Spain* (abridged), with introduction by Mary Maples Dunn (New York: Alfred A. Knopf, 1972).

3. Leticia Mayer Celis, *Entre el infierno de una realidad y el cielo de un imaginario: Estadística y comunidad científica en el México de la primera mitad del siglo XIX* (México: El Colegio de México, 1999).

4. Leticia Reina, *Las rebeliones campesinas en México (1819–1906)* (México: Siglo Veintiuno, 1980). See chapter 3, "The Guerrilla War of the Huasteca: 1846–1848," of Mark Saad Saka's "Social Justice! Huatecan Unrest and the Uprising of 1879" (PhD diss., University of Houston, 1998).

5. E. P. Thompson, "The Moral Economy of the English Crowd in the Eighteenth Century," *Past and Present* 50 (February 1971): 76–136.

6. Guy P. C. Thomson, "Bulwarks of Patriotic Liberalism: The National Guard, Philharmonic Corps and Patriotic Juntas in Mexico, 1847–1888," *Journal of Latin American Studies* 22 (1990): 31–68; "Popular Aspects of Liberalism in Mexico, 1848–1888," *Bulletin of Latin American Research* 10, no. 3 (1991): 265–92; Guy P. C. Thomson and David LaFrance, *Patriotism, Politics and Popular Liberalism in Nineteenth-Century Mexico: Juan Francisco Lucas and the Puebla Sierra* (Wilmington, DE: SR Books, 1999); and Alan Knight, "El liberalismo mexicano desde la Reforma hasta la Revolución. Una interpretación," *Historia mexicana* 35 (1985): 59–85.

7. Intense local attitudes, representing closed communities, form one of the principal arguments of Eric Van Young's *The Other Rebellion: Popular Violence, Ideology, and the Mexican Struggle for Independence, 1810–1821* (Stanford: Stanford University Press, 2003).

8. Geography is essential to the development of collective memory in the theories of Maurice Halbwachs. See *On Collective Memory*.

9. Ola Apenas, *Mapas antiguos del Valle del México*, facsimile (México: 1984; originally published in 1947), 11, 13, 22, 24, 28.

10. Antonio Saborit, "Cuaresmas porfirianas," *Historias* 15 (October–December 1986): 72–73; Raymond B. Craib, *Cartographic Mexico: A History of State Fixations and Fugitive Landscapes* (Durham, NC: Duke University Press, 2004).

11. Quiñónez, *Mexicanos en su tinta.*

12. For the discussion of later caricatures, see Esther Acevedo, *Una historia en quinientas caricaturas: Constantino Escalente en La Orquesta* (México: Instituto Nacional de Antropologia e Historia, 1994).

13. Mayer Celis, *Entre el infierno*, 55.

14. Fernández de Lizardi, *Mangy Parrot*, 11, n. 1.

15. Isabel Quiñónez, "De pronósticos, calendarios y almanaques," in *La república de las letras. Asomos a la cultura escrita del México decimonónico, vol. 2, Publicaciones periódicas y otros impresos,* coord. Belem Clark de Lara and Elisa Speckman Guerra (México: La Universidad Nacional Autónoma de México, 2005), 331–52.

16. Edward Wright-Rios, "Visions of Women: Revelation, Gender, and Catholic Resurgence," in *Religious Culture in Modern Mexico*, ed. Martin Nesvig (Boulder: Rowman and Littlefield, 2007), 7–14.

17. See the advertisement for Ignacio M. Altamirano's *Primer almanaque histórico, artístico, y monumental de la República Mexicana* for 1883 published in *El Pueblo (El Estado de Tlaxcala. Organo oficial del gobierno)* 87 (September 23, 1882): 4.

18. Enrique Florescano, "La creación de la bandera nacional: Un encuentro de tres tradicones;" "Los mitos de identidad colectiva y la reconstrucción del Pasado," "La construcción de identidades colectivas en Mexico: Etnia, estado y nación," *Memoria mexicana* (México: Fondo de Cultura Económica, 1994), part 8.

19. Isabel Fernández and Carmen Nava Nava, "He de comer de esa tuna: Ensayo histórico iconográfico sobre el escudo nacional." Ponencía del año de 1996 como parte de un exposicióna documental se llamaba "la consumación de independencia 175 años" en el Archivo General de la Nación.

20. Quiñónez, *Mexicanos en su tinta*, 68–69.

21. Ibid., 77.

22. *Arte Naïf: Guatemala* (Guatemala: UNESCO, 1998).

23. Interview with Óscar Eduardo Perén, Guatemala, May 21, 2005.

24. Villa-Flores, *Dangerous Speech*, 111–15 for a discussion of the religious and governmental opposition to gambling in the colonial era.

25. Guillermo Tovar de Teresa and Jorge F. Hernández, "Juegos y juguetes en el vierreinato de la Nueva España," in *Juegos y juguetes mexicanos* (México: Fundación Cultural CREMI, 1993), by Luis Gonzales y Gonzalés et al., 51; Enrique García Martín, "Clemente Jacques y Cía, s.a./Pasatimempos Gallo, S.A. de C.V.," *La Sota: Revista de naipefilia y naipologia* 15 (September 1996):

63; and Víctor Ferro Torrellas, "La influencia francesa de los naipes de la Cataluña del siglo XVI," ibid., 65–70.

26. José de J. Nuñez y Dominguez, "Las loterías de figuras en México," *Mexican Folkways 8* (1932): 87–88.

27. *100 años de lotería campechana* (México: Centro de Emisin de Billetes de la Lotería Nacional, 1995), 7–8.

28. Luis Luján Muñoz, "La lotería de figuras en Guatemala" (Guatemala: Serviprensa Centroamericana, 1987), 7, citing Carmen Bravo y Villasanta, *Historia de la literatura infantil española* (Madrid: Doncel, 1972), 71–72.

29. Tovar de Teresa and Hernández, "Juegos y juguetes en el vierreinato," 65.

30. "Cante la lotería como en las ferias," game instructions published with the set by Pasatiempos Gallo, S.A.; *100 años de lotería campechana*, 8.

31. Miguel Ángel Fernández, *Coleccionismo en México* (Monterrey: Museo de Vidrio, 2000), 254, 255, and *100 años de lotería campechana*, 35, 44, 57, and 58, have images of these embroidered game boards.

32. *100 años de lotería campechana*, 8.

33. Ibid., 8–9.

34. García Martín, "Clemente Jacques," *La Sota*, 3–64; interview with Jorge Landín Sánchez, Director, Pasatiempos Gallo, Querétaro, Querétaro, March 17, 1997.

35. Lotería is still played in some public squares such as Pinotepa Nacional, Oaxaca. *100 años de lotería campechana*, 11.

36. Virginia Armella, "Del panal a la vitrina: Investigación sobre los trabajos de cera de México," in Gonzáles y Gónzales et al. *Juegos y juguetes mexicanos* (México: Fundación Cultural CREMI, 1993), 91, 94–95. One example is the Christy Collection in the Victoria and Albert Museum, London.

37. Vincent J. Cincotta, *Zarzuela: The Spanish Lyric Theatre* (Artarmon, NSW: University of Wollongong Press, 2002),182–83.

38. Centro Nacional de los Artes, México, D.F., Biblioteca de los Artes Escencias y Teatrales "Rodolfo Usigli," expediente 90, file 102, paraphrase of list on p. 118.

39. The first recorded *pastorela* was performed in 1586 in Tlajomulco, near Guadalajara. See Antonio de Ciudad Real, *Viajes de fray Alonso Ponce al occidente de México* (Guadalajara: 1968).

40. William H. Beezley, "Altars for Day of the Dead," in *Home Altars of Mexico* (Albuquerque: University of New Mexico, 1997), edited by Dana Salvo, 91–122; Homero Adame Martínez, "Los nacimientos: Una tradición centenaria," *México desconocido* 23, no. 262 (December 1998), 32–39; Tovar de Teresa and Hernández, "Juegos y juguetes en el vierreinato," 57, 60; Armella, "Del panal a la vitrina," 87, 88.

41. For a common representation of the hand of power, see Miguel Ángel Fernández, *Coleccionismo en México* (Monterrey: Museo del Vidrio, 2000), 231.

42. See the 1870 game boards painted on tin, Arizona Historical Society, Cat. 83.19.7.

43. Jack Goody, *The Culture of Flowers* (New York: Cambridge University Press, 1991), 116–17, 122, 130, 136; Aurelia C. Scott, *Otherwise Normal People: Inside the Thorny World of Competitive Rose Gardening* (Chapel Hill: Algonquin Books, 2007), 14.

44. Charlotte de Latour (Mme. Louise Cortambert), *Le langage des fleurs* (Paris: 1819). German translation in 1820 and English translation in 1834; the date of the Spanish translation has not been determined.

45. Goody, *Culture of Flowers*, 282.

46. Ibid., see esp. 289–99.

47. *El patolli del coyote* was another of these games. Decks of cards for use in the gambling halls blossomed during the Bourbon years in Mexico City and remained popular into the twentieth century. See "El arte de la suerte," *Artes de México*, nueva época 13 (Fall 1991), esp. 21, 42, 43; and Miguel Zacarias y Bustos, "Cantar los naipes," 64–74.

48. Fernández de Lizardi, *Mangy Parrot*, 288–89.

49. J. H. Plumb, lecture at the Folger Library, Washington, D.C., March 27, 1979; Plumb offers additional discussion, in his *Georgian Delights: Leisure Time Pursuits in Georgian England* (London: Weidenfeld and Nicolson, 1980); Robert Aguirre, "William Bullock (1773–1849): British Curator of Exotica Visits Mexico," in *The Human Tradition in the Atlantic World*, Karen Racine and Beatriz Gallotti Mamigonian, eds. (Lanham, MD: Rowman and Littlefield, forthcoming).

50. Robert C. Elliott, *The Power of Satire: Magic, Ritual, Art* (Princeton, NJ: Princeton University Press, 1960), 5.

51. James A. Epstein, *Radical Expression: Political Language, Ritual, and Symbol in England, 1790–1850* (New York: Oxford University Press, 1994), 151.

52. Elliott, *Power of Satire*, 88.

53. Tovar de Teresa and Hernández, "Juegos y juguetes en el vierreinato," 73.

54. Stanley Brandes, *Metaphors of Masculinity: Sex and Status in Andalusian Folklore* (Philadelphia: University of Pennsylvania Press, 1980).

55. Timothy J. Mitchell, *Violence and Piety in Spanish Folklore* (Philadelphia: University of Pennsylvania Press, 1988), 96.

56. Iglesias Cabrera and Murray Prisant, *Piel de papel*, 38.

57. James C. Scott, *Weapons of the Weak* (New Haven: Yale University Press, 1985).

58. Mitchell, *Violence and Piety*, 11–25 and 95–97, discusses the folkloric character of Judas burnings in Spain and develops an analysis drawn from the controversial theories of René Girard. Girard emphasizes violence in the creation of cultural institutions and practices and uses "magico-persecutory thought" to refer to what psychoanalysts call projection.

59. Linda Curcio-Nagy sent me these references. See Cristobal Gutiérrez de Medina, *Viaje por mar y tierra de Virrey Marques de Vienna. Aplausos y fiestas en México* (México: UNAM, 1947), 78–79; and for the Monte Paranaso, see Archivo General de la Nación, ramo de hacienda, vol. 251.

60. Because of the ephemeral nature of the figures that are destroyed and the testaments, they are indeed rare. One excellent collection is José Inés Ramírez, *Testamentos de Judas* (Colima: 1994), which provides testaments from a thirty-year period beginning in 1962, for Ciudad de Villa de Alvarez, Colima.

61. William H. Beezley, *Judas at the Jockey Club*, 2nd ed. (Lincoln: University of Nebraska Press, 2003).

62. Patrick Frank, *Posada's Broadsheets: Mexican Popular Imagery, 1890–1910* (Albuquerque: University of New Mexico Press, 1998), 244–45; Elisa Speckman Guerra, "Cuadernillos, pliegos, y hojas sueltas en la imprenta de Antonio Vanegas Arroyo," and Helia Emma Bonilla, "Imágenes de Posada en los impresos de Vanegas Arroyo," in *La república de las letras. Asomos a la cultura escrita del México decimonónico*, vol. 2, *Publicaciones periódicicas y otros impresos*, coord. Belem Clark de Lara and Elisa Speckman Guerra (México: La Universidad Nacional Autónoma de México, 2005), 391–413, 415–36.

63. Fernández de Lizardi, *Mangy Parrot*, 85–86.

64. The drawing forms part the nineteenth-century collection at the Museo Nacional del Arte, Mexico City.

65. Fernández de Lizardi, *Mangy Parrot*, 130 and n. 5.

66. Frank, 71–85.

67. Ibid., 104–18.

68. Kenneth Mills and William B. Taylor, eds., *Colonial Latin America: Documentary History* (Wilmington, DE: SR Books, 1998), 266.

69. Of the several authors who make this point, one in particular is Jorge F. Hernández, "Entre el azar y el vértigo: Juegos y juguetes en el México del siglo XIX," in *Juegos y juguetes mexicanos*, by Luis Gonzáles y Gonzáles et al. (México: Fundación Cultural CREMI, 1993),101–2.

70. Ibid., 113.

71. Fernández, *Coleccionismo*, 68–70.

72. Villa-Flores, *Dangerous Speech*, 112–13, citing Jean-Pierre Etienvre, *Márgenes literarios del juego: Una poética del naipe siglos XVI–XVIII* (London: Tamesis Books, 1990), 100–104, 322–26.

73. Ibid., 240, n. 11, citing David Sidney Parlett, *Oxford Guide to Card Games* (New York: Oxford University Press, 1990), p. 11.

74. Fernández de Lizardi, *Mangy Parrot*, 281.

75. Tovar de Teresa and Hernández, "Juegos y juguetes en el vierreinato," 60–61.

76. Nancy Vogeley, "Introduction," to José Joaquín Fernández de Lizardi, *The Mangy Parrot: The Life and Times of Periquillo Sarniento, Written by Himself for His Children*, translated by David Frye (Indianapolis: Hackett Publishing Company, 2004), xvii.

77. William Rowe and Vivian Schelling, *Memory and Modernity: Popular Culture in Latin America* (New York: Verso, 1991), 33, citing *J. G. Posada: Messenger of Mortality*, ed. Julian Rothstein (London: 1989), 111.

78. Martha Del Río Grimm, "El juego y el juguete en El Paplote Museo del niño," in *Juegos y juguetes mexicanos*, by Luis Gonzalés y Gonzalés et al., (México: Fundación Cultural CREMI, 1993), 136.

## Chapter 3

1. Michael Dibdin, *A Long Finish* (New York: Vintage, 2000; originally published by Pantheon Books, 1998), 152.

2. Thucydides, *The Peloponnesian War*, trans. John H. Finley Jr. (New York: Modern Library, 1951), 331.

3. Eric J. Hobsbawn and Terence Ranger, eds., *The Invention of Tradition* (New York: Cambridge University Press, 1992).

4. Gonzalbo Aizpuru, in *Historia de la vida cotidiana* (21–22), talks about this double pattern of official and community histories, in which the latter includes fantasies, saints, local heroes, and village scamps. This argument builds on Halbwachs, *On Collective Memory*.

5. William H. Beezley and David E. Lorey, eds., *¡Viva Mexico! ¡Viva la Independencia! Celebrations of September 16* (Wilmington, DE: SR Books, 2001); William H. Beezley, Cheryl English Martin, and William E. French, eds., *Rituals of Rule, Rituals of Resistance: Public Celebrations and Popular Culture in Mexico* (Wilmington, DE: SR Books, 1994), xiii–xxxii; Alison Brysk, "'Hearts and Minds': Bringing Symbolic Politics Back In," *Polity* (Summer 1995). Participants in seminars at Pomona, Yale, and Chicago Universities helped me sharpen and expand the explication. I thank them all, especially Alexandra Stern for her incisive commentary.

6. Enrique Florescano, "Les origines de la mémoire nationale: La célébration du triomphe de l'Indépendance en 1821," in *Mémories en devenir Amérique latine XVIe-XXe siècle*, ed. François-Xavier Guerra (Bordeaux: Maison des Pays Ibériques, 1994), 157–76.

7. AHDF: Archivo del Antiguo Ayuntamiento de la Ciudad de Mexico, vol. 1058, exp. 2, 29 Aug. 1822.

8. Manuel Dublán and José María Lozano, *Legislación mexicana; ó, colección completa de las disposiciones legislativas expedidas desde la independencia de la república (1821 hasta 1906)* (México: Dublán y Lozano, 1876–1910), 1822: 559: #283.

9. Stacie G. Widdifield, *The Embodiment of the National in Late Nineteenth-Century Mexican Painting* (Tucson: University of Arizona Press, 1996), 133; Dublán and Lozano, 1822: 660–61: #344.

10. Enrique Krauze, *Siglo de caudillos: Biografía política de México (1810–1910)* (México: Tusquets, 1994), 43–44.

11. Enrique Florescano, *Memory, Myth, and Time in Mexico: From the Aztecs to Independence*, trans. Albert G. Bork (Austin: University of Texas Press, 1994), 216–17.

12. Examining these early celebrations, it is necessary to recognize the work of professors Josefina Vázquez, David Brading, and Richard Warren. See Richard Warren, "The Construction of Independence Day, 1821–1864," paper presented at the conference "Mexico in the Nineteenth Century: A Symposium in Honor of Nettie Lee Benson," Austin, Texas, April 15–16, 1994; Josefina Vázquez K., *Nacionalismo y educación en México* (México: 1970), 32–39; David A. Brading, *The First America: The Spanish Monarchy, Creole Patriots and the Liberal State, 1492–1867* (Cambridge: Cambridge University Press, 1991), 603–72.

13. Michael P. Costeloe, "The Junta Patriótica and the Celebration of Independence in Mexico City, 1825–1855," *Mexican Studies/Estudios Mexicanos* 13, no. 1 (Winter, 1997), 21–53. This essay is available in Beezley and Lorey, eds., *¡Viva Mexico! ¡Viva la Independencia!*, 43–75.

14. "Como se celebró la primera vez el aniversario de la independencia," *El Nacional*, Sept. 16, 1893, reprinted in *Boletin oficial del Consejo Superior de gobierno del Distrito Federal* 13, no. 22 (Sept. 14, 1909).

15. Costeloe, "Junta Patriótica," 25–27.

16. Sergio Rivera Ayala, "Lewd Songs and Dances from the Streets of Eighteenth-Century New Spain," in Beezley, Martin, and French, eds., *Rituals of Rule*, 95–114. Several of the songs that Rivera analyzed are available on *La música prohibida por la Inquisición* by Nesh-Kala (Tlalli, the record label of Radio Educación), recorded on the *Quien canta* program, March 14, 1995.

17. Julio Estrada, ed., *La musica de México*, vol. 1, *Historia, pt. 5 Periodo contemporaneo* (México: UNAM, 1984), 17–18, 39; Gabriel Saldivar, *El Jarabe: Baile popular mexicano* (Puebla: Secretaría de Cultura, 1987); Quiñonez, *Mexicanos en su tinta*, 33–34.

18. Vicente Riva Palacio reported that during the Independence era, acting groups performed mythical and historical episodes or presented icons symbolizing the virtues or vices or characterized personalities from the Old Testament or the gods of mythology on allegorical floats. See *México a través de los siglos*, 16th ed. (México: Editorial Cumbre, 1980), vol. 2, 721–25.

19. See Miguel Soto, "The Monarchist Conspiracy in Mexico, 1845–1846" (PhD diss., University of Texas, 1983).

20. Costeloe, "Junta patriótica," 4, 10. Costeloe provides lists of the September 16 and September 27 orators (23–24, 25).

21. Shannon Baker Tuller, "Santa Anna's Legacy: Caudillismo in Early Republican Mexico" (PhD diss., Texas Christian University, 1999).

22. Amy Baker Salvato, "Recasting a Nation: The Reburial of Agustín de Iturbide" (master's thesis, University of Arizona, 1999), 35–51.

23. Erika Pani, "El proyecto de Estado de Maximiliano a través de la vida cortesana y del ceremonial público," *Historia Mexicana* 45, no. 2 (October–December 1995): 423–61.

24. Ignacio Manuel Altamirano's "Cronica de las fiestas de Septiembre en México y Puebla" was first published in the literary journal *El Renacimiento*; it was reissued by Puebla's Secretaría de Cultura in 1987 as *Lecturas historicas de Puebla, #6.*

25. Discussion of this celebration also appears in William H. Beezley, "New Celebrations of Independence: Puebla (1869) and Mexico City (1883)," in Beezley and Lorey, eds., *¡Viva Mexico! ¡Viva la Independencia!* 131–40.

26. Susan G. Davis provides a helpful guide to parades and processions as social and historical texts in *Parades and Power: Street Theatre in Nineteenth-Century Philadelphia* (Philadelphia: Temple University Press, 1986). Also see Mary Ryan, "The American Parade: Representations of the Nineteenth-Century Social Order," in *The New Cultural History*, ed. Lynn Hunt, 131–53 (Berkeley: University of California Press, 1990).

27. Morales also wrote the music for "Las Flores. Inspiración á la Schottisch," published in 1880, and several operas. Irene Spamer, "Melesio Morales," *Músicos mexicanos de hoy* (México: Editorial Trillas, 2003), 13–14; Roberto L. Mayer, Antonio Rubial García, and Guadalupe Jiménez Codinanch, *México ilustrado. Mapas, planos, grabados e ilustraciones de los siglos XVI al XIX* (México: Fomento Cultural Banamex, 1994), 46, 155, 250.

28. On the militia, see Thomson, "Bulwarks of Patriotic Liberalism," 31–68, and "Popular Aspects of Liberalism." On popular liberalism, see Thomson and David LaFrance, *Patriotism, Politics and Popular Liberalism*; and Knight, "Liberalismo mexicano," 59–85.

29. *Diccionario Porrúa: Historia, biografia y geografia de mexico*, 3rd ed. (México: Editorial Porrúa, 1971), s.v. "Ignacio Zaragoza."

30. Matthew D. Esposito, "Memorializing Modern Mexico: The State Funerals of the Porfirian Era, 1876–1911" (PhD diss., Department of History, Texas Christian University, 1997, 288–89.

31. Aída Mostkoff-Linares, "Foreign Visions and Images of Mexico: One Hundred Years of International Tourism, 1821–1921." (PhD diss., UCLA, 1999), 42–67.

32. Linda Curcio-Nagy, "Giants and Gypsies: Corpus Christi in Colonial Mexico City," in Beezley, Martin, and French, eds., *Rituals of Rule*, 1–26. The history of the *tarasaca* in Corpus Christi processions in Madrid and Sevilla is discussed in J. E. Varey, *Historia de los títeres en España (desde*

*sus origines hasta mediados del siglo XVIII)* (Madrid: Revista de Occidente, 1957), 62–72.

33. Monroy (1836–1882) is best known for his work *Isaac*, praised as a synthesis of academic ideals. Perhaps he was related to Luis Monroy (1845–?), whose work *La muerte de un cautivo* (1872) was highly regarded at the time. Luis also did extremely large religious paintings in 1885, which hang in La Iglesia Valenciana, Guanajuato, Guanajuato.

34. Widdifield, *Embodiment of the National*, 144, 159–60.

35. Ibid., 193–94.

36. Clementina Díaz de Ovando, *Las fiestas patrias en el México de hace un siglo, 1883* (México: Centro de Estudios de Historia de México, Condumex, 1984).

37. Lucio Marmolejo, *Efemérides guanajuatenses* (Guanajuato: Universidad de Guanajuato, 1973), 4:414–21. The exact parade route for both days is included on p. 421.

38. Archivo del Estado de Guanajuato, Ayuntamiento de Guanajuato, Diversiones Públicas, decreto de 26 de febrero de 1881; and Reglamentos, Caja 2, file 163–166, año 1887, Bando de Policia, art. 14.

39. Archivo Histórico del Municipio de Colima, Colima. *El Estado de Colima. Periódico oficial del gobierno* (September 18, 1885), no. 28, pp. 157–59.

40. See the reports of the *junta patriótica* in the Ramo de diversiones civicas, Archivo General Municipal, Guadalajara (hereinafter cited as AGM); all financial amounts are in pesos.

41. AGM, 1887, Caja 1224, Paquete 142, Expediente 109.

42. AGM, 1882, Paquete 150, Expediente 8.

43. AGM, 1892, Caja 1247, Paquete 165, Expediente 39, Fiestas cívicas y diversiones.

44. This became the slogan of the Porfirian administration generally. See Paul Garner, *Porfirio Díaz* (Harlow, England: Pearson Education, 2001).

45. Vernon L. Lidtke, *The Alternative Culture: Socialist Labor in Imperial Germany* (New York: Oxford University Press, 1985), 75–101.

46. Roger D. Abrahams argues that in the United States, nineteenth-century parades quickly became advertisements for business, building on the frontier tradition of organizing parades to show off newly arrived products from the East. See Abrahams, "The Language of Festivals: Celebrating the Economy," in *Celebration: Studies in Festivity and Ritual*, ed. Victor Turner (Washington, DC: Smithsonian Institution Press, 1982), 161–77; Tony Morgan, "Proletarians, Politicos, and Patriarchs: The Use and Abuse of Cultural Customs in the Early Industrialization of Mexico City, 1880–1910," in Beezley, Martin, and French., eds., *Rituals of Rule*, 151–72. On the general topic of the development of the commercial character of holidays in the United States, see Leigh

Eric Schmidt, "The Commercialization of the Calendar: American Holidays and the Culture of Consumption, 1870–1030," *Journal of American History* 78, no. 3 (December 1991), 887–916.

47. El Archivo del Estado de Guanajuato, Ayuntamiento de Guanajuato, Paseos Públicos, p. 2; *El periódico oficial del gobierno del Estado de Guanajuato* 11, no. 66 (September 1883).

48. Ellen M. Litwicki, *America's Public Holidays, 1865–1920* (Washington, DC: Smithsonian Institution Press, 2000).

49. Ryan, "American Parade," 137–38; Hanna Fenichel Pitkin, *The Concept of Representation* (Berkeley: University of California Press, 1967).

50. For Carmen's influence on Díaz, see Mrs. Alec Tweedee, *The Maker of Modern Mexico: Porfirio Diaz* (New York: John Lane, 1906), the chapter entitled "The Influence of a Woman," 286–304. Carmen, who deserves study, has been ignored by nearly everyone. She lived from January 1862 to June 25, 1944, and only scraps of her activities have been recorded and virtually nothing examined. See the articles about her in *Excelsior*, June 26, 1944, and her obituary in the *New York Times*, June 26, 1944.

51. Colin M. MacLachlan and William H. Beezley, *El Gran Pueblo: A History of Greater Mexico* (Englewood Cliffs, NJ: Prentice-Hall, 1994), 97–99.

52. Juan Francisco Lucas, Diaz's comrade in arms and *cacique* of the Puebla sierra, regularly sent birthday congratulations to the president on August 21. See Thomson and LaFrance, *Patriotism, Politics, and Popular Liberalism*, 312.

53. Pacheco, the secretary of public works, colonization and commerce, organized the competition for the 1889 Mexican Pavilion and, with Díaz and the exposition's board of directors, judged the entries. See María Auxiliadora Fernández, "In the Image of the Other: A Call for Rethinking National Identity," *Center: A Journal for Architecture in America* 7 (1992), 44–45, and "The Representation of National Identity in Mexican Architecture: Two Case Studies (1680 and 1889)" (PhD diss., Columbia University, 1993).

54. Gabriel Villanueva, *Las fiestas en honor del sr. General Porfirio Díaz: Crónica completa* (México: Secretaría de Fomento, 1891), commissioned for the Junta Central Porfirista.

55. Diaz's one-time correspondence with Lucas in Puebla, for example, by the 1890s had been reduced to the president sending the *cacique* printed greetings with a stamped signature. See Thomson and LaFrance, *Patriotism, Politics, and Popular Liberalism*, 313.

56. See Roderic A. Camp, *Recruitment across Two Centuries* (Austin: University of Texas Press, 1995), who shows the changing personnel, from veterans from throughout Mexico to college graduates from Mexico City, of the Porfirian regime in the 1890s. Also see François-Xavier Guerra, *Le Méxique: De l'ancien regime a la Revolution* (Paris: L'Harmattan, 1985), 1:395–403.

57. Villanueva, *Fiestas*, 26.

58. For a complete discussion of Sigüenza y Gongora's arch, see Fernández, "Representation of the National," 1–204, and "Image of the Other," 51. See Linda Curcio-Nagy, "The Ideal and the Real: The Mexico City Triumphal Arch and Political Protest in 1697," paper presented at the Rocky Mountain Council for Latin American Studies, Forth Worth, Texas, February 20, 1994; and Peer Schmidt, "Neoestoicismo y disciplina social en la America Latina del siglo XVII," Conference of Three Nations, Mexico City, October 30, 1994.

59. Teresa Matabuena Peláez, *Algunos usos y conceptos de la fotografía durante el porfiriato* (México: Universidad Iberoamericana, 1991), 105–7.

60. Jean-Paul Aron, *The Art of Eating in France: Manners and Menus in the Nineteenth Century* (New York: Harper and Row, 1975), 77.

61. Ibid., 77–78.

62. For an introduction to the social history of Mexican food, see Jeffrey M. Pilcher, *"¡Que Vivan Tamales!:" The Creation of a Mexican National Cuisine* (Albuquerque: University of New Mexico Press, 1998), especially chapter 3.

63. Hugh Johnson, *Hugh Johnson's Story of Wine* (London: Mitchell Beazley, 1989), 330–341; Natalie MacLean, *Red, White, and Drunk All Over: A Wine-Soaked Journey from Grape to Glass* (New York: Bloomsbury, 2006), 76–111; Dewey Markham, Jr., *1855: A History of the Bordeaux Classification* (New York: John Wiley and Sons, 1998).

64. Jim Concannon, with Tim Patterson, *Concannon: The First One Hundred and Twenty-five Years* (Healdsburg, CA: Andy Katz Photography, 2006), 21, 23.

65. Gabriel Gadsden, *Cavas de México* (México: MVS Editorial, 2003), 30–36.

66. For a suggestive essay, see Sonya Lipsett-Rivera, "Configurations within a Pattern of Violence. The Geography of Sexual Danger in Mexico, 1750–1850," paper presented at the annual meeting of the American Historical Association, January 6–8, 1995, 5–7. The practice of excluding or separating women from the main party reached back to European elite dining in the eighteenth century. English radicals brought women to the table, although they remained silent and subservient. See Epstein, *Radical expression*, 160.

67. Villanueva, *Fiestas*, 34–50.

68. L. E. Anderson, "Edison in Mexico, 1904–1912: A Preliminary Study," *Sound Box* (September 1994 and November 1994). Díaz was persuaded to make a wax recording in August 1909 for the Edison Company, identified as E797-7 in the catalog in the Edison collection. Other correspondence between Thomas B. Connery, the company agent, and others in Mexico with Thomas Edison on recording and the sale of phonographs is contained in the Thomas A. Edison Papers, Rutgers University, New Brunswick, N.J. My thanks to Glen Kuecker and Bob Rosenberg for information on these files.

69. For a thought-provoking essay on the efforts to create new images of both the regime and the nation, see Paolo Riguzzi, "México próspero: Las

dimensiones de la imagen nacional en el porfiriato," *Historias* 20 (April–September 1980): 137–57.

70. Mauricio Tenorio-Trillo, *Mexico at the World's Fairs: Crafting a Modern Nation* (Berkeley: University of California, 1996); Riguzzi, "México próspero," 148–53; Gene Yeager, "Porfirian Commercial Propaganda: Mexico in the World Industry Expositions," *The Americas* 34, no. 2 (October 1977): 230–43; Mark D. Barringer and Matthew D. Esposito, "And the Band Played On: Mexico at the World's Industrial and Cotton Centennial Exposition in New Orleans, 1884–1885," paper presented at the annual meeting of the Southwestern Social Science Association meeting, Dallas, Texas, March 23, 1995.

71. See for example the account by the *Chicago Times* correspondent John F. Finerty, sent in 1879 to accompany and report on an eighty-member American Industrial Deputation visit (Wilbert H. Timmons, ed., *John F. Finerty Reports Porfirian Mexico, 1879* [El Paso: Texas Western Press, 1974]).

72. Barbara A. Tenenbaum, "Streetwise History: The Paseo de la Reforma and the Porfirian State, 1876–1910," in Beezley, Martin, and French, eds., *Rituals of Rule*, 127–71.

73. See William H. Beezley, "The Porfirian Smart Set Anticipates Thorstein Veblen in Guadalajara," in Beezley, Martin, and French, eds., *Rituals of Rule*, 173–90.

74. *El Pueblo* (El Estado de Tlaxcala) (Feb. 4, 1883), 4. The essay discussed the school in Orizaba to argue for a similar free college in Tlaxacala.

75. Fernández, "In the Image of the Other," 44–58, esp. 47, 48, 56; the quotation comes from p. 53. The Mexican government participated in the 1876 Centennial Exhibition in Philadelphia, sending a construction similar to most other nations that combined a triumphal arch. See p. 53.

76. Julie K. Brown, *Contesting Images: Photography and the World's Columbian Exposition* (Tucson: University of Arizona Press, 1994), 28, 41–42, 58–59. On the development and use of photography during this period in Mexico, see Matabuena Peláez, *Fotografía durante el porfiriato*.

77. Frederick Starr Collection, Department of Special Collections, University of Chicago Library, Box 29, "World's Fair, Chicago, 1893, Notebook."

78. Fernández, "Image of the Other," 50.

79. Thorstein Veblen, *The Theory of the Leisure Class: An Economic Study of Institutions* (1889; reprint, New York: Viking, 1934), 118.

80. Mark Wasserman, *Persistent Oligarchs: Elites and Politics in Chihuahua, Mexico, 1910–1940* (Durham, NC: Duke University Press, 1993).

81. See Douglas Sullivan-Gonzalez, "The Struggle for Hegemony: An Analysis of the Mexican Catholic Church, 1876–1911" (unpublished University of Texas seminar paper); Randall Scott Hanson, "Catholic Militants in Mexico:

The *Secretariado Social Mexicano* and *Acción Católica Mexicana, 1920–1946"* (PhD diss., Indiana University, 1994), chapter 1.

82. I. J. Caliccho, s.v. "Monarchia Sicula," *New Catholic Encyclopedia* (Detroit, MI: Thomson-Gale Publishers, 2003), IX, 779.

83. The printed program of the coronation and a description of the celebration sold for twelve centavos. A copy is contained in the Frederick Starr Papers, 1860–1930, UCLA Library, Department of Special Collections, Collection 190, Box 17; Alfred Oscar Coffin, *Land without Chimneys; or, The Byways of Mexico* (Cincinnati: Editor Publishing, 1898), 124–25, discusses the coronation, and T. Philip Terry, *Terry's Mexico: Handbook for Travellers*, 2nd ed. (London: Gay and Hancock, 1909,), 401, also describes the crown.

84. Miguel Rodríguez, *Celebración de "la raza": Una historia comparativa del 12 de Octubre* (México: La Universidad Iberoamericana, 2004), 84.

85. Frederick Starr Papers, UCLA, Box 1, Folder "Prayer Sheets."

86. See William B. Taylor, "The Virgin of Guadalupe in New Spain: An Inquiry into the Social History of Marian Devotion," *American Ethnologist* 14, no. 1 (February 1987): 9–33; the quotation comes from p. 20. Taylor argues that the veneration of the Virgin during the colonial period was more widespread among non-Indians and in Mexico City than among Indians in the countryside. He also argues that this was just one of many powerful religious representations, and he develops the multivocal character of this symbol, showing that it had messages of "accommodation and liberation" that waxed and waned. He further proposes that the Virgin of Guadalupe as the symbol of downtrodden Indian Mexico came as a result of the movement for independence, rather than being a cause for the revolt. See p. 24.

87. Esposito, "Memorializing Modern Mexico," 11–18.

88. Jacinto Barrera Bassols, *Pesquisa sobre un estandarte: Historia de una pieza de museo* (México: Ediciones Sinfiltro, 1995); *Mexican Herald*, November 11, 1895, February 18, 1896; Coffin, *Land without Chimneys*, 116; Matthew D. Esposito, "From Father Hidalgo to Porfirio Díaz: Holidays, Relics, and the Liberal Myth in Mexico, 1876–1900," paper presented at the annual meeting of the Southwestern Social Science Association, San Antonio, Texas, April 1, 1994.

89. *Mexican Herald*, Dec. 13, 1895; Elisabeth Lambert Ortiz, *The Festive Food of Mexico* (London: Kyle Cathie, 1992), 52–53.

90. See Alan Knight, *The Mexican Revolution* (Cambridge: Cambridge University Press, 1986), 2:497.

91. Guerra, *Le Mexique*, 1:306–30. The population of the city grew from 230,000 (1877) to 329,774 (1895) and continued to expand, reaching 344,721 (1900), then 471,066 (1910). See Moisés González Navarro, *Estadísticas sociales del Porfiriato, 1877–1910* (México: Dirección General de Estadística, 1956), 9.

92. To examine the growth of the city, an excellent beginning can be made with Thomas F. Reese and Carol McMichael Reese, "Revolutionary Urban Legacies; Porfirio Díaz's Celebrations of the Centennial of Mexican Independence in 1910," in *Arte, historia e identidad en América: Visiones comparativas*, ed. Gustavo Curiel, Renato González Mello, and Juana Gutiérrez Haces (México: UNAM: 1994), 2:365–67. For an analysis of the land transactions in the new neighborhoods in particular, see Jorge H. Jiménez Muñoz, *La traza de poder: Historia de la política y los urbanos en el Distrito Federal, de sus orígenes a la desaparición del ayuntamiento, 1824–1928* (México: CODEX Editores, 1993); Tenenbaum, "Streetwise History," 127–50; Morgan, "Proletarians, Politicos, and Patriarchs," 151–72; Fernández, "Image of the Other," 50.

93. John Lear, *Workers, Neighbors and Citizens: The Revolution in Mexico City* (Lincoln: University of Nebraska Press, 2001), 13–49; William Schell Jr., *Integral Outsiders: The American Colony in Mexico City, 1876–1911* (Wilmington, DE: SR Books, 2001), and "Yankee Bankers and Builders: The Growth of Mexico City during the Late Porfiriato," 14–15, unpublished, undated essay in the author's possession.

94. Conversation with Miguel Tinker-Salas concerning Porfirian Hermosillo, Claremont Men's College, Claremont, CA, April 28, 1998; Gilbert Joseph and Allen Wells, "Chilango Blueprints and Provincial Growing Pains: Mérida at the Turn of the Century," *Mexican Studies/Estudios Mexicanos* 8 (Summer 1992): 167–215; William R. French, *Peaceful and Working People: The Inculcation of the Capitalist Work Ethic in a Mexican Mining District* (Albuquerque: University of New Mexico Press, 1996).

95. Reese and Reese, "Revolutionary Urban Legacies," 367–70; Emily Wakild, "It Is to Preserve Life, to Work for the Trees: The Steward of Mexico's Forests, Miguel Angel de Quevedo, 1862–1948," *Forest History Today* (Spring/Fall 2006), 4–14.

96. See Paul DiMaggio, "Cultural Entrepreneurship in Nineteenth-Century Boston: The Creation of an Organizational Base for High Culture in America," *Media, Culture and Society* 4 (1982): 33–50; John E. Hodge, "The Construction of the Teatro Colón," *The Americas* 36, no. 2 (October 1979): 235–55; Ronald H. Dolkart, "Elitelore at the Opera: The Teatro Colón of Buenos Aires," *Journal of Latin American Lore* 9, no. 2 (1983): 231–50; John Rosselli, "The Opera Business and the Italian Immigrant Community in Latin America 1820–1930: The Example of Buenos Aires," *Past and Present* 127 (May 1990): 155–82. The difference between upper-class Italian opera and lower-class Italian immigrants to Argentina explains the apparent contradiction in attempting to escape Italians in Buenos Aires by fleeing to Italian opera productions.

97. David Scobey, "Anatomy of the Promenade: The Politics of Bourgeois Sociability in Nineteenth-Century New York," *Social History* 17, no. 2 (May 1992): 203–27, esp. 204 and n. 3.

98. Donna Brown, *Inventing New England: Regional Tourism in the Nineteenth Century* (Washington, DC: Smithsonian Institution Press, 1995). See the chapter "Nantucket, 1870–1890," esp. 107, 117.

99. See the entry on the Museo Nacional de Mexico, *Diccionario Porrúa*, 2:1436–37.

100. Beezley, "Porfirian Smart Set."

101. Helmut Brenner, *Juventino Rosas: His Life, His Work, His Time* (Warren, MI: Harmonie Park Press, 2000).

102. For a clear statement of this development, see French, *Peaceful and Working People.*

103. This is a paraphrase of Enrique Florescano, "La construcción de identidades colectivas en México: Etnia, estado y nación" (Coloquio "México en Francia: Tradición y Modernidad. Actualidad de la Investigación Mexicana en Ciencias Sociales," Paris, Tolosa, Burdeos, May 1995), 18.

104. Reese and Reese, "Revolutionary Urban Legacies," 372–73.

105. Comision Nacional del Centenario de la Independencia, "Programa del Desfile Historico, 15 de Septiembre de 1910."

106. Krauze, *Siglo de caudillos,* 28.

107. Frederick Starr Collection, Special Collections, University of Chicago, Box 19, folder 8.

## Chapter 4

1. Michael Connelly, *Trunk Music* (Boston: Little, Brown, 1997), 157.

2. This list comes from the licenses issued in Tlalpán, Distrito Federal. See AHDF, AHT, Ramo de Licencias, cajas 225–28. These appear typical based on research in other local archives. In June 1891, the Compañia Martínez, reciting "Podre María," had nearly no one in the audience, as the people of Orizaba went to see either the bullfights or another puppet performance by sr. Zane (*El pensamiento liberal* [Orizaba, Ver.], June 21, 1891). My thanks to Raquel Velasco of La Universidad de Veracruz for this citation.

3. See the licenses and descriptions of performances in the Archivo Histórico del Estado de San Luis Potosí (AHSLP), Ayuntamiento de San Luis Potosí, and in *La sombra de Zaragoza, Periódico oficial del govierno del Estado de San Luis Potosí.* The example comes from the latter source, 10, no. 932 (January 5, 1876): 4.

4. Archivo Histórico del Municipio de Colima (AHMC), licencias: 1854, Mayo, Caja 205, expediente 3; 1884, Mayo, Caja 169, posición 11, expediente 31; 1888, Febrero, caja D-177, posición 1, expediente 9; 1890, Enero, D-186, posición 10, expediente D; 1893, Enero, Caja D-192, posición 9, expediente P; 1893, Febrero, Caja D-192, posición 1, expediente 22; 1898, Mayo, Caja D-200, posición 5, expediente E.

5. Archivo Municipal de Dolores Hidalgo, Guanajuato, libro 117 "Recaudación para licencias y multas, 1890–1892," and libro 168, "Auxiliar de licencias."

6. AHMC, *El Estado de Colima. Periódical Oficial (ECPO)* contains municipal statements that record income from licenses for public diversions, and these average between three and four performers a month during the Porfiriato. The Lira Orchestra did not perform during the rainy season or during periods of yellow fever epidemic or during the threat of one. Discussion of second seasons for the orchestra is reported in the *ECPO*, 18, no. 27 (July 4, 1884): 112.

7. Blumenthal, *Puppetry*, 11.

8. David Freedberg, *The Power of Images: Studies in the History and Theory of Response* (Chicago: University of Chicago Press, 1989); Armando de María y Campos, *El teatro mexicano de muñecos* (México: El Nacional, 1941), 7; For examples of articulated figures, see the exhibit at the Museo Nacional de Títere, Huamantla, Tlaxcala. For the history of puppets generally, see Paul McPharlin, *The Puppet Theatre in America: A History* (New York: Harper and Brothers, 1949), 6, 7, 70, 71, 73, 77, 78. For discussion of the European origins of marionettes, pre-columbian examples of puppets, and colonial New Spanish puppet theater, see Iglesias Cabrera and Murray Prisant, *Piel de papel*, 53–59.

9. Peggy Muñoz attributes this account to Roberto Lago, who directed the Teatro Guignol in the Mexican Instituto Nacional de Bellas Artes, in "Puppetry—A Flourishing Art-Form in Mexico," an undated pamphlet from about 1949 that was reprinted for an international puppet conference in Munich in 1966. Susan Kinney of the Center for Puppetry Arts in Atlanta provided me with the pamphlet.

10. Blumenthal, *Puppetry*, 14.

11. De María y Campos, *El teatro mexicano de muñecos*, 11.

12. Varey, *Historia de los títeres en España*, 8–9, 99, 107, 131, 155, 239; Centro Nacional de Los Artes (CNA), Biblioteca, Recortes Periodico, 1994; *La Crónica*, June 6, 1998.

13. The Museo de Rafael Coronel, in Zacatecas, Zacatecas, houses a major collection of the masks used in the Moros y Cristianos performances. According to the museum descriptions, the distinguishing characteristics were, for Moros, dark color and Semitic features, including aquiline nose, abundant hair, beard, and moustache, black eyes, and with what were supposed to be oriental clothes; and for the Christians, clear complexion, blonde hair, beard, and moustache. Also see Michael J. Doudoroff, ed., *Moros y Cristianos in Zacatecas: Text of a Mexican Folk Play*, coll. Juan Bautista Rael (Lawrence, KS: Amadeo Concha Press, 1981).

14. Barreiro and Guijosa, *Títeres mexicanos*, 30–31; for a comparative view, see Alfredo S. Bagalio, *Títeres y titiriteros en el Buenos Aires colonial* (Buenos Aires: Ediciones Ata, 1972).

15. Iglesias Cabrera and Murray Prisant, *Piel de papel*, 53–59.

16. Blumenthal, *Puppetry*, 28–29.

17. CNA, Biblioteca de los Artes Escencias y Teatrales "Rodolfo Usigli," expediente Rosete Aranda; Guillermo Murray Prisant, "En Veracruz," *El Financiero*, January 9, 1992, p. 45.

18. Barreiro and Guijosa, *Títeres mexicanos*, 35.

19. Mendez Aquino, "Teatro del siglo XVI a la mitad del siglo XX," 354–55.

20. Quoting Arturo Fenochio, *El Valle de Tlacolula* (La Concepción, Putla, Oaxaca: Editorial La Hoja, 1953).

21. *Función estraordinario de títeres magicos en el Callejón del Vinagre* (México: Oficina de la testamentaria de Ontiveros, 1828), 8–11, 18–19. My thanks to David Dressing, Curator of Manuscripts and Photographs in the Latin American Library at Tulane University, who located this volume for me.

22. Pilar Amorós and Paco Paricio, *Títeres y titiriteros: El lenguaje de los títeres* (Zaragoza: Mira, 2000), 48.

23. Villa-Flores, *Dangerous Speech*, 113–15.

24. Amorós and Paricio, *Títeres y titiriteros*, 25–26, 53. The authors believe this difference separates puppetry from other plays, movies, and television; Barreiro and Guijosa, *Títeres mexicanos*, 19, 114.

25. Alberto Manguel, *A Reading Diary: A Passionate Reader's Reflections on a Year of Books* (New York: Farrar, Straus and Giroux, 2004), 14.

26. Ibid. Page 203 notes that the Brazilian novelist made this statement in his *Posthumous Memoirs of Blás Cubas* about reading, but in conjunction with theater.

27. Amorós and Paricio, *Títeres y titiriteros*, 53.

28. *Celos del negro con d. Folías*, Galeria del teatro infantial. Colección para niños y títeres, published by Antonio Vanegas Arroyo, Mexican Chapbook Collection, MSS 661 BC, box 1, Center for Southwest Research, General Library, University of New Mexico. A copy of the cover of this chapbook can also be found in the Papers of Frederick Starr, Special Collections, University Library, University of California, Los Angeles.

29. For an introduction to the issues of honor and dueling, see the chapter "Honor and Violent Crime," in Pablo Piccato, *City of Suspects: Crime in Mexico City, 1900–1931* (Durham, NC: Duke University Press, 2001), 77–102.

30. Amorós and Paricio, *Títeres y titiriteros*, 57; the colonial laws on adultery and their enforcement that continued into the nineteenth century are discussed in Fernández de Lizardi, *Mangy Parrot*, 376–78.

31. Luis Reyes de la Maza, *El teatro en México durante el porfirismo* (México: Instituto de Investigaciones Estéticas, 1964), 1:147–48; Iglesias Cabrera and Murray Prisant, *Piel de papel*, 76–80.

32. Blumenthal, *Puppetry*, chapter 8, "Politics," 163–85.

33. Iglesias Cabrera and Murray Prisant, *Piel de papel*, 107–14. The origin of the company was reported also by Juan Flores García, "Tepatitlán [Jalisco] en el tiempo: Los títeres," *Vida parroquial* (Parroquia de San Francisco, Tepatitlán, Jalisco,) July 4, 1999. The Rosete Aranda puppets visited the parish in the 1940s.

34. This is the argument in *El Contenido* (September 1983), 66–81, in El Centro Nacional de Los Artes (CNA), Centro de Investigación Nacional de los Artes, Biblioteca de los Artes Escencias y Teatrales "Rodolfo Usigli"(ACINAET), expediente Francisco Rosete Aranda.

35. Jurado Rojas, *Títeres durante el porfiriato*, 64.

36. Vicente T. Mendoza and Virginia R. R. de Mendoza, *Folklore de la región central de Puebla* (México: Centro Nacional de Investigación, Documentación e Información Musical "Carlos Chávez," 1991), 311.

37. The origins of the company are summarized in the exhibition descriptions for the Rosete Aranda Puppets at the Museo de Rafael Coronel, Zacatecas, Zacatecas, and the pamphlet "Historia de la Compañia de Títeres Rosete Aranda," by Martín Letechipia Alvarado, for the Dirección de Turismo, Zacatecas. The sale of the company later resulted in major disputes, which are reviewed in CNA, Biblioteca, Recortes Periodicos, 1978; *El Excelsior*, July 25, 1978; and Biblioteca de los Artes Escencias y Teatrales "Rodolfo Usigli," expediente Francisco Rosete Aranda.

38. CNA, Biblioteca, Recortes Periodicos, 1994; *El Universal*, July 15, 1994.

39. The account books of the Rosete Aranda family report the routes of their annual tours. These eighteen *libros de contabilidad* are not numbered, but they are identified by date. A typical year of the family's travels is Libro de 1882, Archivo General de Tlaxcala (AGT), Fondo Rosete Aranda (FRA).

40. Reyes de la Maza, *El teatro en México durante el porfirismo*, 1:147–48.

41. Mante and Tavera, "Los títeres en el Norte de México."

42. CNA, Biblioteca de los Artes Escencias y Teatrales "Rodolfo Usigli," expediente Francisco Rosete Aranda, *Contenido* (September 1983).

43. Cyril W. Beaumont, *History of Harlequin* (New York: Benjamin Blom, 1926). In this connection glimmers the slightest possible relationship between Vale Coyote and the famous nineteenth-century puppet El Negrito. Some experts on commedia dell'arte argue that Harlequin had an African origin and that his black half-face mask represents him in the dramas. Was Vale Coyote developed as an artful play on El Negrito? It is a possibility that at this point cannot be ascertained.

44. *El Coyote* existed for eight months in 1880, during the presidential campaign. It has now been republished in book form (no publisher or editor indicated). A similar French marionette from Lyon, called Guignol, represented the experience and politics of local silk workers (*les canuts*). Laurent Mourguet created Guignol, who was continued (and expanded) by subsequent puppeteers. The puppet is displayed in the Musée Gadagne, Musée de l'Histoire de Lyon et du Marionnettes. (My thanks to Steve Vincent, North Carolina State University for this information); Blumenthal, *Puppetry*, 173.

45. Iglesias Cabrera and Murray Prisant, *Piel de papel*, 127.

46. Aurelio de los Reyes, "Del Blanquita, del público y género chico mexicano," *Diálogos* 16, no. 2 (March–April 1980): 29, 31. This form of variety show influenced Mexican films such as Pedro Infante's Allá en el rancho grande, and U.S. musical comedies (p. 31).

47. Cincotta, *Zarzuela*, 7.

48. Both bullfights and cockfights had long traditions in the family's hometown of Huamantla, including the running of the bulls through the streets. See Jurado Rojas, *Títeres durante el Porfiriato*, 66.

49. Hernández, "Entre el azar y el vértigo," 125; Mendoza and Mendoza, *Folklore de la región central de Puebla*, 311.

50. See "La China Poblana," *Artes de México* 66 (2003), for a discussion of the disputed origins, costumes, images, and significance of the China Poblana. For discussion of the China as a national symbol, see the essay by Ricardo Pérez Montfort, "La China Poblana como emblema nacional," 40–49, and the images in the magazine, 42; and Jeanne L. Gillespie, "Gender, Ethnicity and Piety: The Case of the China Poblana," in *Imagination beyond Nation: Latin American Popular Culture*, ed. Eva P. Bueno and Terry Caesar, 19–37 (Pittsburgh: University of Pittsburgh Press, 1998).

51. The issue "La Tehuana" of *Artes de México* 49 (2000), especially the essays "La creación de un símbolo," by Aída Sierra (16–25), and "Mirando hacia el sur," by Miguel Covarrubias (26–37).

52. Ignacio Manuel Altamirano, *Obras completas*, ed. Catalina Sierra Casasús (México: Secretaría de Educación Pública, 1986–87), 11:250. Thanks to Beatriz de Alba-Koch, University of Victoria, for this citation.

53. Barreiro and Guijosa, *Títeres mexicanos*, 84, citing *El crónica de* El Nacional (October 1891).

54. Marco Velázquez and Mary Kay Vaughan, "*Mestizaje* and Musical Nationalism in Mexico," in *The Eagle and the Virgin: Nation and Cultural Revolution in Mexico, 1920–1940*, ed. Mary Kay Vaughan and Stephen E. Lewis (Durham, NC: Duke University Press, 2006), 96.

55. This speech comes from the AGT, FRA. It is also printed in Francisco Rosete Aranda, *La compañía de títeres de los Rosete Aranda* (Tlaxcala: Instituto

Tlaxcalteca de la Cultura, 1983), 75–77. This is the author's translation, with much help, especially from Carmen Nava. In the discussion that follows, the numbers in parentheses refer to the lines of the oration. The interesting Spanish original is included as Appendix 1.

56. Villa-Flores, *Blasphemy*, 113. Also see Larry Scanlon, *Narrative, Authority, and Power* (New York: Cambridge University Press, 1994) 35.

57. E. P. Thompson, "Moral Economy of the English Crowd," 76–136; Guy P. C. Thomson, "Bulwarks of Patriotic Liberalism, 31–68," and "Popular Aspects of Liberalism; Knight, "Liberalismo mexicano."

58. Eugen Weber makes this argument for the rise of French nationalism, the spirit of the public sphere, and civic culture, in his study of military service *Peasants into Frenchmen: The Modernization of Rural France, 1870–1914* (Stanford, CA: Stanford University Press, 1976).

59. For example, see "Un insurgente viejo" to the editors of El Correo, Archivo Histórico del Estado de Zacatecas, Fondo Ayuntamiento de Zacatecas, Series: Correo político, Año 1826, Caja 1, Expediente 1; also published in *El Pregonero*, 2nd época, 2, 6 (Zacatecas, April 2005), 7.

60. Brian F. Connaughton, "Sangre de mártir y ciudadanía. Del héroe magnánimo al espíritu cívico (Veracruz, 1837–1853)," in *La construcción del héroe en España y México (1789–1849)*, ed. Manuel Chust and Víctor Mínguez (València: Universitat de València, 2003), 115.

61. One of the few efforts to evaluate this phenomenon is Lyman L. Johnson, ed., *Death, Dismemberment, and Memory: Body Politics in Latin America* (Albuquerque: University of New Mexico Press, 2004).

62. CNA, Biblioteca, expediente 10696, "Discurso patriótico por Juan Pico de Oro," 2.

63. A significant discussion of liberals and Masons can be found in Rosa María Martínez de Codes, "El impacto de la masonería en la legislación Reformista de la primera generación de liberales en México"; and Jean-Pierre Bastián, "La Francmasonería dividida y el poder liberal en México, 1872–1911," in *Masonería española y América*, vol. 1, coord. José Antonio Ferrer Benimeli (V Simposio Internacional de Historia de la Masonería Españoa, Cáceres, June 16–20, 1991. Zaragoza: Centro de Estudios Históricos de la Masonería, 1993), 129–45, 415–436. My thanks to Patricia Massé for directing me to these articles. For the role of the masons in politics during the Porfiriato, see Garner, *Porfirio Díaz*, 29–31.

64. Saint Catherine of Alexandria, http://www.catholic-forum.com/saints/saintco1.htm. Her feast day was November 25 on the official church calendar until 1969, when the date was removed and the cult was suppressed.

65. Juan Javier Pescador, *De bautizados a fieles difuntos: Familia y mentalidades en una parroquia urbana: Santa Catarina de México, 1568–1820* (México: El Colegio de México, 1992), 17–63.

66. Tovar de Teresa and Hernández, "Juegos y juegetes en el vierreinato," 56.

67. See entry for Catarina de San Juan, in *Diccionario Porrúa*.

68. See entry for Chato, in Francisco J. Santamaria, *Diccionario de mejicanismos* (México: Editorial Porrúa, 1992), 227, 365–66.

69. *The Divine Comedy of Dante Alighieri*, ed. and trans. Robert M. Durling, vol. 1 *Inferno* (New York: Oxford University Press, 1996), 59–60;

70. An extensive collection of Independence Day sermons and speeches is preserved in the Biblioteca Burgoa, Museo de Santo Domingo, Oaxaca, Oaxaca, especially in the pamphlet collection Proyecto Fondo Conventual–Oaxaca. See, for example, José Juan Canseco, "Oración fúnebre patriotico religiosa en las solemnes ecsequias a las ilustres víctimas de la Patría por el cura de la parroquico de San Larenzo Zimatuan, 17 Sept. 1833." Similar unpublished examples for the small towns around the capital can be found in the Archivo Histórico del Distrito Federal, Mexico City, Archivo Histórico de Tlalpán, Ramo de Festividades, 1862, expedientes 13 and 14; and for the celebration of the holiday in San Luis Potosí, see Sergio A. Cañedo Gamboa, *Los festejos septembrinos en San Luis Potosí: Protocolo, discurso y transformaciones, 1824–1847* (San Luis Potosí: El Colegio de San Luis Potosí, 2001). For a survey of Independence Day celebrations in Mexico, see Beezley and Lorey, eds., *¡Viva Mexico! ¡Viva la Independencia!*

71. Antonio Castro Leal, "Estudio preliminar," in *El fistol del diablo*, by Manuel Payno (México: Editorial Porrúa, 1992), xvi–xvii.

72. José Luis Martínez, "México en busca de un expresión," in *Historia general de México—Versión 2000*. (México: El Colegio de México, 2004), 726–27.

73. Carlos Illades, "La representación del pueblo en el segundo romanticismo mexicano," *Signos históricos* 10 (July–December 2003), 31; the puppets also used a version of this phrase in the twentieth-century play *Hidalgo*. CNA, ACINAET.

74. Mayer Celis, *Entre el infierno de una realidad*; Gordon Wright, "Eugène Sue: Master of the Serial Thriller," *Notable or Notorious? A Gallery of Parisians*, 13–28. (Cambridge: Harvard University Press, 1991); Pegasos, entry for Eugène Sue, www.kirjasto.sci.fi/esue.htm consulted on September 14, 2005; Castro Leal, "Estudio preliminar," xvii.

75. Maurice Agulhon, *Marianne into Battle: Republican Imagery and Symbolism in France, 1789–1880*, trans. Janet Lloyd (Cambridge: Cambridge University Press, 1981), passim.

76. High Beam Encyclopedia, entry for Camille Flammarion, http://www.encyclopedia.com/doc/1E1-Flammari.html, consulted December 10, 2004.

77. "1875 in Literature." http://encyclopedia.thefreedictionary.com/1875+in+literature.

78. "Editor's introduction," Robert Graves, *I, Claudius* (New York: Time Reading Program Special Edition, 1965), vii–viii.

79. Marco Arturo Moreno Corral, *Odisea 1874, o El primer viaje internacional de científicos mexicanos* (México: El Fondo Cultural Económica, 1986).

80. Jules Verne's *From the Earth to the Moon* (1869) was the favorite book of Robert H. Goddard, who became the world's first rocket scientist. See Nicolas A. Basbanes, *Every Book Its Reader: The Power of the Printed Word to Stir the World* (New York: HarperCollins, 2005), 14. See Jules Verne, *The City in the Sahara* and *Into the Niger Bend*, trans. by I. O. Evans. Thanks to my colleague Douglas Weiner for this information. Verne became world-famous for his novels, which included *Five Weeks in a Balloon* (1858), *Journey to the Center of the Earth* (1864), *From the Earth to the Moon* (1865), *Around the World in Eighty Days* (1872), *Twenty Thousand Leagues under the Sea* (1870), and *The Mysterious Island* (1875).

81. Lomnitz, *Death and the Idea of Mexico*, 32, 498.

82. This article was reprinted in *ECPO*, 19, no. 6 (February 6, 1885): 24, and the same official publication reprinted obituaries, ibid., no. 23 (June 5, 1885), 91–92.

83. Fernández de Lizardi, *Mangy Parrot*, p. 186.

84. I have translated "siñores comunes" as "familiar men" (93). Iglesias Cabrera and Murray Prisant (*Piel de Papel*, 128) say this is a reference to communists. Certainly there were socialists and anarchists active in the countryside of both Puebla and Tlaxcala with whom the Rosete Aranda may have been familiar. See John M. Hart, *Anarchism and the Mexican Working Class, 1860-1931* (Austin: University of Texas, 1990). Certainly, some in the audience may have made this connection.

85. My thanks to Linda Arnold, Virginia Polytechnic University, for the information on wig usage.

86. On the creation of Hidalgo as the preeminent national hero, see Fausto Ramírez, "Hidalgo en su estudio: La ardua construcción de la imagen del *pater patriae* mexicano," in Chust and Mínguez, eds., *La construcción del héroe*, 189–210.

87. Fernández de Lizardi refers to hair color and virtue in *Mangy Parrot*, 452; El Archivo de Central Integral de Fotografía, Puebla, Puebla, Fototeca de Lorenzo Becerril, Expediente Fietas y Festajos, El Día de Independencia, 1907, shows school kids, with one dressed as Hidalgo, identified by his long white hair. This is the typical representation.

88. CNA, Biblioteca de los Artes Escencias y Teatrales "Rodolfo Usigli," *Hidalgo*.

89. Chust and Mínguez, eds., *La construcción del héroe*, 9.

90. As Cees Nooteboom put it, "Some images have the value of a seal: they accompany all future versions of the *éducation sentimentale*." *Roads to Santiago*, 211.

91. Barreiro and Guijosa, *Títeres mexicanos*, 73–74.

92. Joaquín Pardavé became a fan of the songs. He often went to Huamantla to talk with the family and copied the words and music of seventy of the *coplas*. Later he produced a movie using them, entitled *Los tiempos de don Simón* (Iglesias Cabrera and Murray Prisant, *Piel de papel*, 131).

93. Mercedes Meade de Angulo, "La empresa nacional de automatas de los hermanos Rosete Aranda," Poniencia del Coloquio de Teatro de Tlaxcala, July 1994.

94. The criticism of physicians was common in the nineteenth century. See, for example, Fernández de Lizardi, *Mangy Parrot*, 295–303.

95. "Primera parte de las Coplas de don Simón" (Puebla: Imprenta de Jesús Franco é hijo, 1907), p. 3.

96. Rodney D. Anderson, *Outcasts in Their Own Land: Mexican Industrial Workers, 1906–1911* (DeKalb: Northern Illinois University Press, 1976).

97. Meade de Angulo, "La empresa nacional de automatas."

98. Amorós and Paricio, *Títeres y titiriteros*, 25.

99. For a discussion of the role of puppets in the construction of the identity of social classes in England, see Scott Cutler Shershow, *Puppets and "Popular" Culture* (Ithaca: Cornell University Press, 1995).

100. Mendoza and Mendoza, *Folklore de la región central de Puebla*, 311.

101. "Un día en Monterrey," from José Alvarado, *Luces de la ciudad* (Monterrey: Dirreción General de Investigaciones Humanísticas, 1978), 55–56, reprinted in *Norte de México: Visión histórica de la frontera*, coord. David Piñera Ramírez (Tijuana: Universidad Autónoma de Baja California, 1998), 69.

102. Mante and Tavera, "Titeres en el Norte de México."

103. The standard work on Mexican participation in World's Fairs is Tenorio-Trillo, *Mexico at the World's Fairs*. An example of how local municipalities organized their participation in these international exhibits can be found in AHDF, AHT, Ramo de Exposiciones, Box 101, Expediente 9 "Exposición universal en Nueva Orleans de 1884," and Expediente 20, "Exposición en Buffalo."

104. Libros de contabilidad, ACINAET, FRA. The account books describe the inventory, including backdrops, scenery, and any necessary repairs during the year.

105. *ECPO* 18, no. 27 (July 4, 1884): 112.

106. Pérez Montfort, "La expresión musical popular mexicana del porfiriato a la Revolución. De la piesa académica a la canción revolucionaria," in *Estampas de nacionalismo popular mexicano*, 97–120.

107. Aurelio Tello, "El patrimonio musical de México. Una síntesis aproximativa," in *El patrimonio nacional de México*, coord. Enrique Florescano (México: Consejo Nacional Para la Cultura y las Artes, 2004), 2:86–89, 107.

108. AHSLP, foja suelta, 1891.46, expediente sin número, Tesoreria municipal de la Capital, Recibo Num. 97, San Luis Potosí, December 30, 1891. My thanks to Monserrat Mendez González for this citation; Archivo Municipal de Dolores Hidalgo, Guanajuato. Auxiliar de licencias, 1901–1902, libro 168. Licenses were issued from January to April 1902, to these different puppeteers.

109. *El pensamiento liberal* (Orizaba, Ver.), June 21, 1891, p. 2.

110. Mante and Tavera, "Titeres en el Norte de México."

111. Jurado Rojas, *Títeres durante el Porfiriato*, 78.

112. Blumenthal, *Puppetry*, 21.

113. CNA, Biblioteca, Recortes, 1978, *Uno más uno* (July 24, 1978).

114. Letechipia Alvarado, "Historia de la compañia," 5; for a discussion of the puppet plays of the 1920s and 1930s, see William H. Beezley, "Arte en la calle. Los títeres de la Compañía de Rosete Aranda y la imagen del mexicano," in *La Mirada, mirada. Transculturalidad e imaginarios del México revolucionario, 1910–1945* (México: Instituto de Investigaciones Estéticas de la Universidad Nacional Autónoma de México, forthcoming).

115. Francisca Miranda Silva has written an excellent synopsis of this government program as the introduction to the DVD *Época de oro del teatro guiñol de Bellas Artes, 1932–1965*, produced by CONACULTA under the general direction of Marisa Giménez Cacho. The DVD includes an inventory of the puppets, itineraries of the shows, outlines of the plays, photographs of the puppets, and biographies of the puppeteers.

116. CNA, Biblioteca de los Artes Escencias y Teatrales "Rodolfo Usigli," Expediente Rosete Aranda, Juan Jimenez Izquierdo, "¿Qué pasa con el teatro de títres?" *El Universal*, February 2, 1992, sec. Cultura, p. 2.

117. The catalog of the Museo Nacional de Títere, (MNT).

118. CNA, Biblioteca, Recortes, 1978; *El Universal*, July 23, 1978; Olga Rosete Aranda disputed the origin of the puppets. See *Excelsior*, July 25, 1978. An analysis of the collections at the Center for Puppetry Arts Museum in Atlanta reports that it holds a papier-mâché hand puppet of a *campesino* made by Robert Lago and a set of clay marionettes from Puebla, which might be those of the Rosete Aranda family (Nancy Lohman Staub, "The Center for Puppetry Arts Museum," in Dircks, *American Puppetry*, 79). In addition, Harvard University holds some Mexican puppets in the Ralph C. McGoun Collection of Puppets and Masks (Fredric Woodbridge Wilson, "Puppetry and Related Materials in the Harvard Theatre Collection," in Dircks, *American Puppetry*, 41), and Columbia University reports having a dozen puppets from Mexico (eleven clay "jiggling" puppets and a giraffe) that the author says may come from the Rosete Aranda collection (John Ball "Puppets and 'The Iconography of Drama': The Brander Matthews Collection at Columbia University," in Dircks, *American Puppetry*, 109). In addition, a number of these puppets appear to have become part of the collections of the Museo Nacional

de Antropología; see Maria Eugenia Sánchez Santa Ana, *Muñecas mestizas: Catalogo de las colecciones etnograficas del Museo Nacional de Antropología* (México: INAH, 1992), 39–86.

119. *El Universal*, July 24, 2005), sec. F, p. 1.

120. Jurado Rojas, *Títeres durante el Porfiriato*, 32–33.

121. Martín Letechipia Alvarado, "La carpa de don Heleno Flores: Arte y tradición que se resiste a ceder ante la modernidad," *Imagen*, Sept. 9, 2001, http://201.120.149.127/2003/09/01/cultura1.htm.

122. Iglesias Cabrera and Murray Prisant, *Piel de papel*, 101–2.

123. Ibid., 91–92.

124. See the newspaper *La Defensa*, nos. 182 and 184 (1885), cited in Mante and Tavera, "Titeres en el Norte de México.".

125. Iglesias Cabrera and Murray Prisant, *Piel de papel*, 151–75.

126. AHMC, "Licencias de diversiones," 1884, Mayo 4, Mayo 10, Caja 169, posición 11, expediente 31.

127. Speckman Guerra, "Cuadernillos, pliegos, y hojas sueltas," and Bonilla, "Imágenes de Posada en los impresos de Vanegas Arroyo" ; Iglesias Cabrera and Murray Prisant, *Piel de papel*, 95–96.

128. For example, Guadalupe Posada engraved a lotería game that Venegas Arroyo published in 1890.

129. Researchers working for Frederick Starr collected several of the chapbooks. They are contained in the Frederick Starr Papers, Special Collections, UCLA Library. Correspondence about them is contained in the Frederick Starr Collection, University of Chicago Library. The Posada *calavera* formed part of the exhibit on the Porfiriato at the Museo Nacional del Arte, Mexico City, during the summer of 2003.

130. Piccato, *City of Suspects*, 77–102.

131. James A. Garza, *Imagining an Underworld, Creating a Nation: Sex, Crime, and Vice in Porfirian Mexican City, 1876–1911* (Lincoln: University of Nebraska Press, forthcoming); Patrick Frank, *Posada's Broadsheets*, 19–37, 48–50. Moreover, a number of studies have examined Mexico City crime during the Porfirian regime. Among the most relevant are the collection edited by Claudia Agostoni and Elisa Speckman Guerra, *De normas y transgresiones: Enfermedad y crimen en América Latina (1850–1950)* (México: La Universidad Autónoma de México, 2005), especially the articles by Claudia Agostoni, "Los infinitamente pequeños: Debates y conflictos en torno a la bacteriología (Ciudad de México, siglos XIX a XX)," 167–94, and Elisa Speckman Guerra, "Infancia es destino. Menores delincuentes en la ciudad de México (1884–1910)," 225–54; Jacinto Barrera Bassols, *El caso Villavicencio: Violencia y poder en el porfiriato* (México: Extra Alfacuara, 1997); Claudia Canales, *El poeta, el marqués y el asesino: Historia de un caso judicial* (México: Ediciones Era, 2001).

132. Blumenthal, *Puppetry*, chapter 7, "And Violence," 142–61.

133. Historians of France have given particular attention to these performances as part of public life and civic behavior. Examples include Avner Ben-Amos, *Funerals, Politics, and Memory in Modern France, 1789–1996* (Oxford: Oxford University Press, 2000); Mona Ozouf, *Festivals and the French Revolution*, trans. Alan Sheridan (Cambridge: Harvard University Press, 1988); Charles Rearick, *Pleasures of the Belle Epoque: Entertainment and Festivity in Turn-of-the-Century France* (New Haven: Yale University Press, 1985); and David Troyanski, "Monumental Politics: National History and Local Memory in French *Monuments aux Morts* in the Department of the Aisne since 1870," *French Historical Studies* 15, no. 1 (1987): 121–41.

134. Phyllis T. Dircks, in *American Puppetry*, concludes that puppetry as both cultural index and artistic object has been largely ignored (p. 3).

## Chapter 5

1. Linda A. Curcio-Nagy, *The Great Festivals of Colonial Mexico City: Performing Power and Identity* (Albuquerque: University of New Mexico, 2004).

2. Barreiro and Guijosa, *Títeres mexicanos*, 38.

3. Martínez, "México en busca de su expresión," 707–55.

4. De los Reyes, "Del Blanquita," 31. See the novel, as an example, Luis G. Inclán, *Astucia, el jefe de los Hermanos de la Hoja o los charros contrabandistas de la Rama*.

5. Rafael Barajas Durán, "Retrato de un siglo. ¿Cómo ser mexicano en el XIX?" in *Espejo mexicano*, coord. Enrique Florescano (México: Consejo Nacional para la Cultura y las Artes, 2002), 140–41.

6. Barajas Durán, "Retrato de un siglo," 116–77; for a discussion of foreigners and their views of Mexico, see Stacie Widdifield, "El impulso de Humboldt y la mirada extranjera sobre México," in *Hacia otra historia del arte en México: De la estructuración colonial a la exigencia nacional (1780–1860)*, coord. Esther Acevedo (México: El Consejo Nacional de la Cultura y Las Artes, 2001), I, 257–72.

7. Mayer Celis, *Entre el infierno de una realidad*.

8. Martínez, "México en busca de su expresión," 738–55.

## Appendix

1. Iglesias Cabrera and Murray Prisant, *Piel de papel*, 127–28.

# BIBLIOGRAPHY

## Archival Collections

Archivo de Central Integral de Fotografía, Puebla, Puebla
    Expediente fiestas y festajos, el Día de Independencia, 1907
    Fototeca de Lorenzo Becerril
Archivo del Estado de Guanajuato
    Ayuntamiento de Guanajuato
        Bando de policia
        Diversiones públicas
        Paseos públicos
        Reglamentos
Archivo General de la Nación
    Ramo de hacienda, vol. 251
Archivo General de Tlaxcala (AGT)
    Fondo Rosete Aranda (FRA)
        Libros de contabilidad
Archivo General Municipal, Guadalajara (AGM)
    Ramo de diversiones cívicas
    Ramo de fiestas cívicas y diversiones
Archivo Histórico del Distrito Federal (AHDF)
    El Antiguo Ayuntamiento de la Ciudad de México, vol. 1058, exp. 2, 29
    Aug. 1822
    El Archivo del Antiguo Ayuntamiento de la Ciudad de México
    El Archivo Histórico de Tlalpán (AHT)
        Ramo de exposiciones
        Ramo de festividades
        Ramo de licencias

Archivo Histórico del Estado de San Luis Potosí (AHSLP)
Ayuntamiento de San Luis Potosí
Archivo Histórico del Estado de Zacatecas, Fondo Ayuntamiento de Zacatecas
Archivo Histórico del Municipio de Colima, Colima (AHMC)
Archivo Histórico Municipal de la Ciudad de Oaxaca, Manuel R. Palacios, fondo "independencia," 7 boxes
Archivo Municipal de Dolores Hidalgo, Guanajuato
"Auxiliar de licencias"
"Recaudación para licencias y multas"
Arizona Historical Society, Tucson
Lottery Card Collection, Catalog. 83.19.7
Biblioteca Burgoa, Museo de Santo Domingo, Oaxaca, Oaxaca
Proyecto Fondo Conventual–Oaxaca
Centro de Investigación Nacional, Centro Nacional de los Artes, México, D.F. (CNA)
Biblioteca, Recortes Periodicos
Biblioteca de los Artes Escencias y Teatrales "Rodolfo Usigli" (ACINAET)
Expediente Francisco Rosete Aranda
Museo de Rafael Coronel, Zacatecas, Zacatecas
Museo Nacional de los Artes
Jesús Martínez Cerrion drawing "El Borracho," 1901
Museo Nacional de Títere, Huamantla, Tlaxcala
Rutgers University, New Brunswick, NJ
Thomas A. Edison Papers
Universidad Nacional Autónoma de México
Colección LaFragua, "Seis Noches de Títeres Mágicos"
University of California–Los Angeles Library, Department of Special Collections
Frederick Starr Papers, 1860–1930
University of Chicago Library, Department of Special Collections
Frederick Starr Collection
University of New Mexico, Center for Southwest Research, General Library
Mexican Chapbook Collection, MSS 661 BC

## Other Works

Abrahams, Roger D. "The Language of Festivals: Celebrating the Economy." In *Celebration: Studies in Festivity and Ritual*, edited by Victor Turner. Washington, DC: Smithsonian Institution Press, 1982.

Acevedo, Esther, coord. *Hacia otra historia del arte en México*. Vol. 1, *De la estructuración colonial a la exigencia nacional (1780–1860)*. México: Consejo Nacional para la Cultura y las Artes, 2001.

——. *Una historia en quinientas caricaturas: Constantino Escalente en La Orquesta*. México: Instituto Nacional de Antropología e Historia, 1994.

Adame Martínez, Homero. "Los nacimientos: Una tradición centenaria." *México desconocido* 23, no. 262 (December 1998): 32–39.

Aguirre, Robert. "William Bullock (1773–1849): British Curator of Exotica Visits Mexico." In *The Human Tradition in the Atlantic World*, edited by Karen Racine and Beatriz Gallotti Mamigonian. Boulder: Rowman and Littlefield, forthcoming.

Agulhon, Maurice. *Marianne into Battle: Republican Imagery and Symbolism in France, 1789–1880*. Translated by Janet Lloyd. Cambridge: Cambridge University Press, 1981.

Alonso, Ana Maria. *Thread of Blood: Colonialism, Revolution, and Gender on Mexico's Northern Frontier*. Tucson: University of Arizona Press, 1995.

Altamirano, Ignacio Manuel. "Crónica de las fiestas de Septiembre en México y Puebla." First published in *El Renacimiento*; reissued by Puebla's Secretaría de Cultura in 1987 as *Lecturas historicas de Puebla*, #6.

——. *Obras completas*. Edited by Catalina Sierra Casasús. México: Secretaría de Educación Pública, 1986–87.

Amorós, Pilar, and Paco Paricio. *Títeres y titiriteros: El lenguaje de los títeres*. Zaragoza: Mira, 2000.

Anderson, Benedict. *Imagined Communities*. Rev. ed. New York: Verso, 1991.

Anderson, L. E. "Edison in Mexico, 1904–1912: A Preliminary Study." *Sound Box* (September and November 1994).

Anderson, Rodney D. *Outcasts in Their Own Land: Mexican Industrial Workers, 1906–1911*. DeKalb: Northern Illinois University Press, 1976.

Anthony, Vincent. "A Snapshot of Puppeteers of the United States and Canada." In Dircks, ed., *American Puppetry*, 9–21.

Apenas, Ola. *Mapas antiguos del Valle del México*. Facsimile. México: 1984. Originally published 1947.

Armella, Virginia. "Del panal a la vitrina: Investigación sobre los trabajos de cera de México." In Gonzáles y Gonzáles et al., *Juegos y juguetes mexicanos*, 77–98.

Aron, Jean-Paul. *The Art of Eating in France: Manners and Menus in the Nineteenth Century*. New York: Harper and Row, 1975.

*Arte Naïf: Guatemala*. Guatemala: UNESCO, 1998.

*Artes de México*. Issue "El arte de la suerte," nueva época 13 (Fall 1991).

Bagalio, Alfredo S. *Títeres y titiriteros en el Buenos Aires colonial*. Buenos Aires: Ediciones Ata, 1972.

Baker Tuller, Shannon. "Santa Anna's Legacy: Caudillismo in Early Republican Mexico." PhD diss., History Department, Texas Christian University, 1999.

Ball, John. "Puppets and 'The Iconography of Drama': The Brander Matthews Collection at Columbia University." In Dircks, ed., *American Puppetry*, 105–17.

Barajas Durán, Rafael. "Retrato de un siglo. ¿Cómo ser mexicano en el XIX?" In *Espejo mexicano*, coord. Enrique Florescano. México: Consejo Nacional para la Cultura y las Artes, 2002.

Barreiro, Juan José, and Mancela Guijosa. *Títeres mexicanos: Memoria y retrato de autómatas, fantoches y otros artistas ambulantes.* México: Grupo Roche Syntex de México, 1997.

Barrera Bassols, Jacinto. *El caso Villavicencio: Violencia y poder en el porfiriato.* México: Extra Alfacuara, 1997.

———. *Pesquisa sobre un estandarte: Historia de una pieza de museo.* México: Ediciones Sinfiltro, 1995.

Barringer, Mark D., and Matthew D. Esposito. "And the Band Played On: Mexico at the World's Industrial and Cotton Centennial Exposition in New Orleans, 1884–1885." Paper presented at the annual meeting of the Southwestern Social Science Association, Dallas, Texas, March 23, 1995.

Basbanes, Nicolas A. *Every Book Its Reader: The Power of the Printed Word to Stir the World.* New York: HarperCollins, 2005.

Bastián, Jean-Pierre. "La Francmasonería dividida y el poder liberal en México, 1872–1911." In Ferrer Benimeli, *Masonería española y América*, 1:415–36.

Beaumont, Cyril W. *History of Harlequin.* New York: Benjamin Blom, 1926.

Beezley, William H. "Altars for Day of the Dead." In *Home Altars of Mexico*, edited by Ramón A. Gutiérrez. Albuquerque: University of New Mexico Press, 1997.

———. "Arte en la calle. Los títeres de la Compañía de Rosete Aranda y la imagen del mexicano." In *La Mirada, mirada. Transculturalidad e imaginarios del México revolucionario, 1910–1945.* México: Instituto de Investigaciones Estéticas de la Universidad Nacional Autónoma de México, forthcoming.

———. *Judas at the Jockey Club.* 2nd ed. Lincoln: University of Nebraska Press, 2003.

———. "New Celebrations of Independence: Puebla (1869) and Mexico City (1883)." In Beezley and Lorey, eds., *¡Viva Mexico! ¡Viva la Independencia! Celebrations of September 16.* Wilmington, DE: SR Books, 2001.

———. "The Porfirian Smart Set Anticipates Thorstein Veblen in Guadalajara." In Beezley, Martin, and French, eds., *Rituals of Rule*, 173–90.

Beezley, William H., Cheryl English Martin, and William E. French, eds. *Rituals of Rule, Rituals of Resistance: Public Celebrations and Popular Culture in Mexico.* Wilmington, DE: SR Books, 1994.

Beezley, William H., David E. Lorey, eds. *¡Viva Mexico! ¡Viva la Independencia! Celebrations of September 16.* Wilmington, DE: SR Books, 2001.

Ben-Amos, Avner. *Funerals, Politics, and Memory in Modern France, 1789–1996*. Oxford: Oxford University Press, 2000.

Benjamin, Thomas. "A Vigorous Mexico Arising: Mexico's Twentieth of November Commemorations." Paper presented at the Ninth Conference of Mexican, United States, and Canadian Historians, Mexico City, October 27–29, 1994.

Blumenthal, Eileen. *Puppetry: A World History*. New York: Harry N. Abrams, 2005.

*Boletín oficial del Consejo Superior de gobierno del Distrito Federal* 13, no. 22 (September 14, 1909).

Brading, David A. *The First America: The Spanish Monarchy, Creole Patriots and the Liberal State, 1492–1867*. Cambridge: Cambridge University Press, 1991.

Brandes, Stanley. *Metaphors of Masculinity: Sex and Status in Andalusian Folklore*. Philadelphia: University of Pennsylvania Press, 1980.

Bremer, Catherine. "Defying U.S., Mexicans Flock to Buy 'Racist' Stamps." Reuters, July 1, 2005.

Brenner, Helmut. *Juventino Rosas: His Life, His Work, His Time*. Warren, MI: Harmonie Park Press, 2000.

Brown, Donna. *Inventing New England: Regional Tourism in the Nineteenth Century*. Washington, DC: Smithsonian Institution Press, 1995.

Brown, Julie K. *Contesting Images: Photography and the World's Columbian Exposition*. Tucson: University of Arizona Press, 1994.

Brysk, Alison. "'Hearts and Minds': Bringing Symbolic Politics Back In." *Polity* 27, no. 4 (Summer 1995): 559–85.

*100 años de lotería campechana*. México: Centro de Emisin de Billetes de la Lotería Nacional, 1995.

Camp, Roderic A. Camp. *Recruitment across Two Centuries*. Austin: University of Texas Press, 1995.

Cañedo Gamboa, Sergio A. *Los festejos septembrinos en San Luis Potosí: Protocolo, discurso y transformaciones, 1824–1847*. San Luis Potosí: El Colegio de San Luis Potosí, 2001.

Castro Leal, Antonio. "Estudio preliminar." In *El fistol del diablo*, by Manuel Payno. México: Editorial Porrúa, 1992.

"La China Poblana." *Artes de México* 66 (2003).

Chust, Manuel, and Victor Mínguez, eds. *La construcción del héroe en España y México (1789–1849)*. València: Universitat de València, 2003.

Cincotta, Vincent J. *Zarzuela: The Spanish Lyric Theatre*. Artarmon, NSW: University of Wollongong Press, 2002.

Coffin, Alfred Oscar. *Land without Chimneys; or, The Byways of Mexico*. Cincinnati: Editor Publishing, 1898.

Comisión Nacional del Centenario de la Independencia. "Programa del Desfile Histórico, 15 de Septiembre de 1910."

Concannon, Jim. *Concannon: The First One Hundred and Twenty-five Years.* Healdsburg, CA: Andy Katz Photography, 2006.

Connaughton, Brian F. "Sangre de mártir y ciudadanía. Del héroe magnánimo al espíritu cívico (Veracruz, 1837–1853)." In *La construcción del héroe en España y México (1789–1849)*, edited by Manuel Chust and Víctor Mínguez. (València: Universitat de València, 2003), 115–32.

Connelly, Michael. *Trunk Music.* Boston: Little, Brown, 1997.

Costeloe, Michael P. "The Junta Patriótica and the Celebration of Independence in Mexico City, 1825–1855." *Mexican Studies/Estudios Mexicanos* 13, no. 1 (Winter 1997): 21–53.

Covarrubias, Miguel. "Mirando hacia el sur." *Artes de México* 49 (2000): 26–37.

Craib, Raymond B. *Cartographic Mexico: A History of State Fixations and Fugitive Landscapes.* Durham, NC: Duke University Press, 2004.

Curcio-Nagy, Linda. "Giants and Gypsies: Corpus Christi in Colonial Mexico City." In Beezley, Martin, and French, eds., *Rituals of Rule*, 1–26.

———. *The Great Festivals of Colonial Mexico City: Performing Power and Identity.* Albuquerque: University of New Mexico, 2004.

———. "The Ideal and the Real: The Mexico City Triumphal Arch and Political Protest in 1697." Paper presented at the Rocky Mountain Council for Latin American Studies, Fort Worth, Texas, February 20, 1994.

Davis, Susan G. *Parades and Power: Street Theatre in Nineteenth-Century Philadelphia.* Philadelphia: Temple University Press, 1986.

de los Reyes, Aurelio. "Del Blanquita, del público y género chico mexicano." *Diálogos* 16, no. 2 (March–April 1980): 29, 31.

Del Río Grimm, Martha. "El juego y el juguete en El Papalote Museo del Niño." In Gonzáles y Gonzáles et al., *Juegos y juguetes mexicanos*, 133–51.

Dibdin, Michael. *A Long Finish.* New York: Vintage, 2000. Originally published by Pantheon Books, 1998.

*Diccionario Porrúa: História, biografía y geografía de México.* 3rd ed. México: Editorial Porrúa, 1971.

DiMaggio, Paul. "Cultural Entrepreneurship in Nineteenth-Century Boston: The Creation of an Organizational Base for High Culture in America." *Media, Culture and Society* 4 (1982): 33–50.

Dircks, Phyllis T., ed. *American Puppetry: Collections, History and Performance.* Jefferson, NC: McFarland, 2004.

Dolkart, Ronald H. "Elitelore at the Opera: The Teatro Colón of Buenos Aires." *Journal of Latin American Lore* 9, no. 2 (1983): 231–50.

Doudoroff, Michael J., ed. *Moros y Cristianos in Zacatecas: Text of a Mexican Folk Play*, collected by Juan Bautista Rael. Lawrence, KS: Amadeo Concha Press, 1981.

Dublán, Manuel, and José María Lozano. *Legislación mexicana; ó, colección completa de las disposiciones legislativas expedidas desde la independencia de la república (1821 hasta 1906)*. México: Dublán y Lozano, 1876–1910.

Dunning, John. *The Bookwoman's Last Fling*. New York: Scribner, 2006.

Elliott, Robert C. *The Power of Satire: Magic, Ritual, Art*. Princeton, NJ: Princeton University Press, 1960.

Epstein, James A. *Radical Expression: Political Language, Ritual, and Symbol in England, 1790–1850*. New York: Oxford University Press, 1994.

Esposito, Matthew D. "From Father Hidalgo to Porfirio Díaz: Holidays, Relics, and the Liberal Myth in Mexico, 1876–1900." Paper presented at the annual meeting of the Southwestern Social Science Association, San Antonio, Texas, April 1, 1994.

———. "Memorializing Modern Mexico: The State Funerals of the Porfirian Era, 1876–1911." PhD diss., Department of History, Texas Christian University, 1997.

Estrada, Julio, ed. *La musica de México*. Vol. 1, Historia, pt. 5 *Periodo contemporaneo*. México: UNAM, 1984.

Fausto Ramírez. "Hidalgo en su estudio: La ardua construcción de la imagen del *pater patriae* mexicano." In Chust and Mínguez, eds., *La construcción del héroe*, 189–210.

Fenochio, Arturo. *El Valle de Tlacolula*. La Concepción, Putla, Oaxaca: Editorial La Hoja, 1953.

Fernández, Isabel, and Carmen Nava Nava. "He de comer de esa tuna: Ensayo histórico iconográfico sobre el escudo nacional." Paper (1996) presented as part of a documentary exposition, La Consumación de Independencia 175 Años, in the Archivo General de la Nación.

Fernández, María Auxiliadora. "In the Image of the Other: A Call for Rethinking National Identity." *Center: A Journal for Architecture in America* 7 (1992): 44–45.

———. "The Representation of National Identity in Mexican Architecture: Two Case Studies (1680 and 1889)." PhD diss., Department of Art History, Columbia University, 1993.

Fernández, Miguel Ángel. *Coleccionismo en México*. Monterrey: Museo de Vidrio, 2000.

Fernández de Lizardi, José Joaquín. *The Mangy Parrot: The Life and Times of Periquillo Sarniento, Written by Himself for His Children*. Translated by David Frye. Indianapolis: Hackett, 2004.

Ferrer Benimeli, José Antonio, coord. *Masonería española y América*. Vol. 1. V Simposio Internacional de Historia de la Masonsería Española, Cáceres, June 16–20, 1991. Zaragoza: Centro de Estudios Históricos de la Masonería, 1993.

Ferro Torrellas, Víctor. "La influencia francesa de los naipes de la Cataluña del siglo XVI." *La Sota: Revista de naipefilia y naipología* 15 (September 1996): 12–16.

Florescano, Enrique. *Bandera mexicana: Breve historia de su formación y simbolismo*. México: Santilana, 2000.

———. *Memoria mexicana*. México: Fondo de Cultura Económica, 1994.

———. *Memory, Myth, and Time in Mexico: From the Aztecs to Independence*. Translated by Albert G. Bork. Austin: University of Texas Press, 1994.

———. "Les origines de la mémoire nationale: La célébration du triomphe de l'Indépendance en 1821." In *Mémories en devenir Amérique Latine XVIe–XXe siècle*, edited by François-Xavier Guerra. Bordeaux: Maison des Pays Ibériques, 1994.

Frank, Patrick. *Posada's Broadsheets: Mexican Popular Imagery, 1890–1910*. Albuquerque: University of New Mexico Press, 1998.

Freedberg, David. *The Power of Images: Studies in the History and Theory of Response*. Chicago: University of Chicago Press, 1989.

French, William R. *Peaceful and Working People: The Inculcation of the Capitalist Work Ethic in a Mexican Mining District*. Albuquerque: University of New Mexico Press, 1996.

*Función estraordinario de títeres magicos en el Callejon del Vinagre*. México: Oficina de la Testamentaria de Ontiveros, 1828.

Gadsden, Gabriel. *Cavas de México*. México: MVS Editorial, 2003.

García Martín, Enrique. "Clemente Jacques y Cía, s.a./Pasatiempos Gallo, S.A. de C.V." *La Sota: Revista de naipefilia y naipología* 15 (September 1996).

Garner, Paul. *Porfirio Díaz*. Harlow, Eng.: Pearson Education, 2001.

Garza, James A. *Imagining an Underworld, Creating a Nation: Sex, Crime, and Vice in Porfirian Mexican City, 1876–1911*. Lincoln: University of Nebraska Press, 2008.

Gillespie, Jeanne L. "Gender, Ethnicity and Piety: The Case of the China Poblana." In *Imagination beyond Nation: Latin American Popular Culture*, edited by Eva P. Bueno and Terry Caesar. Pittsburgh: University of Pittsburgh Press, 1998.

Gonzalbo Aizpuru, Pilar. "Introducción." In *Historia de la vida cotidiana*. México: El Colegio de México, 2006.

Gonzáles y Gonzáles, Luis, et al. *Juegos y juguetes mexicanos*. México: Fundación Cultural CREMI, 1993.

González Navarro, Moisés. *Estadísticas sociales del Porfiriato, 1877–1910*. México: Dirección General de Estadística, 1956.

Goody, Jack. *The Culture of Flowers*. New York: Cambridge University Press, 1991.

Goytisolo, Juan. *Realms of Strife: The Memoirs of Juan Goytisolo, 1957–1982*. Translated by Peter Bush. San Francisco: North Point Press, 1990.

Greenleaf, Stephen. *Southern Cross*. New York: Bantam Books, 1995.

Gutiérrez de Medina, Cristobal. *Viaje por mar y tierra de Virrey Marques de Vienna. Aplausos y fiestas en México*. México: UNAM, 1947.

Halbwachs, Maurice. *On Collective Memory*. Edited and translated by Lewis A. Coser. Chicago: University of Chicago Press, 1992.

Hanson, Randall Scott. "Catholic Militants in Mexico: The *Secretariado Social Mexicano* and *Acción Católica Mexicana, 1920–1946*." PhD diss., Department of History, Indiana University, 1994.

Hart, John M. *Anarchism and the Mexican Working Class, 1860–1931*. Austin: University of Texas, 1990.

Hernández, Jorge F. "Entre el azar y el vértigo: juegos y juguetes en el México del siglo XIX." In Gonzalés y Gonzalés et al., *Juegos y juguetes mexicanos*, 99–131.

Hobsbawn, Eric J., and Terence Ranger, eds. *The Invention of Tradition*. New York: Cambridge University Press, 1992.

Hodge, John E. "The Construction of the Teatro Colón." *The Americas* 36, no. 2 (October 1979): 235–55.

Humboldt, Alexander von. *Political Essay on the Kingdom of New Spain* (abridged), with introduction by Mary Maples Dunn. New York: Alfred A. Knopf, 1972.

Hutton, Patrick H. *History as an Art of Memory*. Hanover: University of Vermont, 1993.

Iglesias Cabrera, Sonia, and Guillermo Murray Prisant. *Piel de papel, manos de palo; historia de los títeres en México*. México: Espasa-calpe Mexicana, 1995.

Illades, Carlos. "La representación del pueblo en el segundo romanticismo mexicano." *Signos históricos* 10, no. 5 (July–December 2003): 16–36.

Inclán, Luis G. *Astucia, el jefe de los Hermanos de la Hoja o los charros contrabandistas de la Rama*. México: Porrúa, 1973.

Ingham, John M. *Mary, Michael, and Lucifer: Folk Catholicism in Central Mexico*. Austin: University of Texas Press, 1986.

Jaffary, Nora E. *False Mystics: Deviant Orthodoxy in Colonial Mexico*. Lincoln: University of Nebraska Press, 2004.

Jiménez Muñoz, Jorge H. *La traza de poder: Historia de la política y los urbanos en el Distrito Federal, de sus orígenes a la desaparición del ayuntamiento, 1824–1928*. México: CODEX Editores, 1993.

Johnson, Hugh. *Hugh Johnson's Story of Wine*. London: Mitchell Beazley, 1989.

Johnson, Lyman L., ed. *Death, Dismemberment, and Memory: Body Politics in Latin America*. Albuquerque: University of New Mexico Press, 2004.

Joseph, Gilbert, and Allen Wells. "Chilango Blueprints and Provincial Growing Pains: Mérida at the Turn of the Century." *Mexican Studies/Estudios Mexicanos* 8 (Summer 1992): 167–215.

Jurado Rojas, Yolanda. *El teatro de títeres durante el porfiriato: Un estudio histórico y literario*. Puebla: Benemérita Universidad Autónoma de Puebla, 2004.

Knight, Alan. "El liberalismo mexicano desde la Reforma hasta la Revolución. Una interpretacion." *Historia mexicana* 35 (1985): 59–85.

——. *The Mexican Revolution*. Vol. 2 (Cambridge: Cambridge University Press, 1986).

Krauze, Enrique. *Siglo de caudillos: Biografía política de México (1810–1910)*. México: Tusquets, 1994.

Lacy, Elaine C. "The Centennial Celebrations of 1921 and North American Historians." Paper presented at the Ninth Conference of Mexican, United States, and Canadian Historians, Mexico City, October 27–29, 1994.

Latour, Charlotte de (Mme. Louise Cortambert). *Le langage des fleurs*. Paris: 1819.

Lear, John Robert. *Workers, Neighbors, and Citizens: The Revolution in Mexico City*. Lincoln: University of Nebraska Press, 2001.

León, Nicolás. *El Negrito poeta mexicano y sus populares versos*. México: 1912.

Lidtke, Vernon L. *The Alternative Culture: Socialist Labor in Imperial Germany*. New York: Oxford University Press, 1985.

Lipsett-Rivera, Sonya. "Configurations within a Pattern of Violence. The Geography of Sexual Danger in Mexico, 1750–1850." Paper presented at the annual meeting of the American Historical Association, Chicago, January 6–8, 1995.

Litwicki, Ellen M. *America's Public Holidays, 1865–1920*. Washington, DC: Smithsonian Institution Press, 2000.

Lohman Staub, Nancy. "The Center for Puppetry Arts Museum." In Dircks, *American Puppetry*, 73–86.

Lomnitz, Claudio. *Death and the Idea of Mexico*. New York: Zone Books, 2005.

Lorey, David E. "The Meaning of Patriotic Festivities in Post-Revolutionary Mexico." Paper presented at the Ninth Conference of Mexican, United States, and Canadian Historians, Mexico City, October 27–29, 1994.

Luján Muñoz, Luis. "La lotería de figuras en Guatemala." Guatemala: Serviprensa Centroamericana, 1987.

MacLachlan, Colin M., and William H. Beezley. *El Gran Pueblo: A History of Greater Mexico*. Englewood Cliffs, NJ: Prentice-Hall, 1994.

MacLean, Natalie. *Red, White, and Drunk All Over: A Wine-Soaked Journey from Grape to Glass*. New York: Bloomsbury, 2006.

Manguel, Alberto. *A Reading Diary: A Passionate Reader's Reflections on a Year of Books*. New York: Farrar, Straus and Giroux, 2004.

María y Campos, Armando de. *El teatro mexicano de muñecos*. México: El Nacional, 1941.

Markham, Dewey Jr. *1855: A History of the Bordeaux Classification*. New York: John Wiley and Sons, 1998.

Marmolejo, Lucio. *Efemérides guanajuatenses.* Guanajuato: Universidad de Guanajuato, 1973.

Martínez, José Luis. "México en busca de un expresión." In *Historia general de México—Versión 2000.* México: El Colegio de México, 2004.

Martínez de Codes, Rosa María. "El impacto de la masonería en la legislación reformista de la primera generación de liberales en México." In Benimeli, coord., *Masonería española y América,* 1:219–76.

Matabuena Peláez, Teresa. *Algunos usos y conceptos de la fotografía durante el porfiriato.* México: Universidad Iberoamericana, 1991.

Mayer, Roberto L., Antonio Rubial García, and Guadalupe Jiménez Codinanch. *México ilustrado. Mapas, planos, grabados e ilustraciones de los siglos XVI al XIX.* México: Fomento Cultural Banamex, 1994.

Mayer Celis, Leticia. *Entre el infierno de una realidad y el cielo de un imaginario: Estadística y comunidad científica en el México de la primera mitad del siglo XIX.* México: El Colegio de México, 1999.

McPharlin, Paul. *The Puppet Theatre in America: A History.* New York: Harper and Brothers, 1949.

Meade de Angulo, Mercedes. "La empresa nacional de automatas de los hermanos Rosete Aranda." Poniencia del Coloquio de Teatro de Tlaxcala, July 1994.

Mendez Aquino, Alejandro. "El teatro del siglo XVI a la mitad del siglo XX." In *Historia del arte de Oaxaca,* vol. 2: *Colonia y siglo XIX,* coord. Margarita Dalton and Verónica Loera y Chávez Castro. Oaxaca: Gobierno del Estado de Oaxaca, 1997.

Mendoza, Vicente T., and Virginia R. R. de Mendoza. *Folklore de la región central de Puebla.* México: Centro Nacional de Investigación, Documentación e Información Musical "Carlos Chávez," 1991.

Mills, Kenneth, and William B. Taylor, eds., *Colonial Latin America: Documentary History.* Wilmington, DE: SR Books, 1998.

Miranda Silva, Francisca. "Introducción." In *Epoca de oro del teatro guiñol de Bellas Artes, 1932–1965.* DVD. Under the general direction of Marisa Giménez Cacho. Produced by CONACULTA.

Mitchell, Timothy J. *Violence and Piety in Spanish Folklore.* Philadelphia: University of Pennsylvania Press, 1988.

Montes Moctezuma, Eduardo. *El Negrito poeta mexicano y el dominicano: ¿Realidad o fantasía?* México: 1982.

Moreno, Daniel. "La epoca independiente entre la Independencia y la Reforma. *Artes de México* 18, no. 147 (1971): 227–33.

———. "Mito y realidad del Negrito poeta." *Artes de México* 18, no. 147 (1971): 9–18, 109–10.

Moreno Corral, Marco Arturo. *Odisea 1874, o el primer viaje internacional de científicos mexicanos.* México: El Fondo Cultural Económica, 1986.

Morgan, Tony. "Proletarians, Politicos, and Patriarchs: The Use and Abuse of Cultural Customs in the Early Industrialization of Mexico City, 1880–1910." In Beezley, Martin, and French, eds., *Rituals of Rule*, 151–72.

Mostkoff-Linares, Aída. "Foreign Visions and Images of Mexico: One Hundred Years of International Tourism, 1821–1921." PhD diss., Department of History, UCLA, 1999.

Muñoz, Peggy. "Puppetry—A Flourishing Art-Form in Mexico." Undated pamphlet from about 1949. Reprinted for an international puppet conference in Munich in 1966.

Murray Prisant, Guillermo. "En Veracruz," *El Financiero*, January 9, 1992, p. 45.

Nesh-Kala. *La música prohibida por la Inquisición*. Tlalli (the record label of Radio Educación), recorded on the Quien canta program, March 14, 1995.

Nooteboom, Cees. *Roads to Santiago: A Modern-Day Pilgrimage through Spain*. Translated by Ina Rilke. New York: Harvest Books, 1992.

Nuñez y Dominguez, José de J. "Las loterías de figuras en México." *Mexican Folkways* 8 (1932): 87–106.

Ortiz, Elisabeth Lambert. *The Festive Food of Mexico*. London: Kyle Cathie, 1992.

Ozouf, Mona. *Festivals and the French Revolution*. Translated by Alan Sheridan. Cambridge: Harvard University Press, 1988.

Pani, Erika. "El proyecto de estado de Maximiliano a través de la vida cortesana y del ceremonial público." *Historia Mexicana* 45, no. 2 (October–December 1995): 423–61.

Parlett, David Sidney. *Oxford Guide to Card Games*. New York: Oxford University Press, 1991.

Pérez Montfort, Ricardo. *Estampas de nacionalismo popular mexicano: Diez ensayos sobre cultura popular y nacionalismo*. 2nd ed. México: Centro de Estudios Superiores en Antropología Social, 2003.

*El periódico oficial del gobierno del Estado de Guanajuato* 11, no. 66 (1883).

Pescador, Juan Javier. *De bautizados a fieles difuntos: Familia y mentalidades en una parroquia urbana: Santa Catarina de México, 1568–1820*. México: El Colegio de México, 1992.

Piccato, Pablo. *City of Suspects: Crime in Mexico City, 1900–1931*. Durham, NC: Duke University Press, 2001.

Pilcher, Jeffrey M. *"¡Que Vivan Tamales!": The Creation of a Mexican National Cuisine*. Albuquerque: University of New Mexico Press, 1998.

Piñera Ramírez, Dávid, ed. *Norte de México: Visión histórica de la frontera*. Tijuana: Universidad Autónoma de Baja California, 1998.

Pitkin, Hanna Fenichel. *The Concept of Representation*. Berkeley: University of California Press, 1967.

Plasencia de la Parra, Enrique. "Conmemoración de la hazaña épica de los

Niños Héroes: Su origen, desarrollo y simbolismos." *Historia mexicana* 45 (1995): 241–79.

Plumb, J. H. Lecture at the Folger Library, Washington, DC, March 27, 1979.

Prieto, Guillermo. *Memorias de mis tiempos*. 5th ed. Vol. 4. México: Ediciones Patria, 1968.

"Primera parte de las Coplas de don Simón." Puebla: Imprenta de Jesús Franco é hijo, 1907.

*El Pueblo* (El Estado de Tlaxcala. Organo oficial del gobierno) 87 (Sept. 23, 1882).

Quiñónez, Isabel. "De pronósticos, calendarios y almanaques." In *La república de las letras. Asomos a la cultura escrita del México decimonónico. Vol. 2, Publicaciones periódicicas y otros impresos*, coord. Belem Clark de Lara and Elisa Speckman Guerra. México: La Universidad Nacional Autónoma de México, 2005.

———. *Mexicanos en su tinta: Calendarios*. México: Instituto Nacional de Antropología e Historia, 1994.

Ramírez, José Inés. *Testamentos de Judas*. Colima, Col., 1994.

Rearick, Charles. *Pleasures of the Belle Epoque: Entertainment and Festivity in Turn-of-the-Century France*. New Haven: Yale University Press, 1985.

Reese, Thomas F., and Carol McMichael Reese. "Revolutionary Urban Legacies; Porfirio Díaz's Celebrations of the Centennial of Mexican Independence in 1910." In *Arte, historia e identidad en América: Visiones comparativas*, edited by Gustavo Curiel, Renato González Mello, and Juana Gutiérrez Haces. México: UNAM, 1994.

Reina, Leticia. *Las rebeliones campesinas en México (1819–1906)*. México: Siglo Veintiuno, 1980.

Reyes de la Maza, Luis. *El teatro en México durante el porfirismo*. México: Instituto de Investigaciones Estéticas, 1964.

———. *El teatro en México entre la Reforma y el Imperio (1858–1861)*. México: Imprenta Universitaria, 1958.

Rico Mansard, Luisa Fernanda. *Exhibir para educar: Objetos, colecciones y museos de la ciudad de México (1790–1910)*. México: Ediciones Pomares, 2004.

Riguzzi, Paolo. "México próspero: Las dimensiones de la imagen nacional en el porfiriato." *Historias* 20 (April–September 1980): 137–57.

Riva Palacio, Vicente. *México a través de los siglos*. 16th ed. Vol. 2. México: Editorial Cumbre, 1980.

Rivera Ayala, Sergio. "Lewd Songs and Dances from the Streets of Eighteenth-Century New Spain." In Beezley, Martin, and French, eds., *Rituals of Rule*, 95–114.

Roach, Joseph. *Cities of the Dead: Circum-Atlantic Performance*. New York: Columbia University Press, 1986.

Rodríguez, Miguel. *Celebración de "la raza": Una historia comparativa del 12 de Octubre*. México: La Universidad Iberoamericana, 2004.

Rosete Aranda, Francisco. *La compañía de títeres de los Rosete Aranda*. Tlaxcala: Instituto Tlaxcalteca de la Cultura, 1983.

Rosselli, John. "The Opera Business and the Italian Immigrant Community in Latin America 1820–1930. The Example of Buenos Aires." *Past and Present* 127 (May 1990): 155–82.

Rowe, William, and Vivian Schelling. *Memory and Modernity: Popular Culture in Latin America*. New York: Verso, 1991.

Ryan, Mary. "The American Parade: Representations of the Nineteenth-Century Social Order. In *The New Cultural History*, edited by Lynn Hunt. Berkeley: University of California Press, 1990.

Saborit, Antonio. "Cuaresmas porfirianas." *Historias* 15 (October–December, 1986).

Saka, Mark Saad. "Social Justice! Huatecan Unrest and the Uprising of 1879." PhD diss., Department of History, University of Houston, 1998.

Saldivar, Gabriel. *El Jarabe: Baile popular mexicano*. Puebla: Secretaría de Cultura, 1987.

Sallis, James. *Black Hornet*. New York: Avon Books, 1996.

Salvato, Amy Baker. "Recasting a Nation: The Reburial of Agustín de Iturbide." M.A. thesis, Center for Latin American Studies, University of Arizona, 1999.

Sánchez Santa Ana, María Eugenia. *Muñecas mestizas: Catálogo de las colecciones etnográficas del Museo Nacional de Antropología*. México: INAH, 1992.

Santamaria, Francisco J. *Diccionario de mejicanismos*. México: Editorial Porrúa, 1992.

Satterthwait, Walter. *Accustomed to the Dark*. Toronto: Worldwide, 1998.

Scanlon, Larry. *Narrative, Authority, and Power: The Medieval Exemplum and the Chaucerian Tradition*. New York: Cambridge University Press, 1994.

Schell, William, Jr. *Integral Outsiders: The American Colony in Mexico City, 1876–1911*. Wilmington, DE: SR Books, 2001.

———. "Yankee Bankers and Builders: The Growth of Mexico City during the Late Porfiriato." Unpublished, undated essay in the author's possession.

Schmidt, Leigh Eric. "The Commercialization of the Calendar: American Holidays and the Culture of Consumption, 1870–1930." *Journal of American History* 78, no. 3 (December 1991): 887–916.

Schmidt, Peer. "Neoestoicismo y disciplina social en la America Latina del siglo XVII." Paper presented at the Conference of Three Nations, Mexico City, October 30, 1994.

Scobey, David. "Anatomy of the Promenade: The Politics of Bourgeois Sociability in Nineteenth-Century New York." *Social History* 17, no. 2 (May 1992): 203–27.

Scott, Aurelia C. *Otherwise Normal People: Inside the Thorny World of Competitive Rose Gardening*. Chapel Hill: Algonquin Books, 2007.

Scott, James C. *Seeing like a State: How Certain Schemes to Improve the Human Condition Have Failed*. New Haven: Yale University Press, 1999.

———. *Weapons of the Weak*. New Haven: Yale University Press, 1985.

Semo, Ilán, coord. *La rueda del azar: Juegos y jugadores en la historia de México*. México: Ediciones Obraje, 2000.

Shershow, Scott Cutler. *Puppets and "Popular" Culture*. Ithaca, NY: Cornell University Press, 1995.

Soto, Miguel. "The Monarchist Conspiracy in Mexico, 1845–1846." PhD diss., Department of History, University of Texas, 1983.

Spamer, Irene. *Músicos mexicanos de hoy*. México: Editorial Trillas, 2003.

Speckman Guerra, Elisa. "Cuadernillos, pliegos, y hojas sueltas en la imprenta de Antonio Vanegas Arroyo." In *La república de las letras. Asomos a la cultura escrita del México decimonónico*, vol. 2, *Publicaciones periódicas y otros impresos*, coord. Belem Clark de Lara and Elisa Speckman Guerra (México: La Universidad Nacional Autónoma de México, 2005).

———. "Infancia es destino. Menores delincuentes en la ciudad de México (1884–1910)." In *De normas y transgresiones: Enfermedad y crimen en América Latina (1850–1950)*, ed. Claudia Agostoni and Elisa Speckman Guerra. México: La Universidad Autónoma de México, 2005.

Sullivan-Gonzalez, Douglas. "The Struggle for Hegemony: An Analysis of the Mexican Catholic Church, 1876–1911." Unpublished University of Texas seminar paper in author's possession.

Swortzell, Lowell. "A Short View of American Puppetry." In Dircks, *American Puppetry*, 22–46.

Taylor, William B. "The Virgin of Guadalupe in New Spain: An Inquiry into the Social History of Marian Devotion." *American Ethnologist* 14, no. 1 (February 1987): 9–33.

Tello, Aurelio. "El patrimonio musical de México. Una síntesis aproximativa." In *El patrimonio nacional de México*. Vol. 2. Coord. Enrique Florescano. México: Consejo Nacional Para la Cultura y las Artes, 2004.

Tenenbaum, Barbara A. "Streetwise History: The Paseo de la Reforma and the Porfirian State, 1876–1910." In Beezley, Martin, and French, eds., *Rituals of Rule*, 127–71.

Tenorio-Trillo, Mauricio. *Mexico at the World's Fairs: Crafting a Modern Nation*. Berkeley: University of California Press, 1996.

Terry, T. Philip. *Terry's Mexico: Handbook for Travellers*. 2nd ed. London: Gay and Hancock, 1909.

Thompson, E. P. "The Moral Economy of the English Crowd in the Eighteenth Century." *Past and Present* 50 (February 1971): 76–136.

Thomson, Guy P. C. "Bulwarks of Patriotic Liberalism: The National Guard, Philharmonic Corps and Patriotic Juntas in Mexico, 1847–1888." *Journal of Latin American Studies* 22 (1990): 31–68.

——. "Popular Aspects of Liberalism in Mexico, 1848–1888," *Bulletin of Latin American Research* 10, no. 3 (1991): 265–92.

Thomson, Guy P. C., and David LaFrance. *Patriotism, Politics, and Popular Liberalism in Nineteenth-Century Mexico: Juan Francisco Lucas and the Puebla Sierra.* Wilmington, DE: SR Books, 1999.

Thucydides, *The Peloponnesian War.* Translated by John H. Finley Jr. New York: Modern Library, 1951.

Timmons, Wilbert H., ed. *John F. Finerty Reports Porfirian Mexico, 1879.* El Paso: Texas Western Press, 1974.

Torres, Teodoro. *El humorismo y la sátira en México.* México: Editora Mexicana, 1943.

——. "El Negrito poeta." In Torres, *El humorismo y la sátira en México*, 149–55.

Tovar de Teresa, Guillermo, and Jorge F. Hernández. "Juegos y juguetes en el vierreinato de la Nueva España." In Gonzáles y Gonzáles et al., *Juegos y juguetes mexicanos*, 47–75.

Trouillot, Michel-Rolph. *Silencing the Past: Power and the Production of History.* Boston: Beacon Press, 1995.

Troyanski, David. "Monumental Politics: National History and Local Memory in French *Monuments aux Morts* in the Department of the Aisne since 1870." *French Historical Studies* 15, no. 1 (1987): 121–41.

Tweedee, Mrs. Alec. *The Maker of Modern Mexico: Porfirio Diaz.* New York: John Lane, 1906.

Van Young, Eric. *The Other Rebellion: Popular Violence, Ideology, and the Mexican Struggle for Independence, 1810–1821.* Stanford, CA: Stanford University Press, 2003.

Varey, J. E. *Historia de los títeres en España (desde sus origines hasta mediados del siglo XVIII).* Madrid: Revista de Occidente, 1957.

Vázquez K., Josefina. *Nacionalismo y educación en México.* México: 1970.

Vázquez Mantecón, Álvaro. "La república Ludens." *La rueda del azar: Juegos y jugadores en la historia de México*, coord. Ilán Semo. México: Ediciones Obraje, 2000.

Veblen, Thorstein. *The Theory of the Leisure Class: An Economic Study of Institutions.* 1889. Reprinted by Viking, New York, 1934.

Velázquez, Marco, and Mary Kay Vaughan. "*Mestizaje* and Musical Nationalism in Mexico." In *The Eagle and the Virgin: Nation and Cultural Revolution in Mexico, 1920–1940*, edited by Mary Kay Vaughan and Stephen E. Lewis. Durham, NC: Duke University Press, 2006.

Villa-Flores, Javier. *Dangerous Speech: A Social History of Blasphemy in Colonial Spanish America.* Tucson: University of Arizona Press, 2006.

Villanueva, Gabriel. *Las fiestas en honor del sr. General Porfirio Díaz: crónica completa*. México: Secretaría de Fomento, 1891.

Villegas, Victor Manuel. *Arte popular de Guanajuato*. México: Banco Nacional de Fomento Cooperativo, 1964.

Vinson, Ben, III. *Bearing Arms for His Majesty: The Free-Colored Militia in Colonial Mexico*. Stanford, CA: Stanford University Press, 2001.

Wakild, Emily. "It Is to Preserve Life, to Work for the Trees: The Steward of Mexico's Forests, Miguel Angel de Quevedo, 1862–1948." *Forest History Today* (Spring/Fall 2006): 4–14.

Warren, Richard. "The Construction of Independence Day, 1821–1864." Paper presented at the conference "Mexico in the Nineteenth Century: A Symposium in Honor of Nettie Lee Benson," Austin, Texas, April 15–16, 1994.

Wasserman, Mark. *Persistent Oligarchs: Elites and Politics in Chihuahua, Mexico, 1910–1940*. Durham, NC: Duke University Press, 1993.

Weber, Eugen. *Peasants into Frenchmen: The Modernization of Rural France, 1870–1914*. Stanford, CA: Stanford University Press, 1976.

Widdifield, Stacie Graham. *The Embodiment of the National in Late Nineteenth-Century Mexican Painting*. Tucson: University of Arizona Press, 1996.

——. "El impulso de Humboldt y la mirada extranjera sobre México." In *Hacia otra historia del arte en México: De la estructuración colonial a la exigencia nacional (1780–1860)*. Coord. Esther Acevedo. México: El Consejo Nacional de la Cultura y las Artes, 2001.

——. "National Art and Identity in Mexico, 1869–1881: Images of Indians and Heroes." PhD diss., Department of Art History, UCLA, 1986.

Wilson, Fredric Woodbridge. "Puppetry and Related Materials in the Harvard Theatre Collection." In Dircks, ed., *American Puppetry*, 39–57.

Wright, Gordon. "Eugène Sue: Master of the Serial Thriller." In *Notable or Notorious? A Gallery of Parisians*, by Gordon Wright. Cambridge: Harvard University Press, 1991.

Wright-Rios, Edward. "Visions of Women: Revelation, Gender, and Catholic Resurgence." In *Religious Culture in Modern Mexico*. Edited by Martin Nesvig. Boulder: Rowman and Littlefield, 2007.

Yeager, Gene. "Porfirian Commercial Propaganda: Mexico in the World Industry Expositions." *Americas* 34, no. 2 (October 1977): 230–43.

Zacarias y Bustos, Miguel. "Cantar los naipes." *Artes de México*, nueva época 13 (Fall 1991): 64–74.

Zorrilla, José. *El drama del alma. Algo sobre México y Maximiliano. Poesía en dos partes con notas en prosa y comentarios de un loco*. Burgos: D. T. Arnaix, 1867.

——. *Memorias del tiempo mexicano*. Edited by Pablo Mora. México: CONACULTA, 1998.

# INDEX

# ABOUT THE AUTHOR

William H. Beezley established a reputation as one of the pioneer cultural historians of Mexico with the publication of his well-known book *Judas at the Jockey Club and Other Episodes of Porfirian Mexico*. His investigations into both Mexican and Latin American history have resulted in thirteen books, including the standard *Oxford History of Mexico*, edited with Michael C. Meyer. He and Judy Ewell focused on the lives of ordinary people in the past in their widely used text *The Human Tradition in Latin America*, which resulted in a series of books on the human tradition in other places and other times. Beezley is currently completing a concise history of Mexicans in the Revolution with Colin MacLachlan. Recently, his research has turned to wine in Latin America, and he has appeared as a guest on the Emmy Award–winning program *The Desert Speaks*, to discuss wine in Baja California del Norte and in Chile. He has begun a book on the Malbec varietal in the Americas. His Mexican investigations now focus on popular culture, especially sports and music, of the 1950s. As professor of history, he teaches at the University of Arizona.

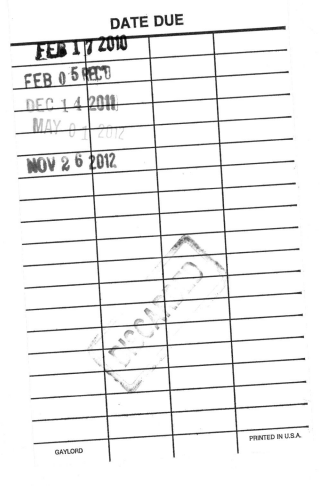